D-Day to Berlin

Victory in Europe Day by Day

10

D-Day to Berlin

Victory in Europe Day by Day

This edition published in 2013 by
Pen & Sword Military
An imprint of
Pen & Sword Books Ltd
47 Church Street
Barnsley
South Yorkshire
S70 2AS

ISBN: 978-1-78346-233-9

Produced by
Windmill Books Ltd
First Floor
9-17 St. Albans Place
London N1 ONX

General Editor: Peter Darman
Designer: Jerry Udall
Picture Research: Andrew Webb
Design Manager: Keith Davis
Editorial Director: Lindsey Lowe

All images from the Robert Hunt Library except: Antony Shaw: 133;
CodyImages/TRH 132, 137, 138, 143, 147, 165, 172.

Windmill books has made every effort to contact copyright holders.
For any further information please contact:
smortimer@windmillbooks.co.uk

Printed in Indonesia

Pages 2–3: Some of the first assault troops to hit the beachhead in Normandy, France, on June 6, 1944.

Contents

Introduction

The Allied invasion of Europe in June 1944 and the subsequent campaigns across France, Belgium, Holland, and Germany remains one of the great military feats of all time. From June 6, 1944, to May 5, 1945, the experienced German armed forces in western Europe were utterly defeated by armies most of whose soldiers had never seen combat before. Operation Overlord, landing an entire army on a hostile shore and then breaking through intense German resistance, was the biggest single episode, but as the campaign carried on there were many battles that tested the Allies to the full—hard, unsuccessful fighting to penetrate the German lines at Arnhem, and bitter and successful defense against the German counter attack in the Ardennes, for example.

In the end, the result was a glorious, overwhelming victory, but there is no doubt that there were difficulties along the way. Early on, an initial problem was the reluctance of the UK government and high command to commit to the invasion that the US leadership wanted to organize as early as 1942. There were many reasons for this reluctance. First, the British argued that an amphibious landing was very risky, and pointed to the failure of the Dieppe raid of August 1942; this test landing on the French coast had been a disaster. Britain preferred a strategy of deploying forces in the Mediterranean, claiming that attacks via the "soft underbelly" of the Axis—Italy—would be very effective, especially when coupled with bombing of German industrial centers.

In spite of British misgivings, the countdown to D-Day began in January 1943. At the Casablanca Conference in Morocco the Allies took several key decisions. They agreed to establish a new body known as COSSAC (Chief of Staff to the Supreme Allied Commander) to plan the invasion of Europe. The Allies also decided that a massive transfer of US troops and equipment to Britain—Operation Bolero—would begin.

COSSAC's Plans

COSSAC was led by Lieutenant-General Frederick Morgan. The key question for COSSAC was where to launch the attack. The target area had to be within range of fighter aircraft from southern England that would be needed to provide air cover. After the initial landings, it was also important to land follow-up troops at least as quickly as German reinforcements could arrive—and Morgan's team initially thought the best plan was to capture a port. They soon realized, however, that the Germans would plan to destroy any ports as soon as an invasion began. So the alternative was to find a long stretch of wide, gently sloping beaches. For this, the French coast in Normandy was promising. It had good beaches that were not as well defended as those farther north. They were also close to the port of Cherbourg. However, invading Normandy also presented some problems. It was relatively far from the vital fighter bases. It was also on a wide part of the English Channel, so the invading troops would have to endure a long sea crossing. If the Allies did not quickly capture Cherbourg, it might also be difficult to land supplies and reinforcements. COSSAC's key to solving this logistical problem were two technological innovations: the creation of two small artificial harbors, code-named Mulberries, that could be floated into position after the first assaults, and the rapid construction of a pipe line, code-named PLUTO (Pipe Line Under the Ocean) to carry fuel across the Channel from England.

▲ ***German Field Marshal Erwin Rommel observes the coast. The hero of North Africa commanded the Channel defenses.***

COSSAC's initial plan for a landing in Normandy was approved by the Allied leaders at the Quadrant Conference in Quebec, Canada, in August 1943. In February 1944, COSSAC became part of SHAEF (Supreme Headquarters Allied Expeditionary Force), under the command of US General Dwight D. Eisenhower. He and other senior commanders, particularly British General Bernard Montgomery who would directly command the troops that went ashore in the first few days, modified the plans. Instead of landing on three beaches, they would land at five beaches across a 60-mile (96km) front. US forces would target two

▶ ***The major Allied leaders—from left to right, Stalin, Roosevelt, and Churchill—agreed at a conference in Casablanca to put plans in train for an invasion of northern Europe, which would take pressure off the Soviet forces on the Eastern Front.***

beaches, code-named Utah and Omaha. The British would land at two others, Gold and Sword. Juno Beach was allocated to Canadian forces.

There were five critical elements in the preparation for the landings. The first was the detailed reconnaissance and study of the beaches, knowing about tidal conditions, likely weather patterns, German defenses (such as underwater obstacles), etc. This process continued through 1943 and the first months of 1944, before the invasion date was set for June 5, 1944.

The second element was keeping the invasion plans secret. There was an extreme security blanket over southern Britain, and false information also misled the Germans about the site of the landings. Fake radio signals convinced the Germans that the assault would take place in the Pas-de-Calais, farther north along the French coast from Normandy, in July.

The third element was the build up of troops in the UK, which had been going on for two years, and the movement of these troops across the Channel in one of the largest fleet ever assembled. UK Admiral Sir Bertram Ramsey and his naval team performed the greatest organizational feat in naval history in getting the different fleets and their escorts together and swiftly clearing the minefields the Germans had laid in the Channel.

The fourth piece of the jigsaw was weakening the German forces in France, without letting them know where the attack would take place. From early April, Allied aircraft dropped some 200,000 tons of bombs on northern France, wrecking communications. They bombed railroads and airfields, coastal defenses, radar stations, and military compounds. The French Resistance also carried out acts of sabotage.

Finally, the preparation of the soldiers for the landings themselves involved not merely training in how to leap off landing craft onto sandy beaches but also creating special armored vehicles ("Funnies") to perform critical tasks such as covering ditches or using flails to clear a swift path through minefields. In addition there was the planning and training necessary for the co-ordination of all the elements involved, from naval gunfire to parachute troops, from landing craft to infantry teams with bunker-blasting equipment.

German strategic debates

The Germans knew, of course, that an invasion would come, but disagreed about their best strategy. The Atlantic Wall was enormously reinforced in the first few months of 1944. As with the Allies there was some disagreement over strategy: should the major armored forces be based along the coast or kept concentrated inland to strike in unison when the target area had been identified? German reactions to the landings were hampered by Hitler's firm belief that the main Allied landing would come near Pas-de-Calais.

▲ ***US Landing Craft Tanks are loaded up from the vast fleet of vehicles assembled in southern England.***

Eisenhower gives the "Go" order

On May 29, 1944, Allied troops began moving to the ports along the south coast of England where they would board their ships. By June 3, everything was ready. The next day, however, the weather changed for the worse, with high winds and low clouds. That evening Eisenhower's weather expert, Group Captain James Stagg, offered some hope. Starting on the afternoon of the next day, June 5, there would be an improvement in the weather. It would last for about 24 hours. On the morning of June 5, Stagg confirmed his forecast. Within a few hours, some 7000 warships and landing craft were heading for Normandy. The largest amphibious operation in history was about to begin—the prelude to the great campaign in western Europe that brought the war in Europe to a successful conclusion.

▼ ***British troops train for D-Day by using ladders to cross the kind of barbed-wire defenses they were likely to face on the beaches.***

The Early Hours

▲ ***Troops of a German mortar platoon. Wehrmacht infantry had to rely on mortars because of a field gun shortage.***

00:00 HOURS

GERMAN DEFENSES, *NORMANDY*
The first German units to face the Allied invasion will be the six infantry and three panzer divisions posted in Normandy. They are concentrated in the Cotentin Peninsula, protecting the port of Cherbourg, and along the Calvados Coast, from the River Vire, in the west, to the River Dives, 10 miles (16km) east of Caen. The divisions vary widely in their equipment, personnel, and fighting effectiveness.

The Cotentin is held by the 243rd, 709th and 91st Divisions. The 243rd is spread out along the west coast of the peninsula. Officially, the division is supposed to be motorized, but by June 6 only six infantry companies have been issued with trucks, and the division artillery is drawn by teams of horses. The 709th is posted along the east coast of the Cotentin, from Cherbourg to Carentan, and is a static unit, having no transport at all. Its main role is to garrison Cherbourg. The 709th consists of poorly trained, overage soldiers and a large number of Osttruppen (Eastern troops) from the conquered lands of Eastern Europe and the Soviet Union.

The 91st Division defends the southern part of peninsula from the River Merderet west to the coast. It arrived in the Cotentin in late May with the specific task of countering airborne landings. Despite its training, the 91st is not a frontline division, being barely six months old and made up of conscripts. It is, however, well stocked with

▼ *A Panzer IV of the SS "Hitler Youth" Panzer Division in northern France. Note how young the crew are.*

artillery, having three battalions of 105mm and 155mm guns.

Supporting these divisions around Carentan is the 6th Parachute Infantry Regiment, part of the 2nd Parachute Division, which in May began to be transferred from Brittany. The 6th is an élite unit of volunteers, commanded by veteran paratrooper, Colonel Frederick von der Heydte.

The 352nd Division defends the coast from the Vire estuary east for a distance of about 24 miles (38km) to Asnelles-sur-Mer, including the areas around Isigny-sur-Mer and Bayeux. The 352nd has been in this sector since March and has spent most of its time strengthening the coastal defenses. It consists of over 12,000 combat veterans, organized into four grenadier regiments, and supported by five battalions of field, anti-tank, and anti-aircraft artillery which are based a little inland.

◀ *German infantry move into position close to the Orne sector, prior to the Allied parachute drop.*

▲ *A German machine-gun position in Normandy. The weapon is a 7.92mm MG42, an excellent piece of equipment.*

The area north of Caen, from Asnelles past the estuary of the Orne to the River Dives, is the responsibility of the 716th Division. This is another static division organized for defense. It consists of many veterans invalided out of the Eastern Front, as well as two battalions of Eastern European troops. The division is supported by a regiment of artillery, but it has too few soldiers to defend a sector covering over 21 (34km). The division commander has therefore had to concentrate his men around 50 fortified positions: strong along the coast but providing for very little defense inland. The 716th Division forms the right flank of Seventh Army's LXXXIV Corps.

The River Dives forms the boundary between the Seventh and Fifteenth Armies. The most westerly formation of Fifteenth Army is the 711th Division, holding the sector from the Dives to Honfleur. This static division also has a high percentage of former invalids from the Eastern Front, as well as a battalion of Eastern troops. As with all the conscripted units from the East, their loyalty is questionable, but they fulfil a need in manning fortifications.

Supporting these infantry divisions are three panzer divisions, held inland as a mobile reserve. Closest to the coast is the 21st Panzer Division, located east of Caen astride the River Orne, in support of the static 716th Division. The original 21st Panzer was destroyed in Tunisia in 1943, but it was re-constituted with personnel from many different units. Looked on as rather second-rate, the new division is equipped with largely obsolete weapons and captured French vehicles. A far more impressive armored unit is located southeast of Normandy,

▲ ***Paratroopers jump from their transport during training. The parachute jump as a method of massed deployment rose and fell with World War II, since high attrition rates from injury and scattering of forces made it a liability.***

▼ ***Under the cover of darkness, Allied gliders like these swooped down, landing behind enemy lines. The journey was perilous, and many overladen gliders crashed, killing both passengers and pilots.***

▶ ***Strategically important bridges in Normandy, such as this one over the Orne, were key objectives for airborne forces.***

between Le Mans and Orléans. The Panzer Lehr Division includes an armored regiment, an armored artillery regiment, two armored infantry regiments, an anti-tank battalion, and an armoured reconnaissance battalion. It has a total strength of over 14,500 officers and men and 183 tanks, including Panther and Tiger tanks and Jagdpanzer IV and StuG assault guns. The third panzer division near Normandy is the most powerful. On June 6, the 12th SS Panzer Division *Hitlerjugend* (Hitler Youth) is spread over an area about 40 miles (65km) southeast of Caen. It is a new élite division and is made up of 20,000 volunteers, most of whom have come from the Hitler Youth movement. They are committed Nazis, sworn to defend the Reich. The division's order of battle includes a panzer regiment, two panzer-

▼ ***The assault area, showing the various sectors of the beaches. This was the grand plan, though sea and weather conditions in the Channel meant many troops landed away from their designated sectors.***

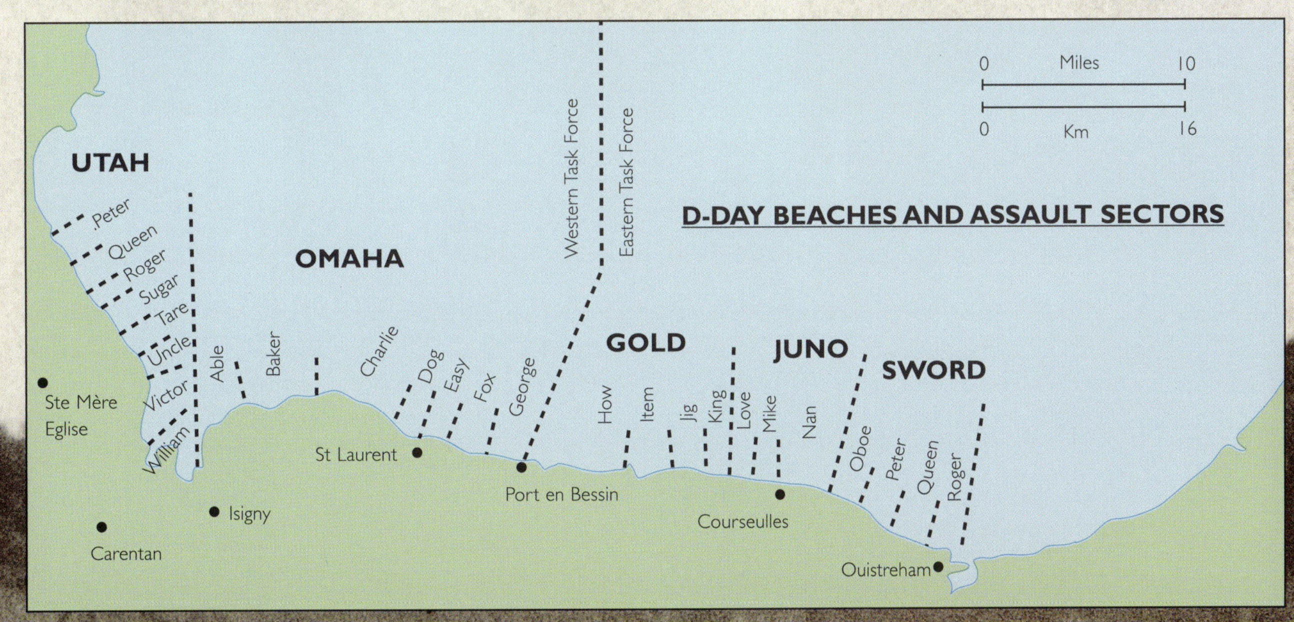

grenadier regiments, and an artillery regiment. It is equipped with Panther tanks, Jagdpanzer IVs and halftracks carrying multiple 20mm flak guns.

The German divisions settle in for another quiet night in Normandy. The Allies are mounting a few air raids, but nothing to be too concerned over. The rough weather in the English Channel gives the region a sense of security. The Allies won't be putting to sea tonight, and in any case the tide is going out and it is a widely held belief that the Allies will only attack at high tide and in daylight, as they did in the Mediterranean theater.

AIRBORNE ASSAULT,
BRITISH SECTOR

The six Horsa gliders carrying Major Howard's troops heading for the Orne River bridges cross the Normandy coast. Separating from their towing aircraft at 6000 ft (1830m) the plywood gliders, each laden with over 15,400lb (7000kg) of men and equipment, sweep over Cabourg, northeast of Caen, at 90 mph (145km/h). One glider becomes separated and veers off toward the Dives River to land about 8 miles (13km) from target; but the rest make a turn west for a glide of 5 miles (8km) to the objective. With no navigational aids other than a stop-watch and a map, the army pilots pick up the Orne Canal at about 1200ft (365m). No. 1 glider crash-lands on the east bank of the canal at about 00:16 hours and plouws straight through a belt of barbed wire before coming to a halt at a road embankment just 140 ft (43m) from the canal bridge. It is followed at one-minute intervals by gliders 2 and 3, which land directly behind.

The platoon from No.1 glider, led by Lieutenant Brotheridge, is the first out, and its men make it up the embankment to the bridge and then split up.

▲ ***German Panzergrenadiers move along the Bocage in Normandy to counter-attack the Allied airdrop. They are supported by a Panther tank.***

▼ ***Panzergrenadiers continue their push toward the Allied paratroopers. The paratroopers have been spread across the French countryside, and are scrambling to organize before German forces get to them in strength.***

▶ ***Lance-Corporals Burton and Barnett, both British paratroopers, guard a crossroads outside the town of Ranville.***

Three men grenade a pillbox on the right while Brotheridge leads the rest of his men in a charge across the bridge to attack the German slit trenches on the far bank. Meanwhile, sappers are already climbing over the underside of the bridge to cut the wires of any demolition explosives. The two platoons from gliders 2 and 3 are also now in action along the east bank, while Brotheridge and his men engage a machine-gun nest to their right. In the face of the sudden onslaught, the garrison, all foreign conscripts, are retreating fast, but their German NCOs are making some show of a fight, and Brotheridge is mortally wounded, before grenades and Bren gun fire silence the machine gun. Men from the two other platoons are now over the bridge and securing the far bank. By 00:22 hours, the canal bridge is almost secure and the sappers have found no explosives. It seems the Germans were wiring the bridge for demolition but had not yet put the charges in place.

Major Howard moves his command post into the pillbox to await news from the platoons in gliders 4, 5 and 6 attacking the river bridge 400 yds (365m) east. The first of these, glider 5, lands at about 00:20 hours. With no sign of the other gliders, Lieutenant Fox leads his platoon straight to the bridge. There is German machine-gun fire from the east bank, which is silenced by a bomb from the platoon's mortar. The defenders run off and Fox crosses the bridge at about 00:21 hours, by which time glider 6, carrying Lieutenant Sweeney and his platoon, has landed. By the time Sweeney's platoon joins Fox, the river bridge is secure. By 00:30 hours, Major Howard is having the radio message "Ham and Jam" sent back to England. It is the call sign that Operation Coup de Main has been a complete success.

With both bridges secure, Howard's priority is defence. News of the attack will have reached the villages of Bénouville and Le Port by now, and Howard's men take their places in the trenches on the west bank of the canal to await the expected German counter-attack. Relief by parachute companies of the 7th Battalion, 5th Parachute Brigade, 6th Airborne, is expected from

▼ ***The Allied deception strategies on D-Day, involving both radar jamming and creating false radar images (red areas) and dummy paratroop drops.***

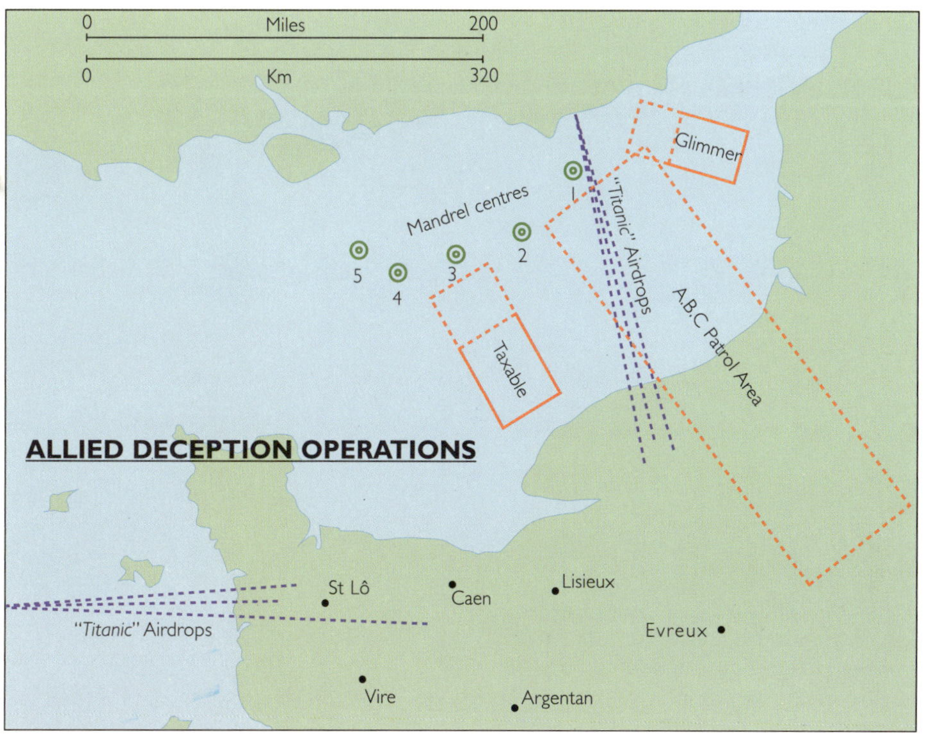

▲ *US paratroopers liaise with a member of the French Resistance about the location of German troop concentrations.*

about 01:00 hours. But until they arrive over the bridge, from their drop zones (DZs) around the villages of Ranville and Bréville, Howard and his men of the "Ox and Bucks" are on their own.

00:30 HOURS

AIRBORNE ASSAULT, *PATHFINDERS*
Transports are now flying in over the Cotentin Peninsula and the area between the Orne and Dives rivers to drop those paratroopers who will act as pathfinders for the three Allied airborne divisions. The pathfinders are meant to land, identify, and mark the DZ for the first airborne troops, now just 30 minutes behind them; but as soon as they fly in, their mission starts to go wrong.

Over the American sector of the Cotentin, pilots fly straight into a cloud bank, which, they discover, covers most of the peninsula. Those aircraft that climb to clear it have to drop the pathfinders without sight of the ground, while those that dive below it are targeted by German flak and forced to scatter. Of the 18 US pathfinder teams, only one lands in the correct place, leaving five DZs unidentified. The British pathfinders of the 22nd Independent Parachute Company are more fortunate. Their drop is also scattered by low cloud and flak, but about half the company finds its way to the three DZs for the leading elements of the 6th Airborne's 5th Parachute Brigade.

AIR CAMPAIGN, *BRITISH SECTOR*
A force of 100 Lancasters and Halifax bombers attack the four concrete casemates of the Merville battery, east of Caen. The raid is meant to support the attack by men of the 9th Parachute Brigade, led by Colonel Terence Otway, scheduled to begin at 02:35 hours. In fact, a reconnaissance party of paratroopers is already on the ground and hears the aircraft release their bombs. It is a terrifying spectacle

▶ *An M-22 Locust light tank emerges from a giant Hamilcar glider. The M-22 was designed to give airborne troops much-needed firepower.*

to watch, but it does the paratroopers little good: the bombs have missed the German battery completely.

00:50 HOURS

AIRBORNE ASSAULT, *BRITISH SECTOR*

The lead aircraft carrying the 5th Parachute Brigade and forward units of Otway's Merville attack force fly in at 120m (400ft). The pathfinders mark the DZ with flares as the Germans nearby realize that something serious is happening. From his command post at the Orne Canal bridge, Major Howard sees their arrival; he recalls later, "We had a first-class view of the division coming in. Searchlights were lighting up the 'chutes and there was a bit of firing going on and you could see tracer bullets going up into the air as they floated down to the ground. It was the most awe-inspiring sight."

01:00 HOURS

DECEPTION, *FORTITUDE SOUTH*

As part of Fortitude South, a large number of deception schemes and electronic warfare operations are in operation over the English Channel and Normandy coast to mask the invasion fleet and draw the Germans away from the airborne DZs. For the past 24 hours Operation Mandrel has been underway. Bombers filled with anti-radar equipment have been flying circuits over the Channel, jamming enemy ground radar, while over the Pas de Calais what are known as ABC patrols are being flown by specially equipped Lancasters to jam and interrupt the radio frequencies used by the German

▲ ***A German soldier inspects the wreckage of a crashed Allied Horsa glider. If not killed in the landing, the Allied troops would have long gone.***

fighter control network. While German radar is being jammed over the real invasion fleet, Operations Taxable and Glimmer are providing German radar with images of two phantom fleets off the coast, at Le Havre and Boulogne: at sea, motor launches tow radar-reflecting balloons, while overhead bombers scatter huge amounts of "Window"—aluminum strips that create a radar shadow over 14 miles (22km) long.

Inland, the SAS's Operation Titanic aims to divert German reserves from the airborne DZ by dropping over 500 dummy paratroopers: man-shaped sandbags, about one-third life size, fitted with small parachutes and explosive gunfire simulators. They are crude, but in the dark, and in large numbers, they have German reserves chasing around looking for Allied "troops". Titanic targets four separate locations: north of the River Seine, east of the River Dives, southwest of Caen, and west of St Lô.

◄ ***A typical Allied Limpet mine. These were placed on railroad lines by French Resistance members to disrupt German military movements.***

01:00 HOURS

AIRBORNE ASSAULT, *US SECTOR*

The first of more than 900 C-47 transport aircraft appears over the Cotentin Peninsula to drop the 101st and 82nd Airborne Divisions into France. But from the moment the planes cross the west coast of the peninsula, the operation begins to descend into chaos. Not only are most of the DZs unmarked, but the transport pilots get lost in the cloud cover, and heavy flak from the German divisions below breaks up their formations. The pilots—not combat-trained—climb, dive, and accelerate away from the gunfire and order their paratroopers to jump at the best opportunity. Transports are shot down, order is lost, and as a result the two divisions are scattered all over the southeast of the peninsula, from the Merderet River to the coast. Some paratroopers drop into the English Channel, while two unfortunate plane-loads of men drop right in the middle of the village of Ste Mère Eglise, to be shot dead with their parachutes still entangled in trees and telegraph wires. Elsewhere, men drown in areas flooded by the Germans precisely to prevent such airborne assaults. Companies, even platoons, are split up, with no idea where they are. But amid the failure of the drop, the paratroopers hold to their tasks. They start to assemble in small groups, get

▼ ***Troops of the 12th SS Panzer Division "Hitler Youth," supported by armor, move through a French village to counter Allied action.***

▲ ***Royal Navy minesweepers, such as these seen in harbor, had been busily clearing a channel for invasion craft to surge toward the beaches.***

their bearings and begin to move north towards the four exits from Utah beach, west to the Merderet and Ste Mère Eglise, and south toward the crossings over the River Douve.

GERMAN DEFENSES, *RESPONSES*
Allied airborne troops have been landing for nearly an hour before the enemy begins to try and organize a response. At about 01:00 hours, the 711th Division goes on alert when British paratroopers mistakenly land close to its headquarters at Pont l'Evêques on the River Dives.

The 716th Division, around Caen, follows suit a few minutes afterward when it receives news that Allied paratroopers are in action east of the Orne. The news is passed up to LXXXIV Corps HQ at St Lô and the LXXXI Corps HQ at Rouen, which both go on alert; but it is not until 01:35 hours that the Seventh Army HQ, at Le Mans, informs Army Group B HQ, near Paris. Rommel's chief of staff, General Speidel, is woken by the call, but decides not to forward the incoming reports to either OB West or General Rommel because as yet he refuses to accept that the Allied attack is anything more than a raid or a diversionary feint. Meanwhile, the commander of the German 6th Parachute Regiment in Périers is also getting reports of the Allied landings around Ste Mère Eglise; but his attempts to contact LXXXIV Corps HQ all fail because the US paratroopers are now busy destroying the German communications network.

The German Navy reacts with a little more efficiency. At 01:30 hours, Vice-Admiral Rieve, commander of the Channel coast, informs Admiral Kranke's HQ in Paris of the American landings. Kranke puts Navy Group West on alert in preparation for action.

01:40 HOURS

AIRBORNE ASSAULT, *REINFORCING*
Fifty-two gliders carrying the first reinforcements and heavy equipment for the 101st Airborne Division are towed into the air from Aldermaston airfield. Their loads are vital to support the

▼ ***A German 88mm flak battery attempts to drive off the Allied bombers pounding the Normandy coast, hours before the first vessels land.***

lightly armed paratroops. They include 16 six-pounder guns, 13 tonnes (13.2 tons) of ammunition and equipment, 24 vehicles, and a small bulldozer. Gliders also carry companies of engineers and medics and the division's HQ staff. There is no communication between the paratroopers scattered across the Cotentin and England, so these men have no idea of what they flying into.

01:30 HOURS

AIRBORNE ASSAULT, BRITISH SECTOR, *GERMAN ATTACK*
As the German Army chain of command attempts to sort out what is going on in Normandy, units of the 716th Division begin the first counter-attack on Major Howard's men at the Orne Canal. Two Panzer IV tanks advance slowly out of Bénouville, heading for the canal bridge, followed by infantry. The lead tank gets to within 50 yds (45m) of the bridge when it is hit by a round from a PIAT and explodes. The burning tank blocks the road and the attack peters out. Shortly afterward the first companies of the 5th Parachute Brigade arrive and take position on the west bank of the canal in preparation for an advance into Bénouville and Le Port.

FRENCH RESISTANCE, *SABOTAGE*
By 01:37 hours the first three SAS and Jedburgh liaison teams have been dropped into Brittany. The first to land is ambushed at the DZ: one French SAS soldier is killed and the rest of the team are captured. The other teams land safely. Throughout northern France the Resistance goes into action against 1050 designated targets, 950 of which will be attacked in the next 24 hours. Cutting rail lines is the priority, especially those needed to reach Normandy by German divisions posted elsewhere in France. The likely routes of two divisions, in particular, have been targeted: the 275th, currently in Redon, 125 miles (200km) to the south-west, and the 2nd SS Panzer Division *Das Reich*, in Toulouse, 450 miles (720km) to the south.

▲ ***Fighters covered the fleet routes (yellow), while tactical and reconnaissance missions were flown far inland. The invasion area was well protected.***

AIRBORNE ASSAULT, *BRITISH FORCES*
Around 01:40 hours, 72 gliders are towed into the air carrying the British 6th Airborne Division headquarters, its commander Major-General Gale, reinforcements, and heavy equip-ment, including anti-tank guns and jeeps. Meanwhile, in France, engineers of the 5th Parachute Brigade are clearing DZs of anti-glider poles and preparing eight landings strips ready for their arrival.

▼ ***British paratroopers from the 6th Airborne Division unload their equipment from a Horsa glider near Ranville. The soldiers here were lucky enough to have experienced a successful landing.***

01:59 HOURS

AIRBORNE ASSAULT, *REINFORCING*
The lift begins of 52 gliders carrying the first reinforcements and heavy equipment for the US 82nd Airborne Division. They carry 16 57mm anti-aircraft guns, 22 jeeps, 10.1 tons (10 tonnes) of ammunition, as well as the head-quarters staff and signalers.

OPERATION NEPTUNE, *MINES*
From 02:00 hours flotillas of minesweepers and their destroyer escorts begin to arrive off the Normandy coast, exactly on schedule. The passage across has, so far, suffered the loss of only one vessel, the US Navy minesweeper *Osprey*, which hit a mine and sank yesterday evening. The mine-sweepers now begin the task of clearing areas offshore prior to the arrival of the five Assault Forces U, O, G, J, and S. This work must be finished in the next three hours, before low water and the turning of the tide at 05:00 hours that will help carry the landing craft and the troops ashore.

Daybreak begins 15 minutes later, with sunrise officially occurring at 06:00 hours. Thirty minutes after that, the first of the assault troops will hit Utah and Omaha beaches at their scheduled H-Hour of 06:30. H-Hours for beaches in the British and Canadian sectors will begin 65 minutes later to catch the tide as it rises, west to east.

As the assault forces exit the cleared channels from England they reassemble in Transport Areas some 6 miles (10km) offshore. The warships tasked with the pre-landing bombardment take station in Fire Support Areas in front, and to the side, of the Transport Areas, with the smaller vessels such as destroyers acting as a screen ahead. From each Transport Area to the coast are cleared boat lanes, which will take the assault craft and landing ships to shore.

▲ ***American landing craft, including DUKW amphibious vehicles carrying supplies, stream toward the shore within hours of the first assault wave.***

▶ ***Flat-bottomed British landing craft like these gave their occupants an uncomfortable ride in choppy waters.***

▶ ***US troops leave England for France. The ambulances in the background must have been a sobering reminder of the fighting and mayhem that awaited them.***

At 02:30 hours, off Utah Beach, the HQ ship of Task Force U, USS *Bayfield,* drops anchor. Its commander, Admiral Moon, issues the order "Lower all landing craft," and within minutes unloading has begun. There is no sign of a reaction from the enemy, but there is real fear that they will launch an E-boat sortie out of Cherbourg.

GERMAN DEFENSES, *RESPONSES*

At 02:15 hours, General Speidel, at Army Group B HQ, receives another phone call. Major-General Pemsel, chief of staff of Seventh Army in Le Mans, tells him that a large-scale Allied air-borne operation is in progress, and that this may be the first moves in the Allied invasion. While some German soldiers have been in action since just after midnight, it seems that the higher up the German chain of command the news travels, the less it is believed. Seventh Army cannot go on full-scale alert without permission from OB West, and Speidel is unwilling to pass the information on at this hour of the morning. Personally, he does not believe it is the start of the invasion, but finally agrees to contact OB West HQ. He receives a reply to his message at about 02:40 hours. Von Rundstedt's staff informs Rommel's chief of staff that the field marshal "does not consider this to be a major operation."

Meanwhile, General Marcks, commander of LXXXIV Corps, is taking action in the face of a rapidly deteriorating situation. The 709th and 91st Divisions and the 915th Infantry Regiment near Bayeux are ordered to move against the airborne troops in the Cotentin. But Marcks's efforts are greatly hindered because many regimental officers are away from their posts attending Seventh Army war games in Rennes, and he cannot ask for help from the panzer divisions: they are held as an army group reserve, controlled from Berlin rather than by local commanders. The situation is particularly exasperating for General Feuchtinger, the commander of the 21st Panzer Division. He is sitting with

▼ ***American LCI (Landing Craft, Infantry) on their way across the Channel. Some 245 LCIs took part in the D-Day landings, half of which were supplied by the US Navy.***

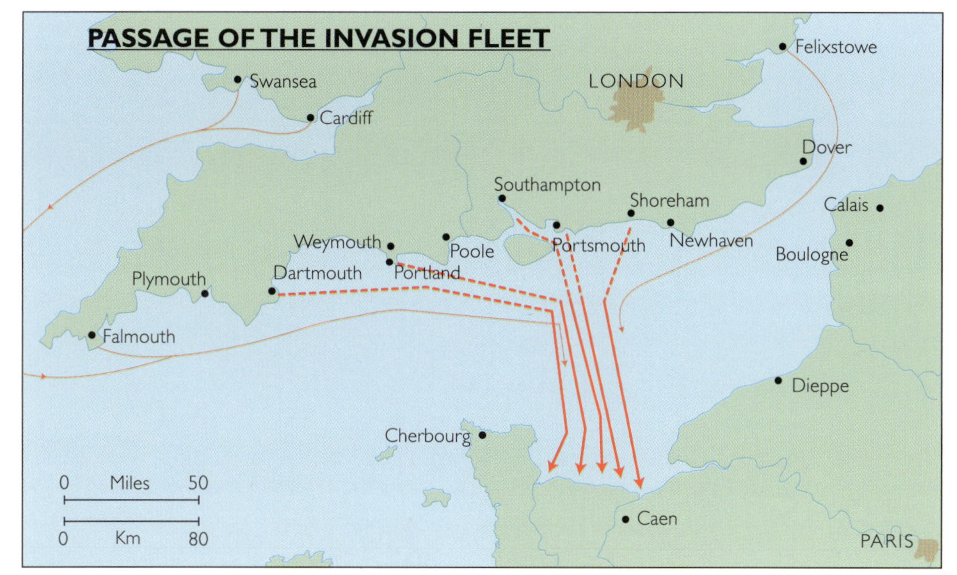

◀ ***The route to victory. The red lines denote the passage of the invasion fleet as it made its way from the many English harbors to the Normandy coast.***

his tanks west of the Orne, watching British airborne troops land in their thousands on the other side of the river, but is unable to move against them because he has no orders.

Out at sea it is at about 03:00 hours when German radar stations along the French coast finally discover the massive Allied invasion fleet crossing the Channel. In response, Admiral Kranke orders the coastal batteries under his command to engage and sends out a flotilla of three E-boats and two armed trawlers to sortie from Le Havre. News of the arrival of the Allied fleet is sent to the U-boat headquarters at Wilhelmshaven, Germany, which puts the boats of Group Landwirt, which is based on the Brittany and Biscay coasts, on alert.

02:50 HOURS

AIRBORNE ASSAULT, *BRITISH SECTOR*
Colonel Otway and men of the 9th Parachute Battalion set off from their DZ toward the Merville battery. The drops and glider landings for this operation have nearly all gone astray, leaving Otway with only 150 men out of the 600 he was planning to use in the attack. To make matters worse, none of the expected heavy equipment has arrived. The battery's defenses were meant to be tackled with mortars, flamethrowers, mine detectors, and scaling ladders; but all the battalion now has are its small arms plus one machine gun and 20 lengths of Bangalore torpedo. Otway is undeterred, and, like so many airborne soldiers this morning, decides to get on with the job anyway. The operation to destroy the guns must be completed by 05:50 hours, when a naval bombardment by cruiser HMS *Arethusa* is to begin.

Farther south, all except 13 of the gliders carrying the 6th Airborne HQ and reinforcements arrive, although 34 glider pilots are killed in the landings. Major-General Gale sets up a divisional HQ in Ranville. From the Orne Canal bridge, companies of the 7th Battalion, 5th Parachute Brigade, begin to attack German positions in Bénouville.

AIR CAMPAIGN, COASTAL TARGETS
As part of the pre-assault bombardment, aircraft of RAF Bomber Command attack enemy concentrations along the invasion coast from 03:14 hours. Over the next 75 minutes the villages of La Pernelle, Maisy, Longues, Mont-Fleury, and Houlgate are all attacked. The raids are heavy, with as many as 100 aircraft taking part in each, which leave the villages in ruin. Maisy is hit with over 508 tons (500 tonnes) of explosive in 14 minutes.

03:54–04:10 HOURS

AIRBORNE ASSAULT, *US SECTOR*
Gliders carrying the reinforcements and heavy equipment for the 101st and 82nd Airborne divisions begin to land. The DZ for the 101st is around the village of Hiesville, almost 6 miles

▶ ***To prevent the Allies from landing and moving easily, the Germans flooded vast areas of rural France. In some places the water was waist deep.***

(10km) from Utah Beach and 3 miles (5km) from the second of the four beach exits. The DZ for the 82nd is northwest of Ste Mère Eglise, between the road and rail line running north from Carentan. Out of the 52 gliders of the 82nd that left England, five actually land on the DZ and 15 others land within a couple of miles. But 22 are destroyed and 12 are badly damaged, many through collision with the sturdy Normandy hedgerows, which prove thicker and higher than intelligence reports had estimated. There are three deaths. Most of the jeeps the the gliders were carrying are destroyed, but 11 still work, as do eight of the anti-aircraft guns.

Of the gliders of the 101st, six land on the DZ with the majority of the others coming in within 2 miles (3km) of it. Five men are killed, including the assistant division commander, Brigadier-General Pratt, and the unfortunate pilots of the glider carrying the bulldozer, which breaks free on landing and smashes through the front of the aircraft, crushing them to death.

Nevertheless, this proves one of the more successful glider drops of the morning, and soon over 100 troops, with six of the surviving anti-tank guns, are establishing themselves around the drop zones.

The paratroopers by this time are beginning to assemble and organize, usually in groups of no more than a dozen men, often from different outfits. To identify friend from foe in the dark, each paratrooper has been issued a "cricket," a

metal toy that makes a clicking sound: one click being met with a two-click answer. The trouble is that men have lost their crickets in the drop and the toy sounds similar to the drawing of a rifle bolt. And the huge numbers of paratroopers wandering around Normandy in the dark is itself a problem. As one paratrooper recalled, "There were so many clicks and counterclicks that night that nobody could tell who was clicking at whom."

OPERATION NEPTUNE, *UTAH*

It is still dark as the transport ships of Task Force U begin to embark the first troops into their assault craft, the flat-bottomed, square-bowed LCA (Landing Craft, Assault), known as "Higgins" boats. These are ideal for landing on a beach, but in the 4ft (1.2m) swell now rising in the channel they make for a less than comfortable ride for soldiers who still have two and half hours to go until H-Hour. The troops embarking are from Companies B, C, F, and E, 2nd Battalion, 8th Infantry Regiment, 4th Division. They will be among the first men ashore on D-Day. Now that embarkation of the LCA is underway, eight LCTs (Landing Craft, Tanks), each carrying four DD (Duplex-Drive) amphibious tanks, form up at the line of departure, 4000 yds (3660m) from the two assault beaches designated as Tare Green and Uncle Red. They will be the first wave of vessels to sail toward Utah, the idea being to have tanks on the beach before the troops arrive. There are planned to be 26 waves of boats in the assault, which will be organized and guided by six control craft. For each beach, there will be one Patrol Craft acting as a primary control vessel, assisted by two LCC (Landing Craft, Control) fitted with radio and radar.

04:15 HOURS

AIRBORNE ASSAULT, *BRITISH SECTOR*

Colonel Otway launches his attack on the Merville battery, despite the fact that three gliders scheduled to land inside the battery perimeter with a company of paratroopers and sappers fail to arrive. However, in one of the few elements of the operation to go as planned, a reconnaissance party has been at work on the outer perimeter for the last couple of hours, cutting gaps in the wire and clearing four paths through the minefield. The enemy garrison is on alert, but unaware that its outer defenses have been breached. Otway decides on a surprise assault, attacking the main gate and the four artillery casemates simultaneously. He is banking on speed, surprise, and aggression to compensate for his lack of manpower and equipment. At 04:15 hours, a squad of seven men create a diversion with a rush on the main gate as Bangalore torpedoes tear two gaps in the inner wire. With a cry of "Everybody in," Otway leads the charge. Two teams of paratroopers break into the casemates with grenades, while a third destroys the machine-gun posts outside. The fighting inside the casemates quickly becomes the type of close-quarter battle the paratroopers are trained to win. Within 25 minutes of the start of the attack, Otway's men have captured the battery. Over 100 of the German garrison are dead, and 22 are prisoners. The paratroopers have taken 70 dead and wounded, reducing the colonel's battalion to 80 out of the 600 who left England last night.

Improvised charges are laid, the demolition explosives having been lost, and the guns—old French 75mm pieces, not the big German artillery guns that were expected—are blown up. With the job done, Otway leads his men on a march south toward the area where the 6th Airborne Division is concentrating its battalions along a ridge of high ground, east of Ranville.

To the southeast of Merville, from 04:00 hours, paratroopers attack six road and rail crossings over the Dives

▼ *As dawn broke in northern France, Allied paratroopers skirmished with German forces, trying to take key strategic junctions and positions.*

STRATEGY & TACTICS

THE LANDING BEACHES AND ASSAULT SECTORS

As laid down in Appendix VIII (Annex B) of the voluminous orders for Operation Neptune, the D-Day assault area covered a distance of 61.7 miles (98.7km) along the Calvados Coast of the Bay of Seine. The coast was divided up into the five assault areas that have gone down in history as the five D-Day beaches: Utah, Omaha, Gold, Juno, and Sword. In fact, this was not how the landing objectives were identified. To make navigation and identification during the assault precise, the orders divide the five areas into sectors, identified phonetically—Able, Baker, Charlie and so on—which were then subdivided into assault beaches, codenamed White, Green, and Red. In this way, the landings on Gold, for example, were to be made over Jig Green, Jig Red, King Green, and King Red.

River. At Bures and Troarn, bridges are demolished by Royal Engineers attached to the 3rd Parachute Squadron, while bridges at Varaville and Robehomme are targeted by men of the squadron's No.3 Troop, attached to the 1st Canadian Parachute Battalion. In one remarkable exploit, at Troarn, nine sappers, in a commandeered medical corps jeep, race through the main street under enemy fire to reach the bridge, which they demolish with explosives before making their get-away. By 09:30 hours, all crossings of the Dives have been cut. Because the Germans have flooded a huge area east of the river, their 711th Division is now isolated from the invasion bridgehead, making the Allied left flank now more secure.

05:00 HOURS

AIRBORNE ASSAULT, *US SECTOR*
After a chaotic drop and several hours wandering in the dark, US paratroopers are beginning to get into the fight, which at first involves them in a series of small actions: ambushing German patrols, clearing villages, and hamlets and establishing roadblocks.

As dawn approaches, men of the 101st Airborne are moving to hold the road exits from Utah Beach. Exit 3, around the village of Audouville-la-Hubert, is secured by Lieutenant-Colonel Robert Cole of the 502nd Regiment and a mixed unit of 75 men who have marched in from the area of Ste Mère Eglise. To the south, men of the 506th Regiment are advancing to secure Exit 2 at Houdenienville and Exit 1 at Pouppeville. Meanwhile, farther south along the Douve River, near Brévands, about 100 men of the 501st Regiment, led by Captain Charles G. Shettle, are dug in and holding the northwest bank, denying the enemy a road crossing and therefore access to the left flank of Utah Beach.

Inland, in the 82nd Airborne area east of the River Merderet, men of the 3rd Battalion, 505th Regiment, led by Lieutenant-Colonel Krause, capture Ste Mère Eglise. Amazingly, they find the German garrison in bed, despite the earlier fighting when US paratroopers landed in the middle of the village! Krause has his men attack the billets with knives and grenades: 30 of the enemy surrender immediately, and 10 are killed when they offer resistance. In support of Krause, the 505th's 2nd Battalion, under Lieutenant Colonel Vandervoort, advances about 2 miles (3km) north of the village to establish a defense line at Neuville-au-Plain, across the main road to Cherbourg.

AIR CAMPAIGN, *COASTAL TARGETS*
Bomber Command begins the last of its pre-dawn attacks, with a raid by 110 Lancasters on Ouistreham, the port north of Caen. As day begins to break, at 05:15 hours, the RAF bombers depart, but the assault is resumed at first light 45 minutes later by the heavy bombers of the US Eighth Army Air Force. They attack targets behind Omaha Beach and the British sector, west of Caen. The area around Utah is tasked to medium bombers of the Ninth Army Air Force, because the lighter bomb loads, to be dropped at lower levels, are likely to be safer for the Allied airborne troops now operating there. This wave of attacks is part of the Joint Fire Plan, designed to suppress coastal defenses as the assault craft come ashore. They will continue until about 08:00 hours, when fighters and fighter-bombers take

▶ ***Allied bombers dropped many tons of bombs onto German positions along the coast and the beaches. However, much of it was poorly targeted.***

▼ ***Young German troops manning an anti-aircraft position pose for a photograph before D-Day. Like many of their comrades, they are barely adults.***

▶ ***German troops lay out barbed wire before D-Day. By dawn of June 6, all such preparations to hinder the Allied invasion were about to be tested.***

over to provide close-air support for the ground troops and fighter cover for the fleet and bridgehead.

OPERATION NEPTUNE, *JUNO AND SWORD*

Around 05:00 hours, the two Royal Navy midget submarines, *X-20* and *X-23*, having arrived 24 hours early for D-Day, finally surface after having spent the best part of the last 72 hours submerged. *X-20* takes up station off Juno, while *X-23* lies off Sword. Their green flashing lights mark the positions of the two beaches. Their presence is important, because the beaches here are flat and almost featureless. There are also several miles of offshore reef and rocky coast on the east side of Juno, to be marked out, for safety.

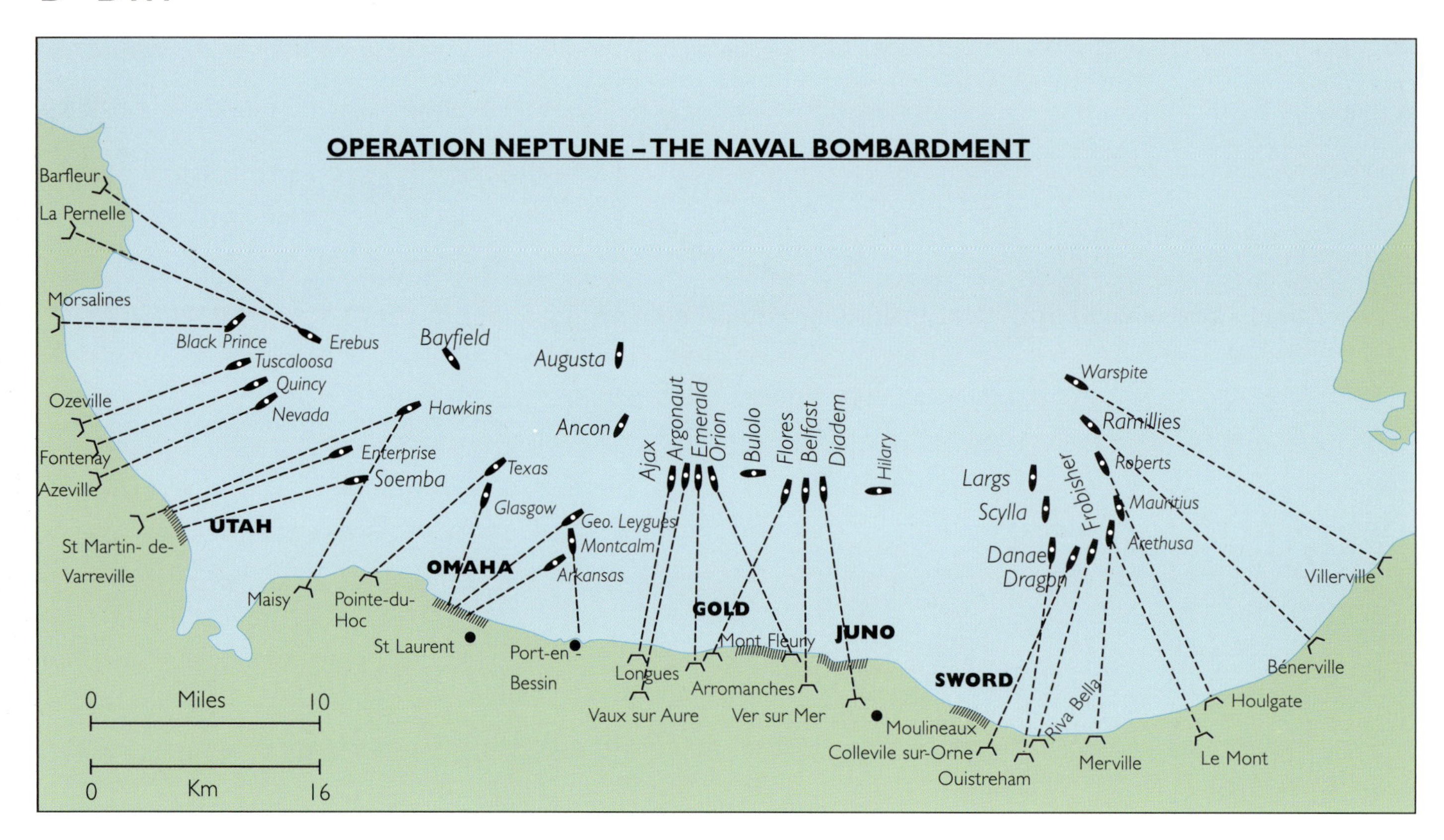

▲ ***The positions of the Allied warships in the bombardment groups. The lines indicate the direction of their bombardment of coastal defenses.***

GERMAN DEFENSES, *U-BOATS*

Also at around 05:00 hours, with a major Allied landing now clearly underway, the U-boats of Group "Landwirt" (Farmer) are ordered into the Channel. A total of 36 boats prepare to set out from Brest, St Nazaire, La Pallice and Lorient, and they include all available snorkel boats: these are submarines fitted with the latest technology, and they are able to remain submerged for long periods.

05:30 HOURS

OPERATION NEPTUNE, *UTAH*

In the middle of Task Force U's assault area are the two tiny islands of St Marcouf, about 4 miles (6km) offshore. They are suspected of holding a German observation post. To clear and

▼ ***Allied ships in the Channel heading for France. Note how each vessel has a barrage balloon above. The balloons were designed to discourage dive-bombing.***

secure them, men of the 4th and 24th Cavalry Squadrons are landed. They do not find any enemy German personnel there, but the soldiers take casualties from the mines and booby traps previously laid by the enemy.

OPERATION NEPTUNE, *SWORD*
German Navy E-boats launch a torpedo attack on Task Force S. Under orders from Navy Group West, three E-boats and two armed trawlers had sortied from Le Havre at 03:48 hours, and by 05:15 hours the E-boats are closing in on the fleet. Taking advantage of a smokescreen laid by the Allies to shield their own ships from the gun batteries at Le Havre, the E-boats begin their attack at 05:30 hours. Torpedoes narrowly miss the battleships *Ramillies* and *Warspite* and the headquarters ship HMS *Largs*; but the Norwegian destroyer *Svenner* is hit amidships. She breaks in two and goes to the bottom, although most of her crew are saved. The E-boats attempt to make their escape, but they are tracked by the radar on HMS *Warspite*, and the warship opens fire, sinking one of the E-boats. Other Allied warships also begin firing, and the cruiser *Arethusa* claims one trawler sunk. This attack is to be the only surface action the German Navy will fight today.

05:36 HOURS

OPERATION NEPTUNE, *UTAH*
The naval bombardment of the Normandy coast begins ahead of schedule to counter German gunfire. For nearly two hours German coastal batteries have been under orders to open fire on the fleet, but, because their targeting radar has been hit by air attack, only as first light approaches can they find targets. Off Utah Beach the US destroyers *Fitch* and *Corry* are shelled at about 05:05 hours, followed soon after by the minesweepers working inshore. The cruiser HMS *Black Prince* returns fire and quickly finds herself targeted. With a battle escalating by the minute, the commander of the Western Task Force Bombardment Group, Admiral Deyo, decides to order all his ships to open fire, 20 minutes ahead of the planned time. By 05:36 hours, Utah and Omaha are under naval bombardment. Off Gold Beach, the bombardment ships are in action even earlier: the cruiser *Orion* opens fire on a battery at Arromanches at 05:10 hours.

At his command post near the Orne Canal bridge, 5 miles (8km) from the coast, Major Howard, whose D-Day was already nearly six hours old, could feel the effects of the naval guns:

"The barrage coming in was quite terrific. It was as though you could feel the whole ground shaking toward the coast, and this was going on like hell. Soon afterward it seemed to get nearer. Well, they were obviously lifting the barrage farther inland as our boats and craft came in, and it was very easy, standing there and hearing all this going on and seeing all the smoke over in that direction, to realize what exactly was happening and keeping our fingers crossed for those poor buggers coming in by sea."

▶ ***The German Goliath was a miniature radio-controlled, motorized vehicle, designed as a remote tank-killer. A number were found near the landing beaches.***

▼ ***The American battleship USS* Nevada *providing naval gunfire support for the US troops about to assault Utah Beach on D-Day.***

▲ ***A French house in ruins. After the landings, the effects of Allied naval and aerial bombardment on the areas near the beachheads could clearly be seen.***

06:30–07:45 HOURS

THE BEACH ASSAULTS,
US, BRITISH & CANADIAN SECTORS

This short period of time, of one and a quarter hours, marks the H-Hours for the beach assaults themselves. Against the vicissitudes of sea currents and geography, facing unpredictable enemy opposition, and in a situation where the neatly drawn plans so often have to be cast aside in favour of on-the-spot improvisation, Allied seaborne forces attempt to gain a toehold on Nazi-occupied northern Europe. It is fragile hold, to be sure, and by midnight many units will be well short of their D-Day objectives. But it will be enough. (The momentous events of the seaborne assaults on Utah, Omaha, Gold, Juno, and Sword beaches are described in their own separate chapters, below.)

The landings will test how well the airborne forces have prepared the ground in the early morning, while those now vulnerable and scattered airborne troops are eagerly awaiting the arrival of reinforcements and armour from the beaches. The beach landings will also make quite it clear to Hitler's commanders that this is, indeed, the Allied invasion.

THE BRITISH AIRBORNE ASSAULT

KEY
Merville battery
Drop Zones

0 Miles 2
0 Km 3

Ouistreham
Cabourg
Merville
MARSH
W
Y
X
N
V
K
Bénouville
Pegasus Bridge
Bréville
Varaville
Ranville
Caen Canal
Robehomme
River Orne
Colombelles
Bures
Caen
Troarn

◀ ***The British drop zones were spread out northeast of Caen, on both sides of the Orne River and its canal. The famous Pegasus Bridge lay between zones X and Y.***

07:30–24:00 HOURS

AIRBORNE ASSAULT,
BRITISH SECTOR

As the British 3rd Division begins to land on Sword, the 6th Airborne Division is holding the Allied left flank, east of Caen, with five battalions centered on the canal and river bridges of the Orne. The 6th has no artillery, the naval guns offshore can reach only as far south as Le Plein, and its tactical reserve is down to just 60 men.

According to the schedule, units of the 3rd Division are due to be at the Orne two hours after H-Hour; but by 09:00 hours there is no sign of them, and German activity everywhere is increasing. There is street fighting in Bénouville and the bridges are under

▶ ***Dozens of Allied gliders lie abandoned by the troops they were carrying. The three gliders in the center illustrate how close each landing came to disaster.***

constant sniper fire. At about10:00 hours, the Germans make a sortie in two small gunboats down the canal from Ouistreham and a lone fighter-bomber makes a bomb run, though both actions are ineffective.

The situation east of the river stays relatively quiet until about 11:00 hours, when 21st Panzer's Battle Group Von Luck attempts to take Ranville from the south. The two-hour fight ends when the Germans withdraw to regroup.

At 13:30 hours, Lord Lovat's commandos, of the 1st Special Service Brigade (1st SSB), reach the canal, and are deployed in the frontlines. A link has been made with the beachhead, but 6th Airborne's hold remains tenuous throughout the afternoon and evening, as it fights off renewed attacks from Battle Group Von Luck and has to reinforce Bénouville. The division's area is finally secured at about 20:50 hours, with the arrival of 246 gliders bringing in the 6th Air Landing Brigade. It includes three battalions of infantry, together with engineers, light artillery, and a regiment of light tanks.

AIRBORNE ASSAULT, *US SECTOR*

In two separate operations, about 128 gliders land in the Cotentin between 20:50 and 23:00 hours, with ammunition and supplies for the 101st and 82nd Airborne. Among the heavy equipment and reinforcements also brought in are a field artillery regiment with 16 105mm howitzers, medical and signals troops, and nearly 100 jeeps.

OPERATION NEPTUNE, *FOLLOW-UP*

At about 16:00, the lead convoys of the follow-up Task Forces B and L begin to arrive off the Normandy coast to catch the afternoon high tide. Force B arrives off Omaha Beach, carrying regiments of the 1st and 29th Divisions, engineers and headquarters troops. Force L, off Gold and Juno beaches, brings units of the 3rd (Canadian) Division, the 51st (Highland) Division and the tactical HQ of Montgomery's 21st Army Group.

▼ ***The 6th Airborne Division positions east of the Orne were to be reinforced by 12:00 hours by lightly armed commandos such as these.***

On D-Day evening, Montgomery and his staff leave Southwick House to join the HQ. They embark on the destroyer HMS *Faulknor* and sail by 22:00 hours.

GERMAN AIR FORCE, *RESPONSES*
Despite being heavily outnumbered, some units and aircraft of Air Fleet 3 manage to break through the Allied fighter screen in an attempt to disrupt Allied landings. At about 09:00 hours, two FW 190 fighters fly a low-level sortie along the invasion coast from Sword to Omaha. Later in the day, 50 FW 190s of Ground Attack Wing 4 are ordered from eastern France to bases around Tours, south of Normandy. Allied fighters shoot down five aircraft, but enough land to launch three sorties against Sword Beach in the afternoon. They are all driven off with losses. From 22:30 hours, German aircraft, in ones and twos, begin uncoordinated raids on the invasion fleet.

▼ ***British infantry from Sword look on as gliders of the 6th Airborne Division make their main assault at 21:00 hours.***

► ***General "Sepp" Dietrich, commander of I SS Panzer Corps (left, wearing peaked cap). He was caught unawares on D-Day, visiting a unit in Belgium.***

GERMAN DEFENSES, *MOBILIZING*
The landings of US paratroopers in the Cotentin have LXXXIV Corps in St Lô on a state of alert before dawn, and by 08:30 hours its commander, General Marcks, has realized this is an invasion. Along the coast both the 352nd and 716th divisions are being pushed inland and there is news of British tanks active north of Bayeux and Caen.

At the Paris HQ of OB West, Field Marshal von Rundstedt can get no orders from OKW—because Hitler is asleep—and finally acts on his own initiative. He hands control of the 21st Panzer Division to the Seventh Army and Marcks's corps, finally freeing division commander General Feuchtinger from his eight-hour wait for orders to move against the British. Meanwhile, at the chateau at La Roche-Guyon, HQ of Army Group B, chief of staff General Speidel phones Rommel at his home in Germany with the news. The field marshal sets off immediately, but does not reach his headquarters until 21:30 hours.

During the afternoon, OKW finally rises from its stupor: 12th SS Panzer and Panzer Lehr are taken out of reserve and placed under the control of Seventh Army, with orders to advance west toward Caen for an attack on June 7. Command of the panzers is taken away from LXXXIV Corps, with the arrival near Normandy of I SS Panzer Corps

▲ ***The smashed remains of a British Horsa glider that landed on D-Day.***

HQ under Lieutenant-General Josef "Sepp" Dietrich.

At 16:53 hours, with nine Allied divisions now ashore, Hitler sends his first message of the day to von Rund-stedt. It emphasizes "the desire of the Supreme Commander [Hitler] to have the enemy in the bridgehead annihilated by the evening of 6 June," and concludes: "The beachhead must be cleaned up not later than tonight."

DECISIVE MOMENTS

HOW THE WORLD LEARNED OF D-DAY

The Nazi regime itself first told the world about D-Day; and US newspapers first published that news. Nazi Propaganda minister Joseph Goebbels, spotting an opportunity if the landings were defeated on the beaches, had the news transmitted from Berlin via his TransOcean News Agency at 07:00 hours. The Associated Press, working seven hours behind Berlin, picked this up, and the *New York Times* had a special edition on the city's streets only 90 minutes after the Omaha landing began.

In Britain, with news tightly controlled by SHAEF, the public learned of D-Day only at 09:30 hours, when the BBC broadcast SHAEF's terse "Communiqué No.1": "Allied naval forces, supported by strong air forces, began landing Allied armies this morning on the coast of northern France." Meanwhile, journalists from the free world were locked in a Ministry of Information building. They were given four press conferences during the day, but could not leave the building without escort, and had to submit their stories for censoring before publication.

June 6 Utah Beach

American troops made good progress on Utah, meeting light resistance from poorly armed German soldiers. Engineers had cleared the beach by noon. Company strength attacks took out enemy strongpoints, and troops waded neck-deep through fields flooded by the Germans. By midnight on June 6, 23,000 men had landed at Utah, plus 1700 tanks, guns, and trucks, with only 197 casualties suffered.

▲ *An Allied rocket ship, essentially a converted LCT, fires high-explosive ordnance onto German positions. These craft were top-secret before D-Day.*

H-Hour: 06:30 Hours

At 05:30 hours the first waves of landing craft from Task Force U are on their way toward beaches Uncle Red and Tare Green, which form a front of about 2200 yds (2010m). In the lead are eight LCTs (Landing Craft, Tanks), which carry 32 DD (Duplex-Drive) tanks of the 70th Tank Battalion, scheduled for launch 5000yds (4575m) offshore. Behind them are assault craft

▶ *A US battleship pounds enemy positions on the shore, as an LCT, carrying reinforcements of US troops, heads for Utah Beach.*

▲ ***Wading through the surf, US troops make their way onto Utah Beach to support the advance parties that had landed before them.***

carrying companies of the 1st and 2nd Battalion, 8th Infantry Regiment, and a detachment of engineers. These specialists, organized into eight-man Underwater Demolition Teams (UDTs), are tasked with blowing up beach obstacles ahead of the rising tide, clearing safe areas for the succeeding waves of invasion craft to beach.

As the assault troops close in on the beaches, the Joint Fire Plan moves into its next phase. The naval bombardment lifts, and soon afterward 270 Marauder medium bombers of the Ninth Army Air Force make a bomb run on enemy positions. At sea, close fire support for the troops will be given by LCGs (Landing Craft, Guns), armed with 4.7in guns, which take position on the flanks of the first boat wave. Also on station, about 700 yds (640m) offshore, are converted tank landing craft fitted with rocket launchers, which can blanket 170 yds (155m) of beach with 790 5in rockets launched in salvo.

The boat waves are still several thousand yards from the beach when their landing schedule starts to break down. A strong tidal current is pushing the landing craft off course, and at about 05:45 hours the Patrol Craft acting as the primary control vessel for Tare Red hits a mine and sinks. The LCC (Landing Craft, Control), which are to set up the line of departure, cannot take a bearing on the beach because it is hidden by the dust and smoke of the shore bombardment. They identify the wrong stretch of coast, and the assault craft carrying troops set off to land 1500 yds (1370m) south of the intended beach area.

Meanwhile, the launch plan for the DD tanks has also gone wrong. Having lost their control vessel, the LCT are now behind the first assault wave when they should be in front. The disorganization is made worse when an LCT hits a mine and sinks, taking four DD tanks with it. The commander of the remaining control vessel decides at this point to abandon the schedule and take the remaining LCT inshore and have them launch their tanks about a mile from the beach, to land 15 minutes behind the first assault wave.

At 06:30 hours, exactly on schedule, the 8th Infantry hits Utah Beach. The tide has pushed them even farther south, and they are now 2000yds (1830m) from where they should be. It means companies have lost their assault objectives; but this area proves

▼ ***Captured German prisoners are marched, hands on heads, to a holding pen by troops of the US 4th Infantry.***

▶ ***US soldiers make their way inland from Utah Beach through the fields, which were flooded by German forces in an attempt to prevent glider landings.***

to be a far better proposition. It is less heavily defended, and the companies make it ashore almost unopposed.

In the first wave is the assistant commander of the 4th Infantry Division, Brigadier-General Theodore Roosevelt. The general has volunteered to be among the first men ashore, and it is his command decision on the beach that sets the US Army's campaign in Europe in motion. Realizing that his men have landed in the wrong place, Roosevelt calls an impromptu conference with 8th Infantry's three senior officers. The choice is whether to transport the regiment to where it should be according to the plan or move inland from where it is, which, Roosevelt discovers, is opposite the causeway to Exit 2: in the plan, Victor Green and Victor Red. With DD tanks now landing, UDT engineers blowing up obstacles and troops beginning to advance inland, the decision is effectively made already. In later reports, Roosevelt is reported as giving the order with the words: "We'll start the invasion from right here."

▼ ***A US mobile signaling battery sets up its equipment on the shore of Utah Beach. The equipment was used to signal to shipping out at sea in the Channel.***

By 08:00 hours units of the next infantry regiment, the 22nd, have begun to arrive, while along the shoreline UDT engineers have cleared 700 yds (640m) of beach, and are preparing to blow gaps in the concrete sea wall, to allow vehicles access inland. German resistance along the beachhead has all but collapsed. It is found that the sector has been held by a regiment of Osttruppen (Eastern troops), mainly from Soviet Georgia, who surrender at the first opportunity. There is still some shelling by 88mm artillery, mainly at the landing craft, but save for random mortar fire the build-up of troops and supplies on the beach goes on without hindrance. The third infantry regiment, the 12th, begins to land at 10:30 hours. At 10:45 hours, Admiral Moon, commander of Task Force U, receives a signal from the beachhead: "Landings can be made anywhere on Red Beach ... obstacles no longer obstacles." Six waves of landing craft set off immediately.

The assault battalions begin to move inland to secure the roads from the beachhead, in order to link up with the paratroopers they hope have secured the exits. They are faced with two obstacles. The dunes behind the beach are seeded with tens of thousands of anti-personnel and anti-tank mines, while farther inland an area up to 1 mile (1.6km) wide has been flooded. The 2nd Battalion, 8th Infantry, moves south along the beach road to pick up Exit 1 causeway, which leads to Pouppeville. With support from tanks,

▶ ***Carrying with them all the necessary equipment to take the fight to the Germans, GIs of the US 4th Infantry Division move inland from Utah Beach.***

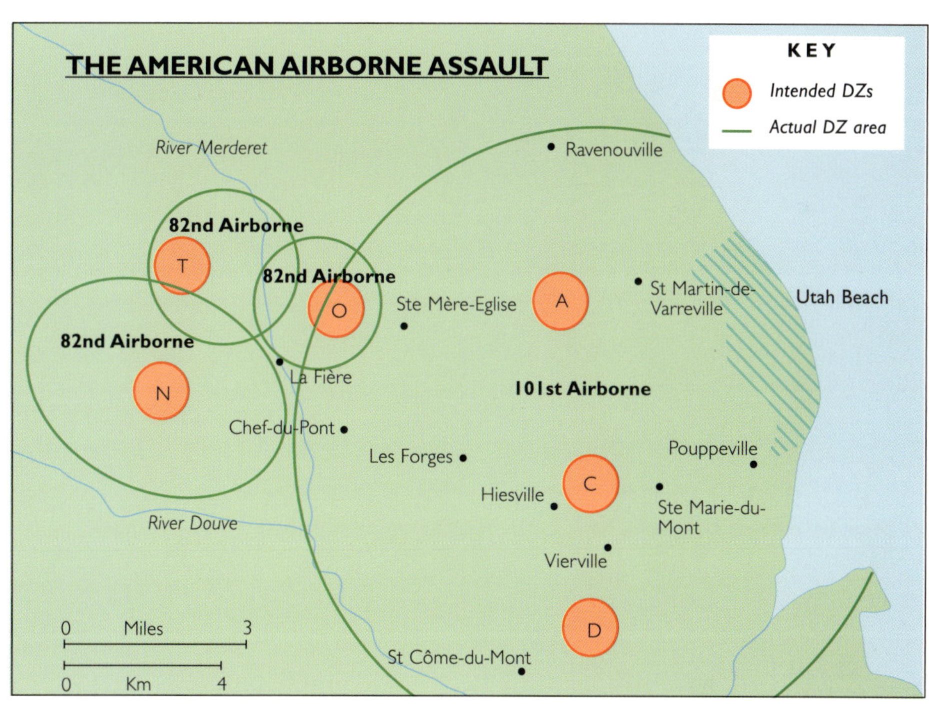

▲ ***The intended drop zones (DZ) for the US airborne forces. However, the area that the parachute and glider forces actually landed in was very wide.***

German strongpoints are easily overrun, but the battalion takes casualties from the anti-personnel mines. At 11:10 hours, the first contact is made between US seaborne forces and the paratroopers when the battalion crosses the causeway and links up with men of the 501st Regiment, 101st Airborne Division, east of Pouppeville. The village has been under attack from a mixed force of paratroopers since about 08:00 hours, and by now is largely in US hands. The 8th Infantry move in to secure it, while the paratroopers advance east to their next objective, the village of Ste Marie-du-Mont. To the north, the 8th Infantry's 3rd and 1st battalions are moving inland to secure the causeways to Exits 2 and 3.

◀ ***A US paratrooper, armed with an M1 Thompson submachine gun, boards his transport the night before the Allied airborne assault.***

By late-morning there is serious congestion on the beachhead. None of the exits has been entirely secured, and vehicles are beginning to back up along the beach roads. This causes difficulties for the beach controllers, the specialist battalions tasked with organizing the movement of assault forces off the beaches. For the colonels commanding the 12th and 22nd Infantry regiments, it means their men cannot use the roads to get inland, making a bad situation worse. They are already a long way south of where they should be, and with time moving on, reaching their D-Day objectives will mean immediate action. The commanders decide to take the difficult option and march their battalions across the flooded country toward the higher ground around the village of St Martin-de-Varreville, due to be in the hands of the 101st Airborne. From there, the 12th will continue on to the area northeast of Ste Mère Eglise, held, according to the plan, by the 82nd Airborne, while the 22nd Infantry will move north to hold the right flank of the bridgehead, between St Germain-de-Varreville and the coast.

The march takes nearly four hours to cover just over 1 miles (1.6km). One sergeant in the 12th Infantry later recalled the experience of the journey: "Aerial reconnaissance had estimated that the flooded area was maybe ankle deep, except in irrigation ditches, which they estimated to be about eighteen inches deep. Well, they made a big mistake. That flooded area was in some places up to your waist and the irrigation ditches were over your head. Some brave souls would swim across the irrigation ditches and throw toggle ropes back and haul the rest of us across."

Despite the difficulties of the march, both regiments make it across the inundated plain without encountering any Germans, save an occasional sniper. Clear of the floods, the 12th Infantry makes a rapid advance through St Martin-de-Varreville, and by dusk, about 22:30 hours, is over 5 miles (8km) inland at Beuzeville-au-Plain northeast of Ste Mère Eglise, and preparing to move north. The 12th Infantry has a battalion of the 502nd Parachute Infantry (of the 101st) on its right. The 22nd Infantry, meanwhile, holds St Germain de Varreville with two battalions, while a third has moved up the beach road to hold a position 4 miles (6km) north of the assault beaches. By nightfall on D-Day, the right flank of the Allied invasion front is being held by seven battalions of infantry.

By midnight on June 6, the 8th Infantry, having gained access to the roads leading from Exits 1,2, and 3, and supported by tanks, are over 6 miles (9km) inland. The 2nd Battalion has moved through the village of St Marie-du-Mont and made contact with the 3rd Battalion from Exit 2 to the north. They have also seized the crossroads of the main Carentan–Cherbourg road at Les Forges and are 2 miles (3km) south of Ste Mère Eglise; but they now face a large pocket of stiff German resistance before they can relieve the paratroopers who have been holding the village for hours. Facing the Germans to the east is the 1st Battalion, which has advanced up the road from Exit 3 through the hamlet of Audouville la Hubert.

The D-Day landings on Utah Beach can be reckoned a qualified success. Over 20,000 troops have been landed, with 1700 vehicles, while the casualty figure for the 4th Division is only 197, of whom 60 have been lost at sea. The Utah bridgehead, however, remains very small and the division's advance is nearly 7 miles (11km) short of the D-Day objective set by 21st Army Group.

AIRBORNE ASSAULT, *UTAH AREA*

At 09:30 hours, three hours after the landings on Utah Beach began, the Germans launch a counterattack south of Ste Mère Eglise, in a bid to retake the village captured at dawn by the 82nd Airborne's 505th Regiment. The 2nd Battalion, under Lieutenant-Colonel Vandervoort, holding a position 2 miles (3km) north of the village at Neuville-au-Plain, is pulled back to strengthen defenses, leaving only a platoon of 42 men to hold Neuville, now under attack from units of the German 1058th Regiment. Out-numbered five to one, the paratroopers hold them off for the next eight hours. But just 16 out of the 42 paratroopers survive the fight. South of the town, the German assault is held, and a company sized counterattack by the paratroopers on a German convoy on the Carentan road secures Ste Mère Eglise for the rest of D-Day.

▼ ***As US forces create a bridgehead, hundreds of extra troops, as well as vehicles and equipment, flood ashore to support the thrust inland. It was a scene of organized chaos.***

▲ ***A knocked-out US Sherman tank, surrounded by the wreckage of other pieces of equipment, lies stricken on Utah Beach.***

To the west of the village, along the Merderet, fighting continues throughout the day. Elements of the 82nd are trying to secure bridges at La Fière and Chef-du-Pont, and make contact with isolated groups of paratroopers holding positions west of the river, around Amfreville, who are under threat from the German 1057th Regiment.

Along the Douve River to the south, units of the 101st are also having difficulty seizing their objectives. One of the most important of these, for the invasion's planners, is the lock gates at la Barquette. By mid-morning, a force led by Captain Shettle holds the north bank of the river, near le Port; but farther upstream paratroopers have met strong opposition from a battalion of the German 1058th Regiment in the town of St Côme-du-Mont. To the south, units of the élite German 6th Parachute Regiment, based in Carentan, are defending the road and rail bridges over the Douve that the 101st is meant to destroy. However, by nightfall a mixed force of 150 paratroopers has succeeded in taking the lock gates and has dug-in on the south bank.

After a chaotic series of drops and landings, the American airborne divisions hold some of their D-Day objectives—but tenuously; and all around they face superior numbers of German forces. Fortunately, the disorganized assault has confused the Germans, who are staying in their fixed positions and not counterattacking. They do not know just how many paratroopers they face and what their objectives are. Aggression in the face of the enemy has hidden the fact that the two airborne divisions are dangerously understrength. Of more than 12,000 para-troopers that boarded in England barely 5000 are organized and facing the enemy at the end of D-Day. The rest are scattered, lost, or dead.

June 6 Omaha Beach

On Omaha US troops struggled to make headway on the beach as intense German machine-gun and mortar fire inflicted enormous losses on the invaders. The amphibious DD tanks designated to take out fortified positions sank like stones, leaving the infantry exposed. Only acts of heroism and supreme bravery forced the Germans back.

06:30 Hours, *H-Hour*

The first minesweepers arrived off Omaha just after midnight, and by 00:55 hours had completed sweeping and identifying the Transport Area with marker buoys. By 02:20 hours, the bombardment warships were arriving, and 30 minutes later the first 16 transport ships of Task Force O, commanded by Rear-Admiral John L. Hall, began dropping anchor 11 miles (17.5km) offshore. The Task Force is anchoring this far from the coast to be out of range of German 155mm guns, believed to be in concrete emplacements on the cliffs of the Pointe-du-Hoc, about 5 miles (8km) west of Vierville-sur-Mer. The guns are reckoned to impose such a threat that a Ranger Group, made up of the 2nd and 5th battalions, are to make an assault to capture and destroy them.

For the assault on Omaha to work, V Corps is relying on overwhelming firepower to break the coastal defenses, allowing the first wave of infantry to land largely unopposed. The bombardment will be provided by air force bombers, naval warships, and DD (Duplex-Drive) tanks, which are due to land five minutes ahead of H-hour. The first assault wave will consist of eight infantry companies, each assaulting one beach sector. On the right are four companies of the 116th Regiment, and on the left four companies of the 16th Regiment. Each has been trained to tackle a specific draw (ravine exit). The plan is not to fight on the beach but to move inland immediately to control the beach exits and secure perimeters around assembly areas near the villages Vierville-sur-Mer, St Laurent, and Colleville. For this reason they are heavily laden with over 60lb (132kg) of equipment, including mortars, flame-throwers, and demolition equipment. There will be no charge up the beach.

Once the draws are secure, engineering equipment will land to

◀ ***The view of Omaha Beach as seen from the deck of USS* Ancon*, the flagship of the landing forces in that sector.***

▶ ***The US battleship USS* Nevada *fires a salvo with her heavy guns at enemy shore batteries on the Cherbourg Peninsula on D-Day.***

clear the shingle bank and anti-tank ditch—tracked vehicles cannot move on the stones of the shingle. This will allow tanks and vehicles to move up the bluffs and advance inland.

The plan goes wrong from the very first. The naval bombardment begins on schedule at 05:50 hours, but the air bombardment, due to strike at 06:00 hours, does not materialize. Five

▲ *American landing craft carrying troops stream toward Omaha Beach. In the background sits USS Augusta, the Western Task Force invasion flagship.*

▼ *The massive guns of USS Nevada fire yet another salvo at German positions along the French coastline.*

STRATEGY & TACTICS

THE CHOICE OF OMAHA

A seaborne assault on Omaha beach was always part of the Allied invasion plan. Even the operation proposed by COSSAC in December 1943, using a limited front of three divisions, envisaged a landing west of Port-en-Bessin, between the villages of Vierville-sur-Mer, St Laurent and Colleville.

The reason was geography. Between the estuary of the River Douve and the village of Arromanches to the east, a distance of 25 miles (40km), the area has the only firm sandy beach suitable for a landing. The beach itself is about 6 miles (9.5km) long and lies in a crescent shape, between cliffs which rise to 100ft (30m). At low tide the beach is about 300yds (275m) wide, and in 1944 was backed by a wide stretch of shingle about 6ft (2m) high. Behind this was a sea wall of wood and stone, a beach road, and area of marshy ground up to 200yds (180m) wide. Rising up from this is a huge escarpment: a series of steep, scrub-covered bluffs over 160ft (50m) high, which dominate the whole beach. For the invasion troops with their vehicles and artillery, the only way off the beach and up to the plateau above was through four small ravines, or draws. Only the most westerly of these had a paved surface and led from the beach road to Vierville, about 0.5 mile (1km) away; the next, near some deserted beach houses at Les Moulin, was a dirt road leading to St Laurent; the third was no more than a dirt track, while the fourth led to Colleville.

To assault this type of ground from the sea posed one of the greatest challenges of the whole D-Day operation; but it was essential the attack succeeded. It held the key to the Allied right flank. With the invasion front extended to Utah Beach, US divisions fighting in the Cotentin Peninsula would be cut off and in danger of being overwhelmed by German units from Brittany—unless the men from Omaha could make it inland and link up with the British sector beginning at Gold Beach, near Arromanches.

hundred heavy bombers of the Eighth Army Air Force miss the coast completely because of low cloud, and drop 1200 tons (1220 tonnes) of bombs 3 miles (5km) inland. At sea, meanwhile, the DD tanks are sinking. Launched 5000yds (4575m) offshore at 05:40 hours, no consideration has been made for the rough seas. A strong tidal current and westerly wind whip up a swell that swamps all but 5 of the 32 first-wave tanks. The rough seas are also pulling the assault craft out of position, and as they approach the beach at 06:30 hours, most of them are over 1000yds (900m) east of where they should be. Meanwhile, the naval bombardment comes to an end after just 40 minutes—not enough time to destroy the German defences. As the landing craft approach the beach at H-hour, the German defenders hold their fire: but as soon as the craft beach and their ramps go down, every German gun on Omaha opens up on the US troops.

It is a slaughter. The infantry land to find not one tank on the beach and all the German defenses intact. Boat-loads of men are killed before they even leave their landing craft. As enemy fire increases, the crews of many assault craft stop too far from shore or hit submerged sandbars, and the troops jump into deep water and drown. Those that do make it ashore,

▶ ***Approaching Omaha Beach, under heavy German machine-gun fire, US troops jump from the ramp of a Coast Guard landing craft and head for shore.***

▼ ***Seen from another landing craft, hundreds of US soldiers struggle to get ashore. On entering the water, many had to abandon their heavy kit to avoid drowning, and arrived on land unarmed.***

STRATEGY & TACTICS

GERMAN DEFENSES AT OMAHA

German commanders had also identified the beach between Vierville and Colleville as a potential landing site, and from April 1944 had been making preparations to defend it. This work turned the already difficult terrain along Omaha Beach into an almost impregnable defensive position.

Along the beach there were three belts of anti-landing obstacles, located between the high and low tidal marks. At the high water line, beyond the shingle embankment, there was a triple belt of barbed wire and mines along the sea wall. Beyond the beach road, the Germans dug an anti-tank ditch 6ft (1.8m) deep. The first bunkers were located on either side of the entrances to four draws (ravines). The draw codenamed D1, which carried the beach road to Vierville, was blocked by a concrete barrier over 12ft (3.6m) thick. The bluffs above were defended with mines, barbed wire, and trip-wired explosive charges. The flat marshy land adjoining the bluffs was also mined.

It was above the beach that German forces concentrated their most powerful defenses. On the crest of the plateau, overlooking the four draws, were eight concrete strongpoints, manned by up to 30 men. They were each equipped with about 10 machine guns and heavier weapons, including 50mm cannon and artillery pieces of 75mm or 88mm calibre. To support these positions, mortars, rocket launchers, and light artillery pieces were located in emplacements inland, while anti-tank guns covered the exits from the draws. These weapons were pre-sighted on positions along the beach and had overlapping fields of fire. The crescent shape of the beach also allowed the positioning of emplacements on the cliffs at either end to provide enfilading fire by artillery and machine guns along the length of the beach. Manning these defenses were about 800 men of the 916th Grenadier Regiment, 352nd Division, who had had three months to prepare their positions. The regiment had a large number of "Osttruppen" conscripts, controlled by a cadre of veteran German NCOs from the Eastern Front. The failure to recognize the presence of the 352nd Division behind Omaha was one of the most serious intelligence deficiencies of the Allied invasion.

▲ ***US assault troops huddle behind the protective front of a landing craft as it nears the beachhead at Omaha. Nerves would have been shredded at the sight of the carnage ahead.***

waterlogged and carrying heavy gear, struggle under fire across the 300 yds (275m) of beach toward the shingle bank, where they try to take shelter behind the beach obstacles. Within minutes of the start of the invasion, the command structure of the assault companies has begun to collapse.

Company A of the 116th, the only company in the first wave to land in the right place, loses all its sergeants and all but one of its officers in the first 10 minutes. Elsewhere, men get ashore only to find themselves lost and out of sight of the beach exits. While survivors, many without weapons, huddle against the shingle bank trying to dig-in, the enemy begins to target them with mortars.

As the first assault wave dies on the beach, the follow-on waves of troops and equipment keep coming. Radio contact with the lead companies has been lost—all the radios have been destroyed—so without news that the first wave has failed, the invasion schedule carries on as planned. Soon, landing craft carrying tanks, vehicles, supplies, even admininstrative and maintenance troops, are coming into land only to hit beach obstacles that remain intact because the engineers sent to destroy them have been killed. Those vehicles that do manage to land either sink in the rising tide or are destroyed within minutes, adding to the chaos. By 08:30 hours, not a man or vehicle has moved off the beach. The plan to take Omaha has collapsed and the invasion is in danger of failing.

A signal has finally gone out from the navy beach controlers suspending the landing of all vehicles, but follow-up units are still coming in, and many

▶ ***Seen here in training, these US troops would not have been prepared for the sights and sounds of Omaha Beach. While they knew the drill, they could not have anticipated the dire situation to come.***

of those troops that make it ashore alive later describe the beach as a vision of Hell. Hundreds of dead and wounded men litter the beach, vehicles and landing craft are burning, as are the bluffs above, set alight by constant explosions. Everywhere there is enemy fire. One captain of the 16th, Fred Hall, remembers particularly "the noise—always the noise, naval gunfire, small arms, artillery, and mortar fire, aircraft overhead, engine noises, the shouting and the cries of the wounded; no wonder some people couldn't handle it."

Offshore, word is finally getting back to the generals in the Task Force that the landings are in deep trouble. First Army commander, General Bradley, begins to consider abandoning Omaha altogether and ordering Task Force O east to land with the British on Gold.

2ND RANGERS, *POINTE-DU-HOC*

As the fighting on Omaha begins, three companies of the 2nd Rangers, led by Colonel James E. Rudder, scale the cliffs of the Pointe-du-Hoc and attack the six huge concrete emplacements there. Intelligence reports say they hold 155mm guns. The Rangers arrive off the Pointe about 40 minutes late, because of the heavy seas, and begin their attack at 07:10 hours. Their LCA (Landing Craft, Assault) land them within 30yds (27m) of the cliff. Each LCA is mounted with three pairs of

▼ ***Crossed rifles in the sand are a comrade's tribute to this American soldier, who was hit while trying to take cover behind a wooden beach obstacle.***

rocket-propeled grapnels, which project ropes and rope ladders onto the cliff edge. The Rangers also carry light 112ft (34m) tubular steel ladders, which they quickly assemble. Using this equipment, the Rangers scale the cliff and within 15 minutes have established themselves on the top in company strength. There is no German resistance. By 07:45 hours, all three companies of Rangers are on the cliff top and Colonel Rudder has been able to establish his command post in a bomb crater.

Assault parties now set off to take the gun emplacements. There is some fighting as they run into small groups of Germans inside, but the action is short-lived. Once inside the emplacements, the Rangers discover that the guns have been removed and replaced with wooden dummies to save them from Allied bombing. Five of them are later discovered by a patrol about 1 mile (1.6km) away, in an orchard, and camouflaged. They are mounted and being prepared to fire. Rangers destroy their breaches with thermal grenades.

With their mission completed, at about 08:30 hours the Rangers move south about 1 mile (1.6km). Here they begin to dig in as they come under increasing sniper fire from German troops, who are beginning to move back in toward the Pointe-du-Hoc. Rudder's command of about 200 is scheduled to be reinforced by 500 men of the 5th Ranger Battalion

▲ ***With order gradually emerging from chaos, US troops organize their German prisoners of war on Omaha.***

▼ ***Surrounded by ammunition boxes, three US soldiers provide covering fire for their comrades up ahead with a .30in M1919 machine gun.***

◀ ***US Army Rangers scale the cliff-face at the Pointe-du-Hoc, just west of the Omaha beachhead.***

together with two more companies of the 2nd Rangers from Omaha. But Rudder's men are unaware of the chaos on the beach and that there are no reinforcements on the way to support them. Rudder discovers this only when a message from the 1st Division eventually gets through in the afternoon, by which time the Rangers are under attack from a full German battalion and are being pushed back toward the Pointe-du-Hoc.

08:30 Hours

As the Omaha plan disintegrates, the infantry, pinned down under enemy fire, begin to advance off the beach. To begin with, this is simply a matter of survival. In the words of Colonel George Taylor, commander of the 16th Infantry: "There are two kinds of people on this beach: the dead and those about to die. So let's get the hell out of here!"

Organization begins to reassert itself among the shattered survivors of the first boat waves, huddled at the sea wall. In small groups, often led by an NCO or junior officer, they blow gaps in the wire and begin to climb up the bluffs. They are helped by the naval destroyers, who come close inshore to deliver fire support.

By 08:30 hours, men of Company C of the 116th, with General Norman Cota, assistant commander of the 29th Division, have made it to the top of the Les Moulins draw toward St Laurent. They are reinforced by the 5th Ranger Battalion, under Colonel Max Schneider: he has managed to land his entire command almost without loss. Farther east, men of the 16th Infantry are on the plateau between the St Laurent and Colleville draws.

To the senior officers on the command ships stationed several miles out, with almost no communication with the shore, the situation is still confused and the outcome looks in doubt. But the men on the beach are making slow, but steady, progress. At 09:50 hours, General Clarence Huebner, commander of the 1st Division, receives a message: "There are too many vehicles on the beach; send combat troops." This is the first optimistic sign of the morning, and Huebner orders the 18th and 115th Infantry Regiments to land on Easy Red, the central beach sector.

At 11:00 hours, forward observers at sea report "men advancing up slope

▶ ***Wounded of the US 3rd Battalion, 16th Infantry Regiment, take shelter from enemy fire under the cliffs at Omaha.***

▶ ***The positions of the German and US forces around Omaha at 23:00 hours on June 6, 1944. Note how little ground had been taken in the east compared to the area around Les Forges.***

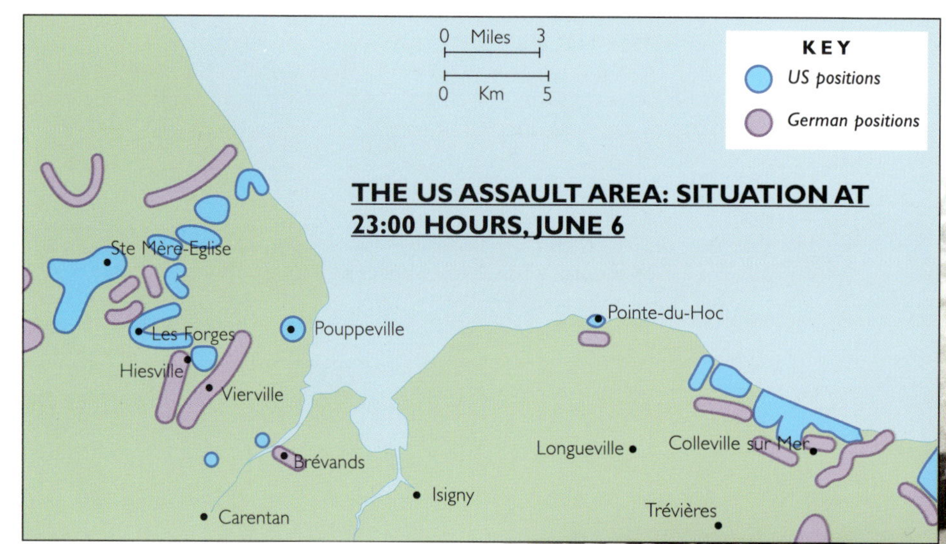

behind Easy Red, men believed ours on skyline." By midday, the US forces have four lodgment areas established on the plateau above the beach, and are beginning to move inland. Although the landing beach is still under heavy fire, and will be for the rest of the day, the draw to St Laurent, codenamed E1, is open to vehicles at 13:00 hours. The afternoon sees attacks on the villages, with the Rangers and sections of the 116th moving west toward Vierville, the 115th approaching St Laurent, and the 16th on the outskirts of Colleville. The last draw in German hands (D1), carrying the beach road to Vierville, falls into US hands at 17:00 hours, when engineers blow up the concrete roadblock.

The commanders of the 1st and 29th Divisions and V Corps finally feel confident enough to proceed with establishing their HQs ashore.

At the end of D-Day, the 1st and 29th Divisions have lost over 4000 men. Those who have made it ashore hold a frontline only 1 mile (1.6km) from the beach, with little more than their personal weapons to defend it. Fifty tanks have been lost, and five battalions of artillery destroyed or lost at sea. Only about 5 percent of the scheduled supplies have landed safely. In spite of all this, the fight for Omaha has broken the frontline strength of the German 352nd Division, while the British attack from Gold Beach has divided its reserve. As night falls, a feared German counterattack fails to materialize.

▼ ***American soldiers round up German prisoners. From here, prisoners would have been passed back into special holding areas.***

▶ *Stepping over wounded comrades and equipment, US GIs move supplies up onto the cliff to re-equip those fighting farther inland.*

▼ *One of the most famous images of D-Day. Men of the US 2nd Infantry Division—one of V Corps's follow-up divisions —make their way inland from Omaha Beach.*

June 6 Gold Beach

On Gold Beach Allied naval gunfire successfully destroyed many German positions, and the DD tanks made it onto the beach by 07:25 hours to support the infantry. Some casualties were suffered, but by Omaha standards they were light. French civilians greeted the British troops with cheers and cascades of flowers. By the evening, the 50th Division had reached the Bayeux–Caen road.

07:25 HOURS, *H-HOUR*

Task Force G, carrying the British 50th (Northumbrian) Division, arrives off the Gold area 10 miles (16km) east of Omaha at 05:30 hours. It assembles 7 miles (11km) from the coast, 4 miles (6km) closer inshore than the US Task Forces. It is hoped this will give the DD (Duplex-Drive) tanks a better chance of landing safely. Underwater reefs offshore will delay H-Hour until 07:25, hours which allows the naval

▲ *British forces assaulting the beach, as seen from a landing craft coming in to drop off more troops.*

▼ *British troops pour ashore on Gold Beach on D-Day. They met little resistance from the German defenders.*

◀ ***The British warship HMS* Ajax*, which took part in the bombardment of German shore batteries on Gold.***

bombardment to begin early. At 05:10 hours, the cruiser HMS *Orion* begins it.

Just before 06:00 hours, a German battery of 155mm guns near Longues fires on the HQ ship, *Bulolo*. Cruisers *Ajax* and *Argonaut* reply. By 08:45 hours, the battery has been silenced with two direct hits on its guns.

The assault sectors of Gold are over 3 miles (5km) wide, and large enough to land four battalions in two brigade groups, side by side: on the left, the 231st Brigade at the village of Le Hamel (Jig Green), and on the right the 69th Brigade at La Rivière (King Green). Both villages are defended with strongpoints and gun emplacements, which enfilade the beach; but the coast in between is defended only at certain points, and it is flat, making it ideal for an assault landing.

In order to break the German beach defenses, which are manned by the 726th Infantry Regiment, the British are relying on the specialist AVREs (Armoured Vehicles, Royal Engineers) of the 79th Armoured Division. The first assault wave will consist of LCTs (Landing Craft, Tanks) carrying six teams of such vehicles, three for each landing sector. The landing craft will motor straight through the beach obstacles and deposit the armor on shore. The AVREs will then cut six paths through the minefields and low dunes to the beach road.

The AVREs are meant to be followed by the DD tanks. But the current and strong winds causing so much havoc on Omaha are also affecting Gold. It is decided to land the DD tanks directly from beached LCTs, thus bringing them in five minutes behind the infantry.

The infantry assault waves come in on time, but the current pulls the 231st Brigade hundreds of metres to the east, and it lands on Jig Red. The left-hand battalion, the 1st Hampshire (1st Hants), meant to land directly at Le Hamel, is forced to spend the morning fighting a German strongpoint farther down the coast, before it advances to take Le Hamel. The battalion is through

▼ ***A Royal Marine commando in action at a roadside. He is firing the Bren light machine gun.***

▲ ***Royal Marine commandos wade ashore. One of them (centre) is carrying a miniature "Wellbike" motorbike.***

the town by mid-afternoon, but Le Hamel is not secured until 20:00 hours. The next battalion, the 1st Dorsets, is luckier, and lands without opposition. It is off the beach within 30 minutes and advances southwest toward the village of Ryes. The brigade objective is Arromanches, 3 miles (5km) west of the beaches. Its capture is vital: it is to be the site for a Mulberry harbor, which is to start arriving tomorrow.

On the left, the 69th Brigade moves on La Rivière. The strongpoint here is held by an entire battalion of nearly 1000 Osttruppen (Eastern troops), but it has taken serious damage from the pre-landing bombardment, and is secured by the 5th East Yorkshire Regiment before 10:00 hours. The 69th's battalions, 6th and 7th Green Howards, move south to take German positions at Ver-sur-Mer and then advance onto a ridge near Meuvaines. The brigade's objective to the east is the town of Creully, on the Seulles, to link up with the Canadians from Juno, while to the south it is to advance about 10 miles (16km) through Crépon to secure the Caen–Bayeux road near St Leger.

From 09:50 hours the landing beaches are secure, and follow-up units and armor begin to land. First to arrive are 300 men of 47 Royal Marine Commando. They are to advance west along the coast, bypassing Arromanches to secure Port-en-Bessin, and link up with US V Corps coming from Omaha.

From 11:00 hours, two more brigades begin landing, to take position between the two assault brigades. Moving in behind the 231st is the 56th, which advances southwest toward the Aure River, north of Bayeux. To the east, the 151st Brigade moves through Meuvaines on the flank of the 69th, toward the Caen–Bayeux road west of St Léger. The infantry is supported by tanks of the 8th Armoured Brigade. During the day, getting the tanks over the landing beaches proves difficult and 100 become bogged down in clay, to be swamped by the rising tide. But the brigade has at least three battalions in action by D-Day afternoon. They are soon joined by lead elements of the 7th Armoured Division, the Desert Rats. Meanwhile, D-Day afternoon sees the arrival of the 50th Division commander, Major-General D.A.H. Graham, and the establishment of the divisional headquarters at Meuvaines.

◀ ***More British commandos disembark from their transport craft. Note how some are carrying bicycles for transport.***

◀ ***An injured British soldier is stretchered off to a medical post by his comrades to receive attention.***

At about 16:00 hours, a German battle group of the 352nd Division from Bayeux—two infantry battalions supported by an anti-tank battalion—launches a counterattack on the 69th Brigade near Bazenville, southwest of Crépon. It is beaten off, with heavy German losses, and the 69th continues south, to end the day around the villages of Rucqueville and Coulombs. It is still about 2 miles (3km) short of St Léger and the Caen-Bayeux road.

By late afternoon, the 1st Hants has arrived at the outskirts of Arromanches. At first bypassing the town, it captures a radar station on the eastern headland intact. With that, and a nearby gun battery, secure, companies prepare to move on the town.

In the words of Major Mott, from B Company: "We expected tanks to stand by, but they never came, so we went in and were met by a dog, which seemed to be German. His masters followed with a white flag. Arromanches was surprisingly full of French people as we had heard they would all be evacuated and out came flowers, tricolors and Union Jacks."

To the east, 47 (RM) Commando has fought its way through La Rosière, and ends the day dug-in on the high ground of Point 72, which is 1 miles (1.6km) south of Port-en-Bessin.

Along the rest of the front, the 56th Brigade has dug-in 2 miles (3km) short of Bayeux, despite the fact that the German LXXXIV Corps actually has no reserves to defend the town. Farther east, the 151st has also stopped short of its objective, and ends the day still 2 miles (3km) north of the Caen-Bayeux road. Despite this seeming lack of urgency in some areas of the advance, on the right flank the 69th secures Creully by nightfall and links up with the 7th Canadian Brigade from Juno.

By the end of D-Day, the Gold lodgment area covers nearly 5 square miles (13 square kilometres), and the whole of the 50th Division—nearly 25,000 men—are safely ashore. The division's right has been secured with the arrival of the Canadians, but the left flank is still open, and there is no sign of the US forces due from that direction. Losses in some battalions have been heavy, with the 1st Hants having suffered some 270 casualties out of the 700 who landed.

▼ ***British troops and commandos file past a Bren gun carrier armored vehicle (left) and a Churchill tank (right).***

June 6 Juno Beach

The Canadians landed behind schedule on Juno, and struggled against the rising tide and submerged mines. Many of the first-wave landing craft were lost as a result. Intense street fighting took place in Courseulles as the 12th SS Panzer Division approached the beachhead.

07:35 & 07:45 Hours, *H-Hours*

At 05:58 hours, Task Force J, under the command of Commodore Geoffrey Oliver, moves out of the cleared channels and begins to assemble 7 miles (11km) from Juno Beach. At about 06:15 hours, the two lead convoys carrying the assault brigades of the 3rd Canadian Division, British I Corps, begin loading troops into landing craft.

As at Gold Beach, the Juno assault sectors are wide enough to allow a two-brigade front of almost 6 miles (10km). On the right, aiming for sector Mike, is the 7th Brigade: the Royal Winnipeg Rifles, the Regina Rifle Regiment, and 1st Battalion, Canadian Scottish Regiment. On the left, heading for sector Nan, is the 8th Brigade: the Queen's Own Rifles of Canada, the French-Canadian Régiment de la Chaudière, and the North Shore (New Brunswick) Regiment. The 7th Brigade

▼ *Canadian troops coming ashore ontoJuno Beach from various landing craft, including LCI (Landing Craft, Infantry) and LCT (Landing Craft, Tank).*

◀ ***The wreckage of a Republic P-47 Thunderbolt, which crashed while giving air support to troops landing on Juno.***

is to land either side of the River Seulles, west of Courseulles, while the 8th Brigade will further east, between Bernières-sur-Mer and St Aubin-sur-Mer. East of 8th Brigade, men of 48 (RM) Commando (of the 4th Special Service Brigade) will land at St Aubin-sur-Mer and advance east along the coast (3km) to Lion-sur-Mer. Here they will link up with the rest of the brigade, consisting of 41 (RM) Commando, landing at Sword Beach.

The German defenses, manned by units of the 716th Infantry Division, are concentrated in the towns, farms, and villas dotted across the flat landscape. The beaches themselves are defended with minefields, anti-tank ditches, and the occasional bunker, and to break through this thinly held defensive line, British I Corps is relying on the specialist armor of the 79th Armoured Division. As had been planned for Gold Beach, squadrons of DD (Duplex-Drive) tanks will motor in at H-5 minutes to engage enemy strongpoints, followed at H-Hour by one LCT (Landing Craft, Tank) group on each landing sector.

Each group carries three teams of the innovative "Hobart's Funnies" to smash through to the beach road. AVREs (Armored Vehicles, Royal Engineers) carrying fascines and light bridges, will make crossings over sea walls and anti-tank ditches, after which flails will clear the minefields, leaving the way open for armored bulldozers to cut new roadways. Any enemy bunkers still causing trouble will be engaged by AVREs firing petard charges: big, low-velocity bombs, nicknamed "flying dustbins" by the tank crews. The assault infantry will land at H+5 minutes and, protected by the armor, move straight inland.

▲ ***Dead German troops left behind by British commandos as they battled through the area.***

Unfortunately, conditions at sea and the coastal geography spoil the timetable. The need for the tide to cover rocks on the approach to the Nan Sector means that H-Hour for the 8th Brigade is delayed by 10 minutes, to 07:45 hours. The late arrival of landing craft across the Channel puts the H-Hour for both sectors back another 10 minutes. As the LCA (Landing Craft, Assault) move from the line of departure toward the beaches, 7th Brigade will be landing at 07:45 hours and 8th Brigade at 07:55 hours. The delays mean that the landing craft are motoring toward beach obstacles that are already being covered by the tide: engineers will not have enough time to clear paths through them before the arrival of follow-on assault waves. As a result, the LCA and their infantry companies take heavy losses.

▼ ***The British battleship HMS Rodney adds her weight of shells to the Allied pounding of enemy positions.***

One wave loses 20 out of 24 craft, while out of one company of the Regina Rifles only 49 men make it to the beach. In all, 90 craft of all types are lost in the day. Heavy seas also disrupt the landings of the DD tanks. Some are delivered as close inshore as 1000yds (915m) by LCT and arrive 20 minutes in front of the infantry, while others are launched 5000yds (4575m) offshore and motor up the beach 20 minutes after H-hour.

Despite the difficulties, the Canadian infantry secure Juno in a series of

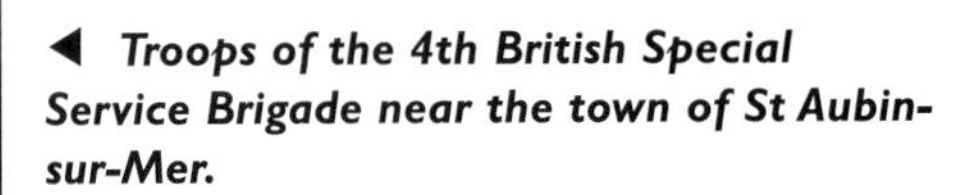

◀ *Troops of the 4th British Special Service Brigade near the town of St Aubin-sur-Mer.*

actions consisting, in the first hours, in house-to-house fighting to clear Courseulles, Bernières, and St Aubin.

On the right, in Mike sector, the Winnipeg Rifles are in action on the Seulles by 08:00 hours. The regiment secures the river bridge and west bank opposite Courseulles, and then moves south and southwest, toward Banville and Ste Croix, with the objective of Creully and a link-up with the British from Gold. On the east bank of the Seulles, the lead companies of the Regina Rifles are onshore by 08:15 hours, moving east toward Courselles, while AVREs set to work and, by 09:00 hours, have two lanes cleared inland for the follow-up waves. Over the next two hours, the Regina Rifles secure Courseulles in a systematic attack, clearing 12 pre-planned sectors. By 11:00 hours, the regiment is moving south toward Reviers. Here, it regroups to await the arrival of the tanks of the 6th Armoured Regiment (1st Hussars) in order to continue the advance to Bretteville l'Orgueilleuse on the Caen–Bayeux Road. With Courseulles secure, the 1st Canadian Scottish Regiment, which has come ashore by 09:30 hours, presses inland and begins marching across country toward Ste Croix to reinforce the Winnipeg Rifles.

In Nan sector, the 8th Brigade runs into trouble at Bernières and St Aubin. On the brigade right, at Nan White, the DD tanks and the AVREs are late, so the Queen's Own Rifles land in front of the Bernières strongpoint without any armoured support. They have to scale the 10ft (3m) sea wall and assault the defenses on their own with little more than their personal weapons and grenades. Naval gunfire assists, but the Queen's Own is not through the village until 09:30 hours, and it remains under partial German control until noon.

This delay, together with the rising tide and the uncleared beach obstacles, creates serious congestion in the Nan sector. Le Régiment de la Chaudière begins to land at 08:30 hours, and is still on the beach, waiting to move through Bernières, at 14:00 hours. More seriously, the follow-up brigade, the 9th, which is to march inland and take the strategically vital Carpiquet airfield, west of Caen, does not begin to land until 10:50 hours. It is unable to move from Bernières until 16:00 hours—too late to secure its D-Day objective. This failure will have serious repercussions for the British Second Army in the coming weeks, as the the enemy reinforces the town with panzers.

Nevertheless, there is some progress around Bernières. By noon, the first self-propeled artillery regiments are ashore and in action, while the division commander, Major-General Keller, lands

▼ *Defenses such as this barbed wire were designed to hinder the Allies.*

◀ *A Canadian soldier peers down the road as Allied armor clears the route ahead of enemy troops.*

and establishes his HQ at about 13:00 hours. By mid-afternoon, to the south of the town, the lead companies of the Chaudière Regiment are 4 miles (6km) inland and in control of Beny-sur-Mer on the Bernières–Caen road.

At Nan Red, the North Shore Regiment tries to secure the brigade's left-flank objectives at St Aubin, with 48 (RM) Commando. The plan is for the Canadians to secure St Aubin before the commandos land at the east end of the village (08:45 hours). Unfortunately, the pre-landing bombardment has missed St Aubin entirely, and German defenses are still intact when the Canadians arrive. The North Shore Regiment is fighting house to house as commandos begin to land. Enfiladed by fire from a German strongpoint in St Aubin, the commandos are pinned down under a sea wall and high earth cliff, suffering heavy casualties. They take most of the day getting off the beach and fighting their way into the neighboring village of Langrune-sur-Mer, instead of racing along the coast. They secure the area only by nightfall, with the help of Canadian armour. Their losses are severe, with over 100 dead, while patrols return from Lion-sur-Mer with news that the coast east toward Sword is still in German hands and that there is no sign of 41 Commando.

The Canadian advance from Juno slows down as the day goes on. This is partly due to congestion on the beach, but also to the German resistance at strongpoints along the coast and a series of small counterattacks, notably by the 726th Regiment at Ste Croix and the 736th Infantry Regiment at Tailleville, south of St Aubin.

To the west, by 17:00 hours the Winnipeg Rifles are consolidating positions around Creully, and have made contact with the British from Gold Beach. Farther south, the 7th Brigade is digging in around Le Fresne-Camilly. A few tanks have advanced as far as Bretteville l'Orgueilleuse on a reconnaissance mission, but, being unsupported, have had to withdraw. The 9th Brigade, meanwhile, has advanced down the Bernières–Caen road to Bény-sur-Mer by 19:00 hours, but has halted at dusk around Villons-les-Buissons, 3 miles (5km) short of the British to the east, and nearly 5 miles (8km) short of Caen to the south. On the beaches, the division has landed 21,500 men, 3200 vehicles, and 2500 ons (2540 tonnes) of supplies, while follow-on units, including the lead elements of the 51st (Highland) Division, are already on shore in preparation for the landings on D+1.

▶ *Troops of the British 13/18th Hussars move through Lion-sur-Mer. The damage to the buildings shows there was heavy fighting earlier in the day.*

EYEWITNESS ACCOUNT

AFTERMATH OF ST AUBIN

By a survivor from 48 (RM) Commando

"One thing we had to do was to clear up the St Aubin beach. It was a shocking sight. Many corpses, some of them badly dismembered, were lying among the rest of the debris of the assault: wrecked and burnt-out tanks; equipment and stores of every sort, scattered on the beach or drifted up along the water's edge; wrecked landing craft broached-to on the beach or in the sea among the beach obstacles. Three of our landing craft were still there, wrecked and abandoned; I never heard what the squadron's casualties were in men. Among all this, several French women were walking about, picking up what tinned food they could find—incredibly they had small children with them, who gazed with indifferent curiosity on the shattered corpses, the broken equipment, and the scattered tins of food."

Extract from: "Haste to the Battle", by Lt. Col. James Moulton, quoted in "D-Day Then and Now", edited by Winston G. Ramsey: Battle of Britain Prints International, 1995.

▲ *The general situation on the ground in the British sector at 23:00 hours, June 6, 1944. Despite sizeable gains during the first day, there was to be determined resistance farther inland.*

▼ *Outside Lion-sur-Mer, men of the 13/18th Hussars get some rest and a chance to eat during a lull in the battle.*

June 6 Sword Beach

The landings on Sword initially went well: Free French commandos took the town of Ouistreham, and by 13:30 hours British commandos under Lord Lovat had seized Hermanville and repulsed General Feuchtiger's 21st Panzer Division. However, the stated objective, Caen, remained in German hands.

▲ *After jumping from a Landing Craft, Infantry, Allied troops wade chest-high though the Channel surf to Sword Beach.*

07:25 Hours, *H-Hour*

At 05:30 hours, the LCA (Landing Craft, Assault) of Task Force S, commanded by Rear-Admiral Arthur G. Talbot, are in the water 7 miles (11km) offshore, and assault companies of the British 3rd Division begin to embark. Their objectives are sectors Queen White and Queen Red, halfway between Lion-sur-Mer to the west and the port town of Ouistreham, and the Orne estuary, to the east. Although the Sword landing area is over 12,000yds (10,970m) wide, only parts of Queen beach have been selected for landing. This is because of low cliffs to the west in sector Peter and a steeply sloping beach in front of sector Roger. This means the landing area for the 3rd Division is 1500yds (1370m) wide, allowing only a limited front of one brigade, consisting of two assault battalions. It also means there is a gap of over 2 miles (3km) between the British landings on Sword and the Canadians at Juno.

▼ ***Huddling together behind a bank of sand, Allied troops take cover from German snipers and machine guns on Sword Beach.***

▲ ***Pushing inland, the first elements of the Sword Beach assault group reach the town of Hermanville-sur-Mer.***

Making the assault is the division's 8th Brigade. On the right, Queen White will be stormed by the 2nd Battalion, East Yorkshire Regiment (East Yorks); on the left, Queen Red will be taken by the 1st Battalion, South Lancashire Regiment (South Lancs). In support will be DD (Duplex-Drive) tanks of the 13/18 Royal Hussars and the AVREs (Armored Vehicles, Royal Engineers) of the 5th Assault Regiment, RE.

Guided into position by the midget submarine *X-23*, 7000yds (6400m) from sector Peter, the first assault waves are closing in on the beach at 06:30 hours. LCTs (Landing Craft,

Tanks) carrying the DD tanks are in the lead, but rough seas mean that the tanks have to be launched at 5000yds (4575m). The LCT carrying the AVREs quickly catch them up, and soon the landing craft are weaving past the DDs, attempting not to run them down. At least one tank is struck and sinks.

Behind the armor, the troops in the LCA are suffering from mixture of sea-sickness and fear, but morale remains high. One major in the East Yorks even reads a patriotic speech to his men from Shakespeare's play *Henry V*.

At 06:45 hours, 72 self-propeled guns in LCTs, coming in behind the troops, begin a "run in shoot" at 10,000yds (9150m) to suppress enemy targets along the beach. They augment other fire-support craft in action, which include three LCG (Landing Craft, Gun) and five multi-rocket-launching LCT(R). Their fire continues for the next 30 minutes, lifting just before the first AVREs hit Queen Red (07:20 hours) to begin clearing four routes off the beach. The first DD tanks arrive soon afterward. Despite the crowded boat lanes and a rough sea, 28 out 40 tanks make it onto the beach and go straight into action. By 07:45 hours, the German positions are silenced.

The East Yorks and South Lancs are on the beach by 07:30 hours, on schedule. The initial assault succeeds, but not far from the beach the East

▶ ***Two soldiers from the South Lancashire Regiment look on as an M4Sherman tank reconnoiters ahead.***

Yorks, coming from Queen Red, run into German resistance at strongpoint WN 20, near la Breche, and the landing schedule begins to slip. Near some beach villas, the strongpoint has 20 positions and is equipped with a 75mm gun, mortars, anti-tank guns, and eight machine guns. The East Yorks spend two hours attacking it, delaying the advance east to Ouistreham. To the right, the South Lancs move off Queen White, and secure the only road leading inland, toward Hermanville-sur-Mer.

From 08:30 hours a second wave of assault units begins to land at Queen Red. These are commandos of the 1st Special Service Brigade (1st SSB), under the command of Lord Lovat. First to land are No. 4 Commando and 170 Free French marines of No.10 (Inter-Allied) Commando, led by Commandant Philippe Kieffer. Both units head east to capture German strongpoints in Ouistreham. They are followed by 41 (RM) Commando, part of 4th Special Service Brigade (4th SSB), which has been landing at Juno. They take the coast road west, to attack through Lion-sur-Mer, and to link up with the 4th SSB and form a united bridgehead with the Canadians. Thirty minutes later, the rest of Lovat's brigade begin to land, played ashore by piper Bill Millin. Led by No. 6 Commando, 1st SSB (with Lovat among the forward units), marches through 8th Brigade, heading southeast through Colleville toward Bénouville and a link-up with the paratroopers of the 6th Airborne Division, east of the Orne.

▼ *Reinforcements land on the Normandy coast to support the first assault groups. In the background, half a dozen LCI (Landing Craft, Infantry) disgorge troops.*

▶ *Dead soldiers from the British and Commonwealth 3rd Division lie where they fell on Sword Beach.*

Meanwhile, reinforcements, which include the 8th Brigade's 1st Suffolk Regiment (Suffolks) and 3rd Division's follow-on brigades (185th, 9th, and the 27th Armoured), are on their way toward the beach. The Suffolks land at 11:00 hours, with the first objective of taking Colleville.

By mid-morning, the South Lancs have secured Hermanville, while the East Yorks have made it to the southern outskirts of Ouistreham. On the right, the Marines of 41 Commando have run into trouble on the eastern outskirts of Lion-sur-Mer and are trying to push their way in with armored support.

Back on the beach, three brigades are trying to land over two beach sectors and move inland over one surfaced road to their assembly areas at

▼ *Looking disheveled and defeated, German prisoners of war are brought in by men of the 13/18th Hussars.*

EYEWITNESS ACCOUNT

THE JOURNEY INTO SWORD

On board the converted American freighter "Battleaxe"

" ... dawn was just breaking and as we looked out over the rough seas we could see a huge red glow on the horizon. This must be France. A destroyer speeding by about 8 miles from us struck a mine and blew up, scattering wreckage in all directions. At 3.30 [03:30 hours] we queued up with our trays for breakfast of porridge, two hard-boiled eggs, four rounds of white bread and butter and jam and a mug of tea. We gave our rifles the once-over, filled the magazines and made sure our ammunition and grenades were ready for use. At 4.45 the word came over the loudspeaker for us to get dressed [for battle]. At 4.50 the captain told us he could see the French coast – a blazing inferno with the Navy shelling it and the RAF bombing it. Then came the order 'Marines of ALC 23 lower away'. Slowly the winches began to turn and we slid down the ship's side and bumped into the stormy sea. We were then 7 miles from shore. We made ourselves as comfortable as possible, some sitting, some standing but all singing. New songs and old – sentimental – patriotic and ballads but we all sang." *(Private Stanley Gardner, Ist Suffolks, 8th Brigade)*

Extract from "Monty's Iron Sides: A History of the British 3rd Division", by Patrick Delaforce, Stroud, Gloucestershire: Alan Sutton, 1995.

Hermanville. The result is heavy congestion, holding up the division's advance south for at least three hours. In the grand plan, 185th Brigade was supposed to be in Caen by midnight; but at noon the brigade is still in Hermanville, 7 miles (11km) to the north, waiting for the arrival of tank support. Finally, brigade commanders lose patience, and its lead battalion, the 1st King's Shropshire Light Infantry (KSLI), starts south toward Beuville.

Farther east, the advance also stalls around Colleville. South of the village the Suffolks come up against a strong-point codenamed Hillman, a battalion HQ of the 736th Infantry Regiment. This huge redoubt is 600yds (550m) wide. It has 12 gun emplacements, concrete walls 9ft (2.7m) thick, a double belt of barbed wire 12 ft (3.6m) wide, and a minefield. It is manned by over 300 men. Allied planners have ignored it, so Hillman has not been hit by either naval or air bombardment, despite being in the direct line of the advance on Caen. It takes the Suffolks until 20:00 hours to take it, with the help of a squadron of tanks, two batteries of artillery and engineers.

South of Hermanville, during the afternoon, a battery of German 88s of

▼ *Additional vehicles and equipment for the 13/18th Hussars are moved onto the beach, ready for the push inland.*

◀ ***Carrying reinforcements for the 6th Airborne Division, which landed on the night of June 5/6, Allied gliders swoop in to land as nightfall approaches on D-Day.***

the 21st Panzer Division at Périers halts the division's advance. Instead of clearing them out, the 185th Brigade sticks to its D-Day task and bypasses the village, heading south through Beuville to Biéville, 4 miles (6.4km) north of Caen, which it reaches at 16:00 hours. By now, tanks of the 27th Armoured Brigade have made it through the Hermanville traffic jams and are operating in the division area south to the 185th's positions. Their arrival does not come a moment too soon; it is now that the 21st Panzer Division launches the only German armored counterattack of D-Day.

Faced with what is, by now, clearly a major Allied landing, the 21st Panzer mobilizes three battle groups. One moves on the paratroopers on the Orne, while the other two, with 70 Mk IV tanks, move north of Caen. The first attack on the 3rd Division, around Biéville, is stopped by the anti-tank guns of the KSLI and supporting armor of the Staffordshire Yeomanry. 21st Panzer loses about 10 tanks but presses on, this time making a flanking move north to Périers, where Battle Group Oppeln expects the battery of German 88s to be in position. To its surprise, the guns have been withdrawn, and a squadron of British tanks now dominates the town from Périers Ridge to the east. Again, the Germans take losses and withdraw. Meanwhile, farther west, Battle Group Rauch has moved north unopposed, into the gap between Juno and Sword.

By 19:00 hours, panzers are in Lion-sur-Mer, and for two hours the Allied invasion front is split in two. However, the German forces cannot exploit the position. Colonel Rauch, the battle group commander, knows he has no support and is faced by a vast invasion fleet. At 21:00 hours, hundreds of Allied gliders are seen overhead, and Rauch, assuming their objective to be Caen, decides to pull back to around Bieville. The gliders are, in fact, reinforcements for the 6th Airborne Division; but the sight of their arrival is enough to end the only chance the Germans will have to throw the Allies back into the sea.

By nightfall, nearly 29,000 troops have landed at Sword, and objectives to the east have been largely secured: Ouistreham and the mouth of the Orne are in Allied hands, and Lovat's commandos have crossed the river into 6th Airborne's area and Le Plein. A battalion of the 185th Brigade (2nd Warwickshire Regiment) has reached the Orne at Blainville and is preparing to move into Bénouville in support of the paratroopers holding the bridges.

Elsewhere, the situation at Sword needs radical improvement. On the right flank, the commandos are not yet through Lion-sur-Mer, while the 8th and 9th Brigades are stuck outside Hermanville and Périers, having failed to advance since early afternoon. There are also no signs of the Canadian forces from Juno. To the south, the 185th Brigade has dug-in 4 miles (6km) short of Caen. There has already been one German panzer attack to hold the town, and more are certainly to come. Caen—an invasion objective—is already looking a hard nut to crack.

D-Day June 7 – 12

The days after the D-Day landings were ones of frustration for the Allies. As the beachhead was consolidated it appeared that the Allied armies would be able to drive inland with relative ease. But organizational and logistical difficulties slowed the advance, and the German High Command at last began to respond to the landings. Though Allied aerial superiority meant the beachhead was secure, a lot of hard fighting lay ahead.

▲ *After landing, Allied engineers set about constructing makeshift airfields for fighters to provide close air support.*

Wednesday, June 7 (D+1)

OPERATION NEPTUNE

From the early hours of the morning U-boats from the Biscay ports and Brittany make a bid to break into the English Channel and attack the Western Task Force lying off the American sector. They are stopped by patrol aircraft of Coastal Command, which through D+1 make 22 contacts and put in seven attacks. *U-955* is confirmed sunk and five other boats are believed damaged. Nevertheless, their attempts to break into the English Channel continue.

On the eastern flank of the invasion fleet, off Sword Beach, the main attack threat comes from the German Air Force based in the Le Havre/River Seine area. To counter this the Eastern Task Force and Task Force S is flanked by the Trout Line: a line of warships and armed landing craft extending 6 miles (10km) out to sea from the Orne estuary. This includes Landing Craft, Flak; Landing Craft, Gun and the so-called Eagle Ships, which are converted vessels, many formerly civilian—including an old paddle

◀ *German air crew "bombing up" a Ju-88. The Luftwaffe was still able to threaten Allied invasion plans and shipping.*

▶ *Numbers of Ju-88s were gradually depleted by Allied bombing raids on airfields and factories.*

steamer—fitted with a large array of anti-aircraft guns.

These defenses do not stop an air attack on HMS *Bulolo*, the headquarters ship of Task Force G. At 06:00 hours she is hit by a bomb. The vessel is saved and she continues to direct landings on Gold Beach.

AIR CAMPAIGN, *NORMANDY*

The Allied air forces are faced with increased German air activity throughout D+1. About 250 sorties are made by German fighters over the beachheads, while there are 50 fighter-bomber attacks on the Sword area. The most serious of these, made by a lone FW 190, hits a beach sector supply dump and blows up 100,000 gallons (450,000 litres) of fuel and 406 tons (400 tonnes) of ammunition. Secondary explosions continue through most of the day.

Luftflotte (Air Fleet) 3 also orders the medium bombers of IX Fleigerkorps (IX Air Corps) into the battle from their bases in northern France. Tonight 130 bombers, including Ju-88s, Ju-188s, and Do-217s—half the Fleigerkorps' strength—attack the invasion fleet but are driven off by anti-aircraft fire and night-fighters.

Allied fighters continue to cover the beachheads with a fighter screen, while offensively the priority is to attack road and rail bridges to the south and west of Normandy over the Loire and Seine rivers. This is to delay the arrival of German reinforcements. But the weather is now deteriorating as the meteorologists predicted on Sunday, and low cloud levels are keeping aircraft at their bases in England. Allied air chief Leigh-Mallory records in his diary: "The weather has interfered with my air programme all day and is seriously upsetting me. The German army is being reinforced and I cannot bomb the reinforcements in daylight."

On a more positive side, airfield construction has already begun at the beachhead. The first is an emergency landing strip at Laurent-sur-Mer off Omaha due for completion on D+2. It will soon be joined by another 89 airfields scheduled for construction by the end of June.

COMMANDERS, *BRITISH AND US*

General Montgomery, on his way to join 21st Army tactical HQ almost doesn't make it to France. HMS *Faulknor* gets lost in the Channel and ends up in the early hours positioned off the Cotentin Peninsula. Dawn sees the destroyer back on course to Juno.

By 06:00 hours the *Faulknor* is with the invasion fleet, and General Bradley is onboard for his first command conference with Montgomery. Dominating their meeting is Omaha Beach and the position of General Gerow's V Corps. As far as is known the bridgehead at Omaha is barely 1 mile (1.6 km) deep and V Corps is still in danger of being pushed back into the sea. The decision is made to give Collins's VII Corps at Utah a new set of priorities. Instead of its headlong drive to Cherbourg, VII Corps is to concentrate its efforts south toward Isigny and Carentan to take the pressure off Omaha and to link up with Gerow. Collins is also to concentrate on getting his forces west of the Merderet River with the aim of reaching the west coast of the Cotentin at Lessay and cutting off Cherbourg from any German reinforcements. Elsewhere, the priorities are to link the British and American beachheads around Port-en-Bessin, close the gap between Juno and Sword, and take Bayeux and Caen. Now the initial Allied forces are ashore the primary concern of the planners is to secure and expand the bridgehead, to allow the space for the follow-up divisions to land and deploy at a faster rate than the Germans can reinforce the area.

◀ *Merchant ships were deliberately scuttled to provide makeshift breakwaters for the vessels unloading on the beach.*

▶ *An aerial view of Allied gliders that landed on D-Day. They look to have had a fortunate landing in a clear field.*

In England, General Eisenhower and Admiral Ramsay leave forward SHAEF HQ at Southwick House to tour the assault area. By 08:00 hours they are on board HMS *Apollo* and on their way across the Channel. Eisenhower's first visit is to General Bradley on board the cruiser USS *Augusta*. He then visits Montgomery on HMS *Faulknor*. Eisenhower's main concern is that the build-up of men and equipment at the beachhead is already behind schedule. Only a quarter of the 14,730 tons (14,500 tonnes) of supplies and 7000 of the planned 14,000 vehicles due by D+1 are ashore, while the total number of troops scheduled—107,000—is 20,000 short.

As the sea is becoming rougher by the hour, it is difficult to see how the situation can be improved. However, the commander of the Eastern Task Force, Admiral Vian, has a solution and orders his LSTs to ground on the beaches and unload their stores directly on to the beach.

Eisenhower is back in Portsmouth by 20:00 hours for meetings with Leigh-Mallory and Spaatz.

THE BUILD-UP

Lead units of the British 7th Armoured Division (of XXX Corps) and 51st (Highland) Division (of I Corps) are arriving at Juno. In the American sector, the 2nd Infantry Division and lead elements of the 2nd Armored Division, both part of US V Corps, begin to land at Omaha. On Utah, lead units of the 90th Division land.

MULBERRY HARBORS

At 12:30 hours the first convoys of the Gooseberry blockships arrive off Omaha Beach at St Laurent and Gold at Arromanches. They will be scuttled bow to stern to create 5 miles (8km) of breakwaters. The Gooseberries are joined during the day by the first of the concrete Bombardons that are sunk to form the outer breakwaters. These measures will prove to be important during the coming days.

▼ *American Landing Ship, Tanks (LSTs) transport ever more men and materiel onto the Omaha beachhead. After beaching themselves, they needed to wait for high tide to leave the area.*

GERMAN DEFENSES

After being taken by surprise on June 6, today the German Army in France begins to organize for battle. OB West divides the front into two. Seventh Army has the western sector from the Cotentin to Bayeux, Panzer Group West has the eastern sector from Bayeux to the River Dives. Seventh Army orders II Parachute Corps from Brittany into the Cotentin with three divisions, the 17th SS Panzergrenadier, 77th Infantry, and 3rd Parachute Division. Panzer Group West assigns I SS Panzer Corps to the Caen area. Of the three panzer divisions which come under its command during the day, 21st Panzer is already heavily engaged defensively east and north of Caen, units of 12th SS are arriving west of the town and attacking north toward the Canadians, and Panzer Lehr is 87 miles (139km) to the southwest around Chartres.

Panzer Lehr's commander, General Fritz Bayerlein, is ordered to move his division immediately for an attack west of Caen tomorrow, despite the general's objections that a move in daylight risks Allied air attack. Over the next 24 hours, Panzer Lehr comes under repeated Allied bombing and loses 130 trucks and fuel tankers, 84 self-propelled guns and halftracks, and 5 tanks before it even reaches the battle front.

THE BEACHHEAD, *UTAH*

On the right flank, moving north along the coast of the Cotentin, two regiments of the 4th Division fail to capture two large German gun emplacements at Crisbeçq and Azeville.

▲ ***Private Boyle of the 6th Durham Light Infantry displays the holes in his helmet caused by shell fragments during battle.***

In the center, a large pocket of German resistance around Turqueville south of St Mère-Eglise, is removed.

North of St Mère-Eglise the German 1058th Regiment renews its counterattack down the Montebourg road. Reinforced with an infantry battalion, 10 self-propelled guns, and artillery, it reaches as far as the outskirts of the village before American tanks make a flanking attack on Neuville and force it back.

West of St Mère-Eglise, at 08:00 hours, the German 1057th Regiment launches a counterattack across the Merderet River at the La Fiere crossing, but is stopped by a company of the 505th Parachute Infantry.

To the south, on the north bank of the Douve River near Carentan, two regiments of the 101st Airborne, the 506th and 501st, kill or capture an entire battalion of German paratroopers of the 6th Parachute Regiment. Out of a unit of nearly 1000, only 25 Germans escape.

During the day, after receiving new instructions from First Army, VII Corps headquarters assigns the task of capturing Carentan to the 101st.

AIRBORNE ASSAULT, *US SECTOR*

Over the Cotentin, the last American glider operations of the invasion begin at about 07:00 hours. Two hundred gliders in four waves deliver reinforcements and supplies to the 82nd and 101st Airborne; the last drop taking place at about 09:00 hours which lands two infantry battalions to the 101st. In contrast to the chaos on D-Day morning, this drop, made in daylight, delivers 90 percent of the two battalions safely, and by 10:30 hours they are assembled and moving against German positions.

THE BEACHHEAD, *OMAHA*

In the western part of the bridgehead, regiments of the 29th Division, the 115th and 116th, spend most of the day consolidating their positions and clearing out pockets of German defenders. After securing St Laurent the 115th moves southwest toward Lôuvieres and Montigny, while the 116th, supported by the newly arrived 175th Regiment, moves along the coast over the bluffs of the Pointe de Raz to try and relieve the Rangers on the Pointe-du-Hoc. By noon they are at St. Pierre du Mont, still 1000yds (915m) short of the Pointe.

Meanwhile, the position of Colonel Rudder's Rangers is perilous. Over a period of 24 hours, counterattacks by the German 914th Regiment have reduced the Ranger force to fewer than 100 men and have forced them gradually back, until by the afternoon of D+1 they hold a strip of cliff only 200yds (180m) wide. Two landing craft manage to deliver their first fresh supplies of food, water, and ammunition, but the Rangers

▲ ***Having been rounded up on the land, German prisoners are loaded onto transport ships to take them back to holding camps in England.***

must hold out until the 116th are able to reach them.

From the eastern end of Omaha Beach, two regiments of the 1st Division, the 16th and 18th, are advancing east to clear Colleville and reach the high ground on the River Aure south of Port-en-Bessin.

THE BEACHHEAD, *GOLD*

The British No. 47 (RM) Commando begins its attack on Port-en-Bessin at dawn. The small port is secured during the early hours of D+2. While heavy fighting goes on, contact is made with a company of the US 16th Regiment from Omaha Beach during the afternoon.

Everywhere in the Gold area, the 50th Division is making good progress. By noon, two battalions of the 56th Brigade have entered Bayeux unopposed. To the east the 151st Brigade advances to the southeast of the town and is astride the Bayeux-Tilly Road. On the flank, 69th Brigade has advanced 5 miles (8km) south from Coulombs, crossing the Bayeux-Caen road at St. Leger, capturing Ducy St. Marguerite and joining up with the Canadians south of the road at Bronay.

THE BEACHHEAD, *JUNO*

The 7th Canadian Brigade crosses the Caen-Bayeux at Bretteville l'Orgueville and pushes on to the railroad at Bronay. To their left, the 9th Canadian Brigade moves west of Caen through Authie toward Carpiquet and its airfield. The Canadians come under artillery fire which halts the advance. The decision is made to retire to defensive positions north of Authie, but as the withdrawal begins at about 14:00 hours, the Canadians come under attack by a reinforced panzergrenadier regiment of the 12th SS Panzer Division. This pushes the Canadians back 3 miles (5km) through Authie and Buron to high ground around les Buissons. The 12th SS Panzer Division begins to arrive in force and concentrates west of Caen. The British Second Army has lost another opportunity to close on the town.

THE BEACHHEAD, *SWORD*

North of Caen, the 185th and 9th Brigades renew their advance toward the town through units of the 21st Panzer Division. The 185th Brigade, while holding a battalion at Bieville, makes a flank attack with two battalions on Lébisey, but is held in heavy fighting and forced to withdraw. The 9th Brigade meanwhile attempts to advance southwest. Périers is taken but the advance is halted outside Cambes. The 8th Brigade meanwhile makes a slow advance west of Hermanville.

East of the Orne River, two commandos of the 1st Special Service Brigade attempt to retake the Merville Battery, but the attack fails with resulting heavy losses.

▼ ***More German prisoners are rounded up by British soldiers and sent back to the beach holding areas.***

▲ *A group of US paratroopers from the 101st Airborne Division in the village of St Marcouf, near Utah Beach. They wait for orders to push on to their next objective.*

THURSDAY, JUNE 8 (D+2)

IN THE ENGLISH CHANNEL
During the night, a Liberator of 224 Squadron, Coastal Command piloted by Flying Officer Kenneth Moore, attacks and sinks *U-629* and *U-373* in the space of 30 minutes.

Meanwhile, German air raids on the invasion fleet go on. At 05:15 hours the frigate HMS *Lawford* is sunk, probably by a Henschel Hs 293 radio-controlled glider bomb, launched from the air by a converted Do-217 bomber. This is one of the first times an anti-ship missile has been used in warfare.

German surface vessels are also in action. During the evening the 5th and 9th E-Boat flotillas sortie from Le Havre. They go north into mid-Channel, avoiding the Trout Line and attack a convoy of 17 landing craft, sinking two of them before they disengage.

Due to enemy action SHAEF warns fishermen from across Europe to return to port and remain there until June 15.

MULBERRY
During the morning the last "Gooseberry" blockships are sunk in position, forming the fixed breakwaters of the two harbours: Mulberry A off St Laurent and Mulberry B off Arromanches. Other elements arrive today having been towed across the Channel by tugs. They include concrete Bombardons—floating breakwaters; "Phoenix" caissons—fixed breakwaters designed to be sunk in position; "Whale" floating piers and "Spud" pier heads. The sea is becoming increasingly rough and the crossing has not been easy. About 40 percent of the "Whales" have been damaged or lost at sea.

COMMANDERS
At Juno Beach, General Montgomery disembarks from HMS *Faulknor* and joins his tactical headquarters ashore. The HQ has been established at Croix sur Mer, but Monty orders it moved closer to the frontline. By the end of the day it is at Cruelly, 10 miles (16km) west of Caen and only 3 miles (5km) from the battle front, between the British XXX and I Corps. The headquarters remains here until June 22. Contact with SHAEF at Southwick House and 21st Army Group base headquarters in London is maintained by radio, and soon staff officers will be flying over every day as Allied forces advance inland.

▶ *The Henschel Hs 293 radio-controlled glider bomb, the first guided missile in the history of warfare, was used in action on June 8.*

▶ ***The town of St Lô took a heavy pounding from Allied bombers before and during the invasion, as they tried to soften up the German garrison based there.***

In the American sector, the US Ninth Air Force and IX Air Force Service Command establish advance headquarters ashore. They join forward supply units that arrived on D-Day.

GERMAN PRISONERS

The first trainload of German Army prisoners from Normandy, consisting of 364 men, arrives from Southampton at a processing center at Kempton Park horse racetrack west of London. From here they will be transferred to permanent camps in the US, Canada, and Great Britain.

Six POW camps are scheduled to be set up in Normandy, but at the beginning of the campaign prisoners are kept on the beaches behind wire and shipped over the Channel in LSTs. Estimates by 21st Army Group of the numbers of Germans it will take in Normandy prove to be wildly optimistic. From D-Day to D+9 the estimate is 500 a day, rising to 1000 a day by D+29. In fact by July 29 (D+53) only 12,153 have been captured.

BRITISH HOME FRONT

In London, General Eisenhower holds his first press conference since June 6. A pre-recorded message by the Supreme Commander was broadcast on D-Day, but this is the first time journalists have had the opportunity to question Eisenhower personally about the progress of the new Second Front.

The information they are given is very limited, with Eisenhower voicing no comment or opinion on the progress of the

operation so far. What he does say is that what he wants most, and indeed is praying for, is good weather. Bad weather is slowing the build-up across the Channel and preventing Allied aircraft from flying and attacking the German divisions as they close on the bridgehead.

THE BRIDGEHEAD, *UTAH*

On Utah, regiments of the 90th Division come ashore to join the lead elements that have been coming ashore since D+1.

To the north, VII Corps makes another attack to silence the German gun emplacements at Crisbecq and Azeville. This combines with a flanking attack by the 82nd Airborne from the area of St Mère-Eglise with the aim of securing a ridge of high ground from Montebourg to Quineville on the coast.

To the south, units of the 101st Airborne are clearing the Germans from north of the Douve River in preparation for the attack on Carentan. On the road north of the town, the village of St Come-du-Mont is occupied during the day after an attack by four infantry battalions supported by light tanks and a battalion of field artillery. The Germans disengage, cross the river and regroup in Carentan, bringing their forces in the town to two battalions of the 6th Parachute Regiment plus elements of the 1058th Regiment.

By nightfall the 101st has three regiments along the Douve ready for the assault on Carentan.

THE BRIDGEHEAD, *OMAHA*

The US 2nd Infantry Division comes ashore at Omaha. Its lead regiments, the 9th and 38th Infantry, are immediately rushed forward into the center of V Corps's line between the 29th and 1st Divisions, their first objective being the village of Trévières. The advance is made without heavy weaponry, most of which is still being unloaded.

As preparations are being made to take Carentan, from the east the 29th Division is attacking Isigny to complete the link-up between Omaha and Utah. Leading the advance is the 175th Infantry. By nightfall it is in Isigny itself, and in the process of securing the town.

Elsewhere in the 29th Division area, units of the 115th and 116th Regiments have pushed south across the Isigny–Bayeux road and on high ground overlooking the River Aure. On the coast, the Rangers on the Pointe-du-Hoc are finally relieved at about midday by a force of the 116th and two companies of tanks.

In the 1st Division's area, regiments are moving south to Formigny on the Isigny–Bayeux road and securing the left flank of the bridgehead, pushing German forces situated around Port-en-Bessin south down the valley of the River Drome.

THE BRIDGEHEAD, *GOLD*

The British 56th Brigade consolidates its position in Bayeux, pushing southwest to block any German advance from St Lô. East of the town, the 151st Brigade advances between the rivers Aure and Seulles, while the 8th Armoured Brigade makes a rapid advance through the 69th Brigade at Coulomb. North of the Bayeux–Caen rail line at Loucelles the tanks engage units of the 12th SS Panzer Division. These are flanked and the 8th Armoured Brigade has advanced as far as Audrieu by nightfall. Its objective is to clear the east bank of the Seulles River toward Tilly-sur-Seulles.

THE BRIDGEHEAD, *JUNO*

The Canadian advance south of the Caen–Bayeux rail line at Putot-en-Bessin is stopped by a counterattack by regiments of the 12th SS Panzer Division moving west. This is part of a larger operation by I SS Panzer Corps for a two-division drive to the coast to capture Courseulles and split the Allied bridgehead in two. 12th SS is operating with 21st Panzer on the right and elements of Panzer Lehr, which is beginning to arrive southwest of Caen.

Within 24 hours of their arrival at Normandy front, units of the 12th SS are reported to be committing war crimes. Today, for example, seven Canadian prisoners are taken to the headquarters of the 25 Panzergrenadier Regiment and executed.

THE BRIDGEHEAD, *SWORD*

The 9th Brigade continues its attack on Cambes while the 8th Brigade continues to close the gap between Sword and Juno to the west. The enemy facing the 185th Brigade north of Caen remains strong, with units of the 716th Division and the 21st Panzer Division.

East of the Orne, the 6th Airborne Division has attempted to advance south from Herouvillette toward St Honorine la Chardonnerette and Escoville, but has failed under increasing pressure from tanks of the 21st Panzer Division and newly arrived units of the 125th Panzergrenadier Division.

◀ ***An American paratroop patrol moves cautiously through the churchyard in St Marcouf, using the high stone wall as cover against enemy fire.***

▼ ***A section of prefabricated port under tow across the Channel, heading for the Normandy coastline.***

FRIDAY, JUNE 9 (D+3)

AIR CAMPAIGN

During the early hours of the morning, 24 Lancaster bombers of 617 Squadron carry out an attack on the Saumur rail tunnel near the River Loire, 125 miles (200km) south of the battle front. Station X at Bletchley Park has decrypted information that the 17th SS Panzergrenadier Division *Götz von Berlichingen* is on the move north by rail and the raid is organized to stop it.

The Lancasters carry one of the biggest weapons in the RAF arsenal, the 12,000lb "Tallboy," ground-penetrating blast bomb. At least 16 "Tallboys" come close to the target and one direct hit seals the tunnel for the rest of the war.

Despite this awesome display of firepower, a panzer battalion of the division is already on its way to face the Americans near Carentan.

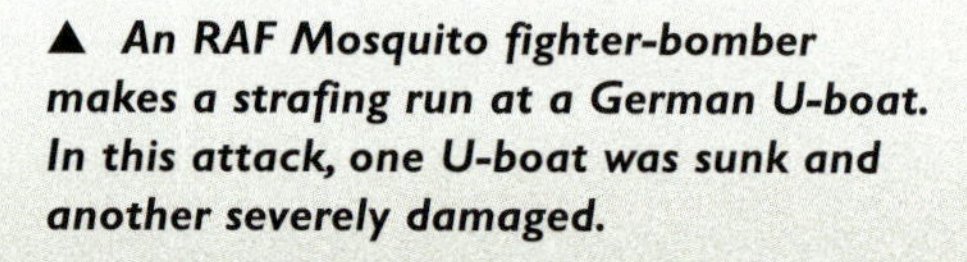

▲ ***An RAF Mosquito fighter-bomber makes a strafing run at a German U-boat. In this attack, one U-boat was sunk and another severely damaged.***

IN THE ENGLISH CHANNEL

Admiral Kranke, commanding Navy Group West, has ordered his last remaining destroyers on the French Atlantic coast, *ZH-1*, *Z-24*, *Z-32*, and *T-24*, to sortie from the Bay of Biscay to Cherbourg, in an attempt to reinforce his tiny surface fleet in Normandy. In the early hours of this morning during the final leg of their journey from Brest, the four German Navy vessels are intercepted by the Royal Navy's 10th Destroyer Flotilla, pre-warned of their arrival through Ultra. Action begins in the dark at about 01:30 hours, and for the next four hours the destroyers fight it out in a running battle. ZH-1 is sunk, *Z-32* is set ablaze and has to beach while the other two German warships, after taking heavy damage, escape back to Brest. From now on Admiral Kranke will have to rely on his E boats.

The U-boats of Group Landwirt are also having a rough time of it. During the day *U-740* is sunk by a Liberator and the decision is made in the face of growing losses to withdraw all boats from the Channel except the six advanced Snorkel types. The remaining

◀ ***Dropping depth charges and firing machine guns, a Sunderland Flying Boat attacks a German U-boat.***

▼ ***A convoy of Allied destroyers patrols the sea to the west of the landing beaches, keeping watch for enemy U-boat activity.***

18 boats of the group are stationed in the Bay of Biscay. Meanwhile, five Snorkel boats from Group Mitte in Norway are ordered to the Channel.

Luftflotte (Air Fleet) 3 is also continuing its attacks on the invasion fleet, and from today begins laying sea mines in the Force U area from low-flying aircraft.

MULBERRY

Surveying of the sites for the two harbors is underway as the first "Phoenix" concrete caissons are flooded and sunk in position off the beachhead. Elsewhere along the coast, the small ports of Port-en-Bessin (on Gold) and Courseulles (on Juno) have now been cleared of obstacles and are open to small landing craft.

BRITISH HOME FRONT

The US Joint Chiefs of Staff, General Marshall, Admiral King, and General Arnold, fly into England for their scheduled meeting with General Eisenhower. Arriving by train in London their first visit is to the British Chiefs of Staff.

On the same day as the Allied chiefs of staff confer, Winston Churchill is writing to Montgomery with his plans to visit the bridgehead in three days time. Having been thwarted in his attempt to be with the fleet on D-Day, the prime minister is not to be denied a visit to Normandy now the troops are ashore. In good humor he writes: "We do not wish in any way to be a burden to you or your headquarters, or in any way to divert your attention from the battle. All we should require is an ADC or a Staff Officer to show us around. We shall bring sandwiches with us."

AT THE BEACHHEAD

General Bradley comes ashore at Omaha to join the headquarters of the US First Army, which has been established a couple of miles inland from the former Ranger positions on the Pointe-du-Hoc.

Off Omaha, landing ships arrive carrying the bulk of the US 2nd Armoured Division, which has been at sea since June 7. Vehicles and tanks begin to be unloaded immediately and are moved to the division assembly area around Mosles, on the Bayeux–Isigny road east of Formigny.

Over St Mère-Eglise, meanwhile, C-47s of the IX Troop Carrier Command begin a small series of drops to keep regiments of the 82nd Airborne supplied. The drops go on for the next four days.

In the British sector the first Graves Registration Unit (GRU) comes ashore. In one of the rare logistics failures of the invasion, manufacturers have failed to deliver 10,000 metal crosses on time, and the GRUs have to improvise wooden crosses

▲ *An RAF ground crew load a 12,000lb "Tallboy" bomb into the bomb bay of a Lancaster II.*

with the help of the British Army's Royal Engineers.

THE BATTLE FRONT, *UTAH*

While the 82nd Airborne is holding down the center of the Utah bridgehead along the Merderet River east of St Mère-Eglise, VII Corps is pushing four regiments north from its right flank toward Montebourg in a line from the river to the coast. German resistance, though, is stiffening and a new defense line held by three regimental battle groups and units from three infantry divisions has been established west from Quinéville, blocking the main road to Montebourg from St Mère-Eglise.

VII Corps makes its first attack left of the road, and by the end of the day has pushed back the Germans at Magneville and Escouville, though the regiments engaged suffer heavy losses.

On the right, the advance is being held up by the German garrisons at Crisbecq and Azeville, which for the last two days have withstood attacks by battalions of the 22nd Infantry. Today, the regiment concentrates its efforts on Azeville. As the Crisbecq position is hit with artillery fire, a fresh battalion approaches Azeville from the west, its weaker point. After breaching the wire and minefield the blockhouse is attacked and the German garrison eventually dislodged after a lucky shot from a flamethrower detonates an ammunition store. Though Crisbecq still remains in German hands, the capture of Azeville at least opens up the route to Quinéville.

To the south, on the Douve River, the 101st Airborne is advancing on Carentan. Its attack on the town will begin tonight. The plan is for a flanking maneuver upriver by the 327th Glider Infantry on the left that will take it through Brevands to attack Carentan from the east, and at the same time link up with V Corps units coming from Isigny. At the same time paratroopers of the 501st, 502nd, and 506th will come down the road from the north, cross the river and then flank the town from the northwest.

OMAHA

The 29th Division having secured Isigny yesterday and having secured its right on the River Vire, begins to advance south with the 175th and 115th Infantry. From the beachhead, the 115th finds crossing points over the flooded River Aure and advances on Colombiere. On its right, the 175th fights its way through La Foret from Isigny and by nightfall is between Lison and la Fortelai, having crossed the Bayeux–Carentan rail line. Meanwhile, patrols of the 29th Division and the 101st Airborne meet at the River Vire.

In the 1st Division area, German resistance on the left flank is collapsing and by the end of the day 26th Infantry is 4 miles (6km) southwest of Bayeux around Agy, with the British 56th Brigade on its left and the US 18th Infantry on its right astride the Bayeux railroad line.

While the flank divisions of V Corps are making good progress, in the centre, the 38th and 9th Regiments, still lacking most of their mortars, machine guns and artillery, are held

▼ ***Troops from the* Hitlerjugend *Division man their 75mm PAK 40 anti-tank gun. The PAK 40 was a highly effective weapon, capable of knocking out all Allied armor.***

at Trévières all day by the remnants of the German 352nd Division.

GOLD

The 8th Armoured Brigade secures Audrieu during the morning. A battalion of the 151st Brigade—the 8th Durham Light Infantry—is brought up in support and advances a mile south to St Pierre on the right bank of the Seulles opposite Tilly. This rapid advance by the 50th Division has left its lead brigades in a salient created near Tilly, and there are reports of growing concentrations of German armor nearby.

JUNO AND SWORD

There are now believed to be three panzer divisions north of Caen, the 12th SS, Panzer Lehr, and 21st Panzer, blocking a direct advance on the town. General Montgomery therefore decides on an attack on the flanks by two of Second Army's follow-up divisions. On the left, the 51st Division will move from the Juno area to east of the Orne. There it will support 6th Airborne and attack south to Cagny, 6 miles (10km) southeast of Caen. On the right, the 7th Armoured Division (XXX Corps) will advance through Tilly to Villers-Bocage and then to Noyers southwest of Caen on the Avranches road, which will be its route east. The operation is codenamed Perch and is scheduled to begin tomorrow.

The arrival of the 51st Division east of the Orne cannot come too soon for the 6th Airborne. This morning Ranville comes under heavy artillery fire, and a battle group of the 21st Panzer moves up from the southwest for another counterattack. In a two-pronged sweep the battle group strikes Longueval and Herouvillette, but both attacks are driven off, with the help of 3rd Division artillery.

▲ ***US soldiers grab some food, whilst the fire set on the hillside in the background is intended to smoke out any snipers.***

▶ ***With a "potato masher" stick grenade to one side, a German paratrooper hidden in a foxhole awaits the Allies.***

▲ *A German paratrooper anti-aircraft battery crew on the lookout for Allied aircraft in Normandy.*

SATURDAY, JUNE 10 (D+4)

THE BATTLE FRONT, *UTAH*

On the right flank of the bridgehead the advance north has stalled after the capture of Azeville yesterday. The 22nd Infantry is meant to attack Quinéville but is still being held by German positions at Crisbecq.

To the west of the Montebourg–St Mère-Eglise Road, the 8th Infantry advance north of Escouville and cross the Montebourg–le Ham road but are stopped short of the railroad line. To the left of the 8th Infantry, the paratroopers of the 505th advance west toward Le Ham, but are stopped half a mile short.

In the center of the bridgehead, for the last four days the 82nd Airborne has been trying to cross the swamps surrounding the flooded Merderet River, with the aim of relieving its units isolated on the west bank since D-Day and beginning VII Corps's delayed advance to cut the Cotentin Peninsula. Action concentrates around the village of la Friere and a causeway running to the south of it. Two battalions are needed to force a crossing, and by the end of today the division has five battalions on the roads running west facing German concentrations in the villages of Amfreville, Le Motey, and Haute-Gueutteville.

Meanwhile, in the attack on Carentan, a causeway crossing is also proving an obstacle to the paratroopers of the 101st Airborne. The flank advance on the left by the 327th Glider Infantry has gone well, though, and all its battalions are across the Douve at Brevands by midday, with lead patrols in contact with units of the 175th Infantry from Isigny during the afternoon. On the right flank, a battalion of the 502nd Parachute

▼ ***Commandos set out to capture a German gun position. Once a gun site had been captured, all the enemy equipment would be destroyed to avoid recapture.***

Infantry spends all day under fire trying to thread its way down the causeway and across its four bridges. By midnight the battalion had companies across the last bridge but was still faced by German positions across the road north of the town.

OMAHA

In the center of the V Corps bridgehead, the 2nd Division succeeds in taking Trévières in the early hours of the morning. The remains of the German 352nd Division is withdrawn to a new defense line northwest of St Lô, allowing the 2nd Division to make an advance of over 5 miles (8km), to a position south of the woods of the Fôret de Cérisy. On the 2nd Division's left, the 1st Division holds a line facing southeast along the Bayeux–St Lô road. At its furthest point, V Corps's lodgment area is now 7 miles (11km) deep, a vast improvement on the dire situation on Wednesday, D+1.

▲ ***British Sherman tanks of the 13/18th Hussars move cross-country in pursuit of German forces.***

GOLD

XXX Corps begins the opening moves of Operation Perch. West of Caen, between the Seulles and Aure rivers, the 7th Armoured Division follows the road south from Bayeux and by 06:30 hours has a brigade in contact with Germans at Buceels 2 miles (3.2km) north of Tilly. In support of the advance, Royal Navy warships begin to target German positions to the south and west. South of Tilly, the village of Hottot comes under bombardment from the battleship HMS *Nelson,* which drops 16in shells on it from 19 miles (30km), while to the west, Lingeveres draws the attention of the cruiser HMS *Orion*. By nightfall the 7th Armoured has Buceels almost secured, while on the division's left, Juaye Mondaye on the Aure has been taken.

Meanwhile, east of the Seulles River, at St Pierre, the 8th Armoured Brigade comes under heavy counterattack, but by the end of the day is holding the northern end of the village.

SWORD

The 51st (Highland) Division is on the move from the Juno area to concentrate east of the River Orne. It is to form the left flank of Operation Perch, but the division is behind schedule. Only two of its three brigades have landed so far, and the division will not be in a position to begin its advance south from the Herouvillette area until June 13 (D+7).

East of the Orne, the Germans are keeping up the pressure on the 6th Airborne Division. At 09:00 hours German infantry begin to advance on Ranville, but they are not supported by armour and are driven off comparatively easily. In the center of the 6th Airborne's positions along the ridge near Breville and St Come, Lovat's 1st Special Service Brigade and the 3rd Parachute Brigade come under attack from units of the German 346th Division supported by self-propeled artillery guns. These positions are in range of the 6in guns of the cruiser HMS *Arethusa*, which help defeat the attack that afternoon.

▲ ***Off the Ile de Batz, a beached German destroyer is left a smoldering hulk after Allied fighter-bombers attacked it with rockets and bombs.***

▼ ***German anti-aircraft gunnery crews rush to their battle stations on hearing the air-raid alarm.***

▲ ***Opening its massive bomb bay, a B-17 Flying Fortress drops thousands of pounds of bombs onto enemy targets below.***

AT THE BEACHHEAD

The US 9th Infantry Division begins to land at Utah, while units of the US 30th Infantry Division begin to land at Omaha. There are now 10 US Army Divisions in Normandy.

In the British sector at St Croix-sur-Mer, north of Cruelly, the RAF opens its first airfield. This is the first RAF base to operate in France since 1940 and begins work today with the refueling of three squadrons of RCAF Spitfires.

AIR CAMPAIGN

Ultra intelligence identifies the location of Panzer Group West's mobile headquarters, 12 miles (19.2km) south of Caen at the Chateau le Cain. At 21:00 hours, four squadrons of Typhoons sweep in to rocket the area and are followed by four squadrons of B-24 Mitchells dropping 500lb bombs. The raid devastates the headquarters, killing 18 staff officers, including the chief of staff General von Dawans and injuring the commander General Geyr von Schweppenburg. Panzer Group West ceases to exist as an operational headquarters and is pulled back to Paris. Command of the sector now passes to I SS Panzer Corps.

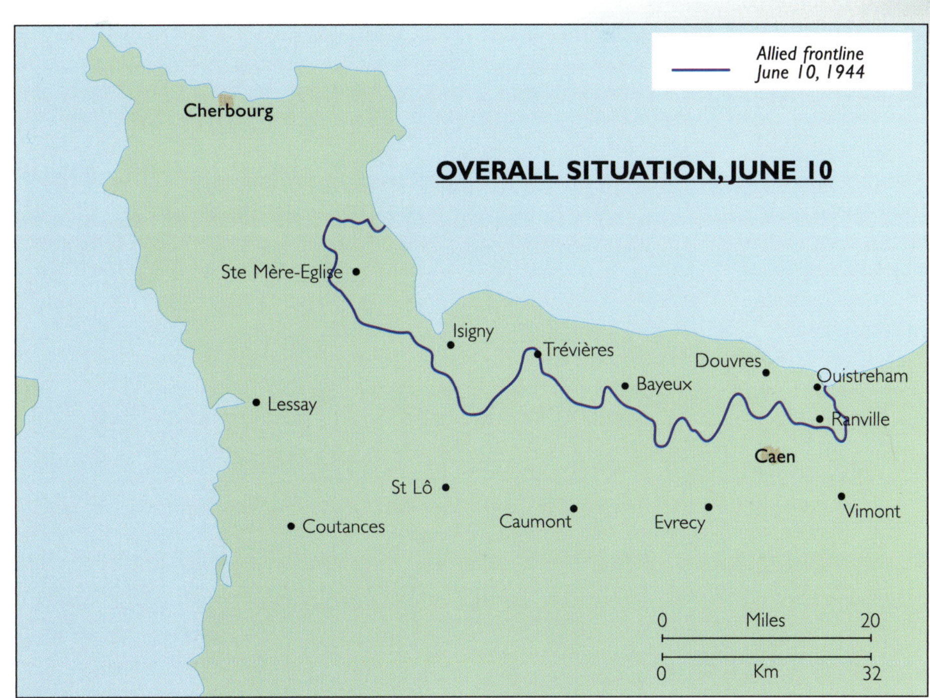

▲ ***The situation on the morning of June 10, 1944, showing the depth of the Allied beachhead only four days after the invasion. From here onwards, however, the fighting would get harder.***

Sunday, June 11 (D+5)

AT THE BEACHHEAD
General Montgomery gives a press conference to journalists at his tactical headquarters at Cruelly; his first since the invasion.

MULBERRY
Two "Whale" floating roadways are under construction in Mulberry A off Omaha beach. Mulberry A is ahead of schedule. It is not due to be operational until June 24 (D+18), but in fact unloads its first LST on June 17 (D+11).

THE BATTLE FRONT, *UTAH*
On VII Corps's right flank, the Germans still hold Quinéville and control a stretch of coast 3 miles (5km) to the south of it, allowing their artillery to keep up a bombardment on Utah Beach. The 22nd Infantry attack on Quinéville has stalled, and the frontline from Montebourg to the coast is only thinly held by the 12th Infantry and the 22nd on its right. Reinforcements are needed, and the arrival of the 9th Division yesterday gives the corps commander, General Gerow, options to put a fresh regiment on the 22nd's right to make a drive up the coast while another attack goes in on Quinéville.

Along the Merderet River, the 82nd Airborne is now supported by the 90th Division, which advanced its two lead regiments over the river crossings from St Mère-Eglise yesterday morning. The 90th's original task was to drive north on the 4th Division's left to capture Cherbourg, but now it is to add its weight to the drive west to cut the peninsula. By nightfall, the division's 357th Regiment is through Le Motey and Amfreville on the St Mère-Eglise–Carteret road and is attacking Les Landes. On its left, the 358th Regiment is at the road junction of Pont-l'Abbe.

At Carentan the German garrison is being reinforced. Two Ost battalions have arrived from LXXXIV Corps and the surviving defenders of Isigny have arrived. To the south, lead units of the 17th SS Panzergrenadier Division are preparing a counterattack. LXXXIV Corps must hold Carentan to stop the link-up of the two US bridgeheads and to prevent an advance southwest through Périers to Coutances, which would outflank St Lô.

Meanwhile the regiments of the 101st are closing in on the town. By midnight

▲ ***General Sir Bernard Montgomery (center) visits a recently captured small port on the French coast.***

▶ ***An M4 Sherman Firefly. Equipped with a 17lb gun, it was arguably the most effective Sherman during the war.***

▲ ***Round a ruined wall in the Normandy village of St Mauvieu, Allied troops move cautiously to avoid snipers and booby-traps.***

▲ ***Scouts from the British 5/7th Gordon Highlanders watch for enemy movement in the woods at Bois-de-Bevent.***

the 502nd Parachute Infantry has three battalions across the causeway to the north, but has taken so many casualties over the past 24 hours it is withdrawn and replaced by the 506th. On the left, the 327th Glider Infantry has now completed its flanking march and is on the eastern outskirts of Carentan along the Taute River, astride the rail line and the Isigny road. The assault will begin before dawn tomorrow reinforced by the 501st Parachute Infantry, advancing on the left of the 327th, and the tanks of the 41st Armored Infantry Regiment (part of the 2nd Armored Division from Omaha) coming down the Isigny road. To coordinate the operation, all units are reorganized into a single task force commanded by Brigadier-General McAuliffe of the 101st Airborne.

OMAHA

In the 29th Division area, units of the 175th and 115th Infantry are now in position along the Elle River south of Isigny. On their left regiments of the 2nd and 1st Divisions are regrouping south and west of the Fôret de Cérisy after their rapid gains of yesterday.

Their lack of progress today is a mistake. Had the two divisions advanced they would have moved into a 10-miles (16km) gap north of Caumont between the Panzer Lehr Division attacking the British at Tilly, south of Bayeux, and the remnants of the 352nd Division northeast of St Lô. The only German unit in the area over the last 24 hours has been a reconnaissance battalion of the 17th SS Panzergrenadier Division. Today this battalion is reinforced by a regiment of the 3rd Parachute Division on the right of the 352nd, but the Caumont Gap still remains largely undefended.

GOLD

The 7th Armoured Division continues its advance between the rivers Aure and Seulles toward Tilly, but its advance is slowing. The British are now entering the Bocage country, with its thick hedgerows that are proving difficult obstacles for tanks but natural defensive positions for the Germans. XXX Corps has brought up infantry brigades in support, and today the 7th Armoured organizes two tank and infantry groups to renew the advance. One attacks Tilly, the other Lingevres to the west on the Tilly–Balleroy road.

At Tilly, the infantry fight its way in, but the tanks are held on the outskirts. By nightfall the British have pulled back to positions to the north, and the Germans still have the village in their possession. At Lingevres, by nightfall the second battle group has advanced as far as woodland to the north, but its position is not secure, and after dark the Germans put in a counterattack. This is beaten off, but the Germans regroup and launch another attack at about midnight. On the road west from Lingevres, units of the 50th Division have captured the crossroads at La Belle Epine by the end of the day.

On the 7th Armoured's right flank, northeast of the St Pierre, there is fighting throughout the day between le Haut d'Audrieu and Cristot. The 69th Brigade, of 50th Division, tries to attack east to Cristot only to be held and counterattacked by units of the 12th SS Panzer Division.

JUNO

On the left of the 69th Brigade, the 3rd Canadian Division takes advantage of the move from St Pierre to strengthen its position south of Bronay and Putot-en-Bessin, after holding off the counterattacks by the 12th SS on June 8. The 2nd Canadian Armoured Brigade, supported by the Queen's Own Rifles, are pushed forward in a hurriedly conceived attack that reaches as far as Le Mesnil Patry. Here, the Canadians are caught between German positions around Cristot and St Mauvieu and subjected to tank and anti-tank fire that inflicts heavy infantry casualties and destroys 37 tanks.

After the action around Le Mesnil, this part of the front stabilizes for the following two weeks. The 3rd Canadian Division will not go on the offensive again until Operation Epsom begins on June 26 (D+20) while the 12th SS, which is now under constant Allied air attack, is forced on to the defensive west of Carpiquet.

▼ ***Fighting through the dense Bocage countryside of northern France, US soldiers moving along a pathway bob and weave as they try to avoid enemy fire.***

▲ ***Propped up against the rubble of a destroyed building, a British soldier of the Durham Light Infantry opens fire with his Bren light machine gun.***

SWORD

After yesterday's heavy counterattack on the 3rd Parachute Brigade at Breville, the frontline here is reinforced by the 5th Black Watch of the 51st Division's 153rd Brigade. The battalion attacks Breville but is met with heavy German fire that inflicts 200 casualties. To the south the remainder of 153rd Brigade advances south in preparation for Operation Perch, and by the end of the day has secured Touffreville, north of the Caen rail line.

GERMAN DEFENCES

Von Rundstedt and Rommel meet in conference in Paris to discuss the serious situation now facing Seventh Army. Their conclusions are sent in two separate reports to Hitler.

Both reports state plainly that units are on the defensive everywhere from the River Orne to the Vire, and because of a lack of infantry, armored units are holding the line and are unable to counterattack in strength. More infantry is needed in Normandy to consolidate the front and free the panzers. Operations should be concentrated on the Americans in the Cotentin to defend Carentan, Montebourg, and Cherbourg. Only then should the weight of the attack be switched east to the British at Caen.

The two officers identify four areas of Allied superiority that may disrupt these plans:

1 Control of the air: "From the long-term point of view this superiority of the enemy air forces will paralyze all movement and control of the battle, and make it impossible to conduct operations."

2 The domination of much of the front by the firepower of Allied warships.

3 The material superiority of the Allied forces. " . . . the spirit and morale [of our] troops are good, but the material superiority of the Anglo-Americans must in the long run have its effect on any troops."

4 The strength and flexibility of the Allied airborne and parachute troops.

Hitler's response is a rejection of what is called the "Cotentin first" proposal. The danger of a breakout by the British through Caen toward Paris is too great. The panzer divisions will therefore concentrate around the key town of Caen. Hitler will accept no large-scale tactical retreats in order to form new defensive lines in northern France, stating in his now infamous remark: "Every man shall fight and die where he stands."

▼ ***Men of the 23rd Hussars warily search trees looking for snipers. Even one good sniper could hold up a sizeable force in the right conditions.***

MONDAY, JUNE 12 (D+6)

AT THE BEACHHEAD

The battle at the beachhead is now becoming one of logistics. A race is on to land fresh troops and supplies faster than the Germans can bring in reinforcements. To increase the unloading capacity over Utah, another two beach sectors have been opened at Sugar Red and Roger White. This nearly triples the capacity of Utah from 1525 tons (1500 tonnes) a day to 4065 tons (4000 tonnes).

On Omaha, Mulberry A nears completion at St Laurent. Meanwhile, army and navy engineers have been working hard to clear the mines and battlefield debris from the beach. They have laid heavy steel mesh over the sand to convert these former killing grounds into hards; landing ramps for the DUKW amphibious trucks and Rhino ferries that shuttle between the shore and the transport vessels, that are now protected from rough seas by the Gooseberry breakwaters.

On Gold the lead brigades of the 49th (West Riding) Division begin to land a day late because of bad weather. The division is assigned to XXX Corps.

COMMANDERS

D+5 is a day of high-level official visits to the bridgehead. The US Joint Chiefs of Staff, Generals Marshall, Arnold, and Admiral King, conclude their visit to the European Theater of Operations with a tour of the American sector, accompanied by General Eisenhower. The party comes over in the destroyer USS *Thomson* from Portsmouth and lands at St Laurent on Omaha and is met by General Bradley. The tour takes them to Bradley's headquarters and then on to Utah by sea, the road through Isigny still being too close the front line. The visit lasts until late afternoon.

The British sector sees the arrival of Winston Churchill and Field Marshal Sir Alan Brooke, Chief of the Imperial General Staff. The prime minister left Portsmouth at 08:00 hours in the destroyer HMS *Kelvin* and lands at 11:00 hours at Courselles on Juno to be met by General Montgomery. The party then visits Montgomery's headquarters at Cruelly for lunch before visiting General Dempsey's Second Army Headquarters and the Mulberry harbour at Arromanches. The prime minister returns to Courseulles and is on his way back to England by late afternoon.

THE BATTLE FRONT, *UTAH*

General Gerow, commanding VII Corps, orders 9th Division's 39th Regiment to join the 22nd Infantry in the attack on Quinéville. So far the 22nd has been trying to do the job on its own.

Moving into position on the right of the 22nd Infantry, the 39th's 2nd and 3rd Battalions move east toward the coast. They find Crisbecq unoccupied, but Fontenay-sur-Mer is garrisoned and is only captured after a fight. The 1st Battalion takes the beach road advancing on Fort St Marcouf.

North of Fontenay, the 22nd Infantry takes fortifications at Ozeville, allowing the 12th Infantry to advance east of Montebourg. By the end of the day the 12th is across the Montebourg road and is on high ground around Les Fieffes Dancel. The German defense line between Montebourg to Quinéville is cracking, but Montebourg itself remains in German hands and its garrison is being reinforced with light tanks and an infantry

▼ ***Fresh off their transport ships, Allied tanks and troops filter through the town of Reviers on their way to the front.***

LOGISTICS

KEEPING THE ARMIES RUNNING

To provide enough fuel for the vehicles, armor, and aircraft during the first two weeks of Overlord, the Eastern Task Force alone transported a 63,000-gallon (286,400-litre) reserve of petrol, oil, and lubricant (POL) on D-Day. By D+6 (June 12) this reserve had grown and the British bridgehead had a stockpile of 1 million gallons (4.6 million litres) of POL, representing a two-day supply for every vehicle ashore. From D+6 petrol began to be landed ashore direct from deep-draught tankers through "Tombola" pipelines and stored in bulk storage tanks, one of which was constructed at Port en Bessin.

battalion. A probing attack into Montebourg from the south by the 8thInfantry is called off during the day when the strength of the enemy garrison is discovered.

West of the River Merderet, the 90th Division and regiments of the 82nd Airborne continue to advance slowly against German opposition now desperate to hold open the roads to Cherbourg. To the south, rapid advances are made across the River Douve by the 82nd Airborne's 508th Parachute Infantry, which attacks before dawn across the river toward Baupte to link with the right flank of the 101st Airborne around Carentan. The German battalion holding thesector flees on first contact and the 508th advances 4 miles (6.5km) to Baupte meeting no resistance, and by 08:00 hours has reached the village.

In Carentan, the defending German garrison, surrounded on three sides by American troops, receives some support after OB West orders a supply drop flown in—the first time the Germans have attempted to do this in Normandy. Before dawn, 18.2 tons (18 tonnes) of artillery and small arms ammunition is dropped by parachute. It arrives too late to affect the outcome of the battle because the garrison commander, Major von der Heydte, has already ordered his men to withdraw south to new defense line.

Overnight, Carentan is prepared for the final American assault by coming under sustained bombardment by naval and land-based artillery. By 02:00 hours the 506th Parachute Infantry are on the move from the causeway, making a flanking march to the west and taking position on Hill 30, which dominates the road southwest to Périers. By 05:00 hours the hill is finally secure and the regiment's 2nd Battalion is ordered into the town. As it fights its way in from the south, the 327th Glider Infantry attacks over the Taute River from the east, supported on its left by the 501st which flanks to the town to the south, reaching Hill 30. By 08:00 hours Carentan is in American hands.

The 506th and 501st now try to sustain the momentum of the attack by advancing from Hill 30 on the line of the Périers road, southwest. Both regiments are stopped within a few hundred yards by von der Heydte's new defense line. During the night the First Army receives information that the Germans are preparing to launch a counterattack in force. General Bradley orders V Corps to have a battalion of

▲ ***Allied ships offload supplies onto waiting trucks at Mulberry B, one of the prefabricated artificial harbors. Mulberry B at Arromanches was used extensively.***

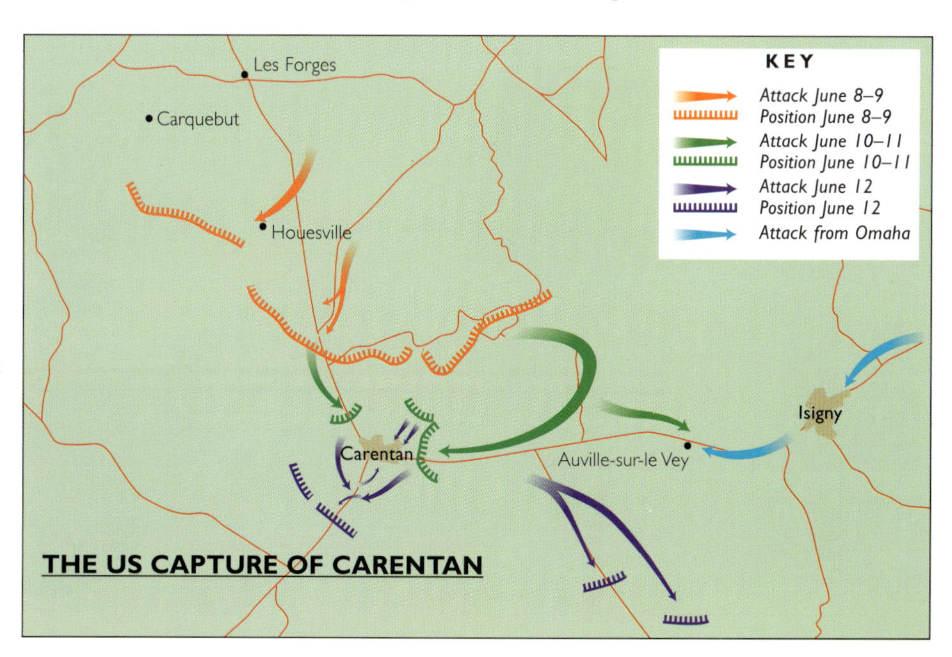

▼ ***The German garrison at Carentan was attacked by the Allies from three sides in a four-day battle, putting up some stiff resistance against the odds.***

▶ *Among the ruins of a French town, US troops clear a path for the trucks of the "Red Ball Express".*

tanks and armored infantry between Isigny and Carentan by dawn ready to stop its progress.

OMAHA

The 2nd and 1st Divisions renew their attacks to the south and west of the Fôret de Cérisy and advance into the Caumont Gap. On the far left of the 1st Division, the 18th and 26th Infantry regiments, moving in support of the British 7th Armoured Division's attack on Villers-Bocage, advance about 4 miles (6.5km) against little resistance and are across the Caumont-St Lô road by the end of the day. The 26th Infantry is in position on the northern outskirts of Caumont, but waits for dawn to begin an assault to clear out companies of the 2nd Panzer Division. South of the forest, the 2nd Division's 9th Infantry moves in support and occupies a ridge near Liteau.

West of the forest, the 2nd Division's 23rd Infantry with the 115th Infantry of the 29th Division on its right begin a slow advance southwest toward St Lô. German resistance intensifies as the Americans move deeper into the bocage. The 115th makes an advance of about 3000yds (2700m) during the morning, but has to withdraw to avoid being surrounded and cut off. The attack on St Lô has been slowed to a halt by the end of its first day.

GOLD

The 7th Armoured Division's advance on Villers-Bocage has been held north of Lingevres and Tilly by Panzer Lehr, which holds strong positions between the rivers Aure and Seulles. Taking advantage of the gap that has opened in the German line around Caumont, tonight 7th Armoured moves its line of advance. Leaving the infantry of the 50th Division to hold the road between La Belle Epine and St Pierre, at 22:00 hours 7th Armoured crosses the Aure and outflanks Panzer Lehr to the west. Meeting little opposition, the advance reaches Livy, 2 miles (3km) northeast of Caumont and only 5 miles (8km) east Villers Bocage, where its lead brigade halts for the night.

SWORD

East of the Orne, the German 346th Infantry Division intensifies its counterattacks around Breville and forward British positions at St Come. At 15:00 hours, after a three hour bombardment, men of the 5th Black Watch and paratroopers of the 3rd Parachute Brigade in St Come are attacked by an infantry battalion of the 858th Regiment supported by assault guns. Holding out in woods and a chateau, the British are reinforced by tanks and a battalion of Canadian paratroopers. The battle goes until 21.00 hours when the Germans withdraw to Breville, which the British promptly start shelling. General Gale, commander of the 6th Airborne, decides to counterattack at once and at 22:00 hours the understrength 12th Battalion of the 5th Parachute Brigade and a squadron of tanks advances east from Amfreville and attacks Breville. By midnight the paratroopers have taken the village, but the cost is appallingly high. Out of 160 officers and men engaged, the 12th Battalion has taken 141 casualties. The German 858th Regiment has also suffered heavily, its 3rd Battalion having only 146 men left out of 564.

◀ *As Churchill continues his tour of the front, enemy planes fly over chased by Allied fighters and engaged by AA guns. Winston undoubtedly enjoyed the show.*

LOGISTICS

THE BUILD-UP IN THE BRIDGEHEAD

A week after D-Day, Tuesday June 13, D+7, 326,547 men, 54,186 vehicles, and 104,400 tons (102,700 tonnes) of supplies had been landed over the five assault beaches.

Until D+4, the cross-Channel convoys bringing in all this materiel were rigidly scheduled under Operation Neptune. After D+5 it was a case of loading in England and unloading in Normandy as fast as possible. Within three weeks of D-Day, 200 vessels including landing craft, landing ships, Liberty ships, and coastal freighters were arriving in the invasion area every day, all bringing in men and supplies for the Second Front, . The vast scale and efficiency of this operation had delivered one million US Army personnel into Normandy by July 5 (D+28).

▼ *A quick-reaction force patrol of the 101st Airborne Division sweeps through the area looking for the snipers that shot their comrades.*

The Battle for Normandy

JUNE 10

WESTERN FRONT, *FRANCE*
The 2nd SS Panzer Division *Das Reich*, moving from its base at Toulouse to join the defensive efforts at Normandy, has been the constant target of members of the French Resistance. In retaliation, the small town of Oradour-sur-Glane is chosen as the target for a brutal reprisal, one the Germans intend to be a lesson to the people of France. The men of the village are herded into barns, the women and children into the church, and the whole town is set on fire. Those who flee are machine-gunned. In total, 642 people are killed, with only 10 able to feign death and escape.

JUNE 13

WESTERN FRONT, *FRANCE*
Lieutenant Michael Wittmann, company commander of the SS 501st Heavy Tank Battalion, destroys 27 tanks and armored vehicles of the British 4th Country of London Yeomanry in a tank battle around the village of Villers-Bocage, Normandy.

JUNE 18

WESTERN FRONT, *FRANCE*
US forces reach the west coast of the Cotentin Peninsula, Normandy, cutting off the German garrison in the port of Cherbourg. Hitler has ordered the garrison to fight to the death, although their sacrifice can have little effect.

JUNE 26

WESTERN FRONT, *FRANCE*
The British launch Operation Epsom, a drive west of Caen. Troops and tanks of the 15th, 43rd, and 11th Armored Divisions make good initial progress, but are then halted following very heavy losses.

JUNE 29

WESTERN FRONT, *FRANCE*
The port of Cherbourg finally surrenders to forces of the US VII Corps. The cost to the US has been 22,000 casualties, while 39,000 Germans defy Hitler's orders to fight to the death and are taken prisoner.

JUNE 30

TECHNOLOGY, *GERMANY*
The Germans have formed the first operational unit equipped with

▲ ***Lieutenant Michael Wittmann, company commander of the SS 501st Heavy Tank Battalion, who created havoc with his Tiger tanks at Villers Bocage.***

▼ *American troops march through bomb-damaged Carentan, the first French city to fall to the invaders after D-Day.*

Messerschmitt Me 262 jet fighters. The unit will be deployed to France in the near future.

AIR WAR, *BRITAIN*
To date, 2000 German V1 "Flying Bombs" have been launched against England, mostly against London. In response, the British have increased the number of anti-aircraft guns, fighter aircraft, and barrage balloons.

JULY 11

POLITICS, *UNITED STATES*
President Franklin D. Roosevelt announces he will run for an unprecedented fourth term in the White House.

JULY 18–22

WESTERN FRONT, *FRANCE*
In the face of fanatical resistance, US troops enter St. Lô. The German 352nd Division is destroyed in the process. On the eastern sector of the front, the British and Canadians launch Operation Goodwood, a drive east of Caen to provoke heavier German concentrations in the area. The aim is to wear down German armor to such an extent that it is of no further value to them. The Allies lose over 100 Sherman tanks in the assault. By the 22nd, however, the British have cleared southern Caen.

JULY 20

POLITICS, *GERMANY*
An attempt is made by German officers to assassinate Adolf Hitler. Count Schenk von Stauffenberg, chief-of-staff to General Friedrich Fromm, plants a bomb near Hitler in a conference room at the Nazi leader's East Prussian headquarters at Rastenburg. The bomb explodes at 1242 hours, after von Stauffenberg has left. The bomb fails to kill Hitler and the conspiracy falls apart. Josef Goebbels, Nazi minister for propaganda, acts quickly to convince the Berlin garrison that Hitler is still alive by linking them by telephone. Fromm, in order to allay suspicions of his own involvement in the plot, has von Stauffenberg executed that same evening.

The failure of the plot results in the arrest, torture, and execution of dozens of suspects in the following months. Field Marshal Erwin Rommel is among the most notable of those senior military figures aware of the conspiracy.

◀ ***Field Marshal Erwin von Witzleben. Involved in the plot to kill Hitler, he was hanged with piano wire at Ploetzenzee.***

JULY 25

WESTERN FRONT, *FRANCE*
Operation Cobra, the Allied breakout from Normandy, begins. Following a massive aerial bombardment, three infantry divisions of General J. Lawton Collins' US VII Corps open a breach in the

▼ ***Hitler shows Mussolini his bomb-damaged conference room following the July assassination attempt.***

▲ ***As enemy defenses buckle, units of the US 4th Armored Division arrives in Coutances on July 30, only to discover that the Germans have already left.***

German line between Marigny and St. Gilles, allowing the armor to get through. Within five days, the US spearhead reaches Avranches, turning the west flank of the German front.

July 30

WESTERN FRONT, *FRANCE*
Avranches falls to the US VIII Corps.

August 8

POLITICS, *GERMANY*
Eight German officers, including Field Marshal Erwin von Witzleben, are hanged at the Ploetzenzee prison in Berlin for their part in the July Bomb Plot against Hitler. They are hanged by piano wire, their last moments recorded on film for Adolf Hitler's amusement. All the condemned go to their deaths with dignity, despite their callous treatment.

August 11

WESTERN FRONT, *FRANCE*
Operation Totalize, the Canadian First Army's offensive toward Falaise, is called off after failing to meet its main objectives.

August 19

WESTERN FRONT, *FRANCE*
Allied units have closed the Falaise pocket two weeks after the Canadian First Army launched Operation Totalize, the unsuccessful attempt to cut off the encircled German troops. Some 30,000 German soldiers escape from the pocket across the Seine River, but an estimated 50,000 more are captured and another 10,000 killed. Inside the pocket, which has been constantly strafed and bombed by Allied aircraft, are hundreds of destroyed and abandoned German vehicles. Canadian, British, and Polish forces coming from

DECISIVE WEAPONS

RESISTANCE

Within those countries and regions overrun by the Germans and Japanese in Word War II, there were those among the various populations who were determined to oppose the occupiers in some way, often at great risk to themselves and their families. This resistance could be active or passive. Passive resistance involved demonstrations, industrial strikes, and slowdowns, the production of underground newspapers and leaflets, and wall slogans. Active resistance involved gathering intelligence, assisting escaped Allied prisoners of war and shot-down aircrews, sabotage, and armed action against occupation forces.

Throughout Europe and the Far East, resistance was never the preserve of any particular political grouping or social class; rather it encompassed a complete cross-section of each country's society.

The dangers of fighting back against occupiers were ever present, and resistance movements were under constant threat from enemy intelligence, collaborators, and informers, with torture and death the usual price of being caught. Ownership of a carrier pigeon, for example, warranted death by firing squad in Europe. In addition, there was often infighting between various resistance groups. In Yugoslavia, the Chetniks and Tito's forces fought each other as well as the Axis occupiers. Nevertheless, with outside help (which was often crucial in keeping the various units going), resistance groups in Europe and the Far East aided the general Allied war effort against the Axis powers.

Jubilant members of the French Resistance near Paris in August 1944, with the Germans in full retreat.

▲ ***US infantry make their way through the ruins of Domfront early in August, after the town had been subjected to artillery and aerial bombardment.***

the north link up with the US First Army driving from Argentan.

AUGUST 23

WESTERN FRONT, *FRANCE*
The US 36th Division takes Grenoble. General Dwight D. Eisenhower, Supreme Commander of the Allied Expeditionary Force, overrules General Bernard Montgomery, commander of the 21st Army Group, regarding the latter's plea for a concentrated thrust through the Low Countries into northern Germany. Eisenhower decides that after the capture of Antwerp—a port vital to the Allies—there will be an American assault toward the Saar by General George Patton's US Third Army.

AUGUST 25

WESTERN FRONT, *FRANCE*
The commander of the German garrison of Paris, General Dietrich von Choltitz, surrenders the city to -Lieutenant Henri Karcher of the French 2nd Armored Division. Choltitz, who has 5000 men, 50 artillery pieces, and a company of tanks under his command, had been ordered by Hitler to ensure that "Paris [does] not fall into the hands of the enemy except as a heap of ruins." Some 500 Resistance members and 127 other civilians are killed in the fighting for the city.

AUGUST 25–26

WESTERN FRONT, *FRANCE*
The British XII and XXX Corps cross the Seine River.

AUGUST 31

WESTERN FRONT, *FRANCE*
The US Third Army spearheads an advance toward the Meuse River as the British XXX Corps secures all the main bridges over the Somme near Amiens.

▶ ***French civilians line the streets of Paris to welcome US troops on a victory parade after the Allied liberation of the French capital on August 25 .***

Cracking the German Defenses

With Allied men and materiel pouring ashore on Normandy, the next priority was breaking out of the peninsula. The Germans still had the invasion forces penned in. Any Allied breakout would have to come against formidable strongpoints—particularly the key strategic town of Caen.

British and Canadian troops came ashore on the eastern flank of the Allied invasion. Their major objective was to swiftly capture Caen and then to push armored divisions inland to complete the German rout. Rommel had other ideas.

For the six weeks following the landings, Montgomery launched the British and Canadian troops forward in a series of set-piece battles of growing intensity, as more forces poured into the bridgehead and became available for action. First he sent forwards the 7th Armoured Division—the famous Desert Rats—on a daring outflanking attack to the west of Caen. German Tiger tanks ambushed the force and sent it reeling back to the bridgehead. Next, the British XXX and VIII Corps began Operation Epsom to envelop Caen, but four Waffen-SS panzer divisions concentrated to hammer them hard. Into July, Montgomery continued to chip away at the Germans until his infantry were at the gates of Caen.

To the west, the Germans were giving the Americans under Bradley a hard time in the difficult bocage country. Rommel was desperate to prevent the Allies capturing the port of Cherbourg, which would considerably ease their logistical problems. The defense was led by

▼ *British and American troops aboard landing craft stream toward the Normandy coastline on D-Day.*

veteran German parachute and Waffen-SS divisions, but there were nowhere near as many German tanks facing the Americans as the British.

SOLID ALLIANCE

During the first two months of the Battle for Normandy, all the Allied ground forces were under the command of Montgomery and his Twenty-First Army Group headquarters. Eisenhower was still back in England and had limited control over the unfolding battle. Monty's conduct of the early phases of the Normandy campaign is still very controversial, as rival Allied generals and their acolytes pushed to demonstrate their contribution to the eventual victory. At the heart of Allied strategy was the need to ensure the British and American alliance remained solid. This was Eisenhower's area of expertise, but some of his subordinates lacked his finesse at soothing egos and forging consensus.

By the end of June the Germans had massed some 10 panzer divisions in Normandy, with more than 1500 tanks and armored vehicles. Even though the British and Americans had more than double this number of tanks, an Allied breakthrough seemed elusive. The Soviets had also just begun a major offensive on the Eastern Front, which ripped the heart out of the German defenses and cost the Wehrmacht a further 500,000 casualties. If the German line in Normandy could be breached, Hitler's Reich would never recover. The Allies had to strike soon.

To break the impasse, Montgomery proposed a new strategy. Rather than attempt a breakthrough along a broad front, the aim would be for the British and Canadians to continue to pin the bulk of the German armor in the east around Caen to allow the Americans to break through on a narrow front in the west. Once through the German defenses, US tanks would swing both west and east to capture the vital Brittany ports and ultimately to defeat the German forces facing the British and Canadians around Caen. Bradley liked the new plan, but fierce German

▲ US troops killed during the initial D-Day assault lie covered on the beach.

▼ A German soldier lies dead outside the pillbox he was manning, overlooking the US landing zone at Utah Beach.

THE JULY BOMB PLOT

Dissident German officers almost succeeded in killing Hitler on July 20, 1944.

Within the German Army there had always been senior officers who distrusted Hitler and believed that it was their duty to remove him from power. However, the Nazi leader's popularity meant that they found it difficult to formulate an effective plan. They were also hampered by the fact that the Allies were demanding the unconditional surrender of Germany, and offered no opportunity to negotiate with a regime that supplanted Hitler.

By 1944, however, a small group of officers believed they had no choice. They were led by Claus Schenk von Stauffenberg, who had been badly wounded in North Africa and had a staff position that brought him into regular contact with Hitler.

The plot was codenamed Operation Valkyrie. On July 20, at a meeting at Hitler's East Prussian headquarters in Rastenburg, Stauffenberg placed a briefcase filled with a kilogram of high explosive under the table. He left the room on the pretext of making a phone call and the bomb then detonated. Stauffenberg then left for Berlin, to carry out the next stage of the plot —to seize power in the capital and neutralize the SS and the Gestapo.

However, the plot failed. The bomb had not killed Hitler. Most of the force was absorbed by the heavy wooden table and just three of his staff died. When Stauffenberg arrived in Berlin, the other conspirators had not been able to take the reins of power. Knowing that Hitler had survived, his supporters in Berlin refused to cave in. Stauffenberg was arrested and shot that same evening.

The aftermath of the plot was brutal. Anyone remotely connected with the plot was arrested, and two active field marshals, Rommel and von Kluge, committed suicide.

◀ ***"I want them to be strung up like butchered cattle," was how Hitler told Freisler he wanted the conspirators dealt with. The convicted men were strangled with piano wire and then hung from meat hooks.***

▼ ***Not all of the conspirators were army officers. Here, Johannes Popitz, Prussian Minister of Finance (second from right) and one of the conspirators, is being sentenced to death. In all, 5000 people were killed in Hitler's revenge for the attack.***

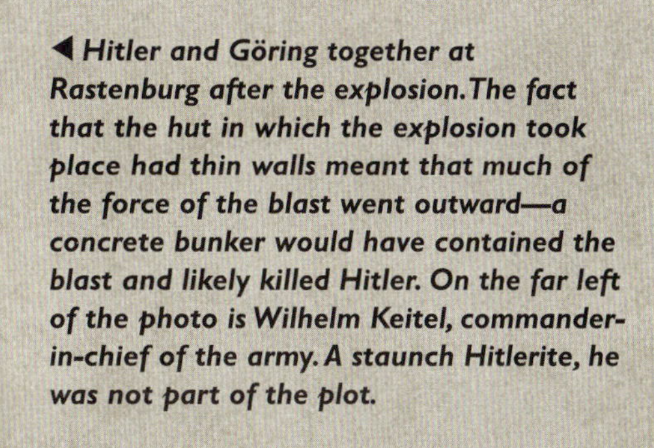

◀ *Hitler and Göring together at Rastenburg after the explosion. The fact that the hut in which the explosion took place had thin walls meant that much of the force of the blast went outward—a concrete bunker would have contained the blast and likely killed Hitler. On the far left of the photo is Wilhelm Keitel, commander-in-chief of the army. A staunch Hitlerite, he was not part of the plot.*

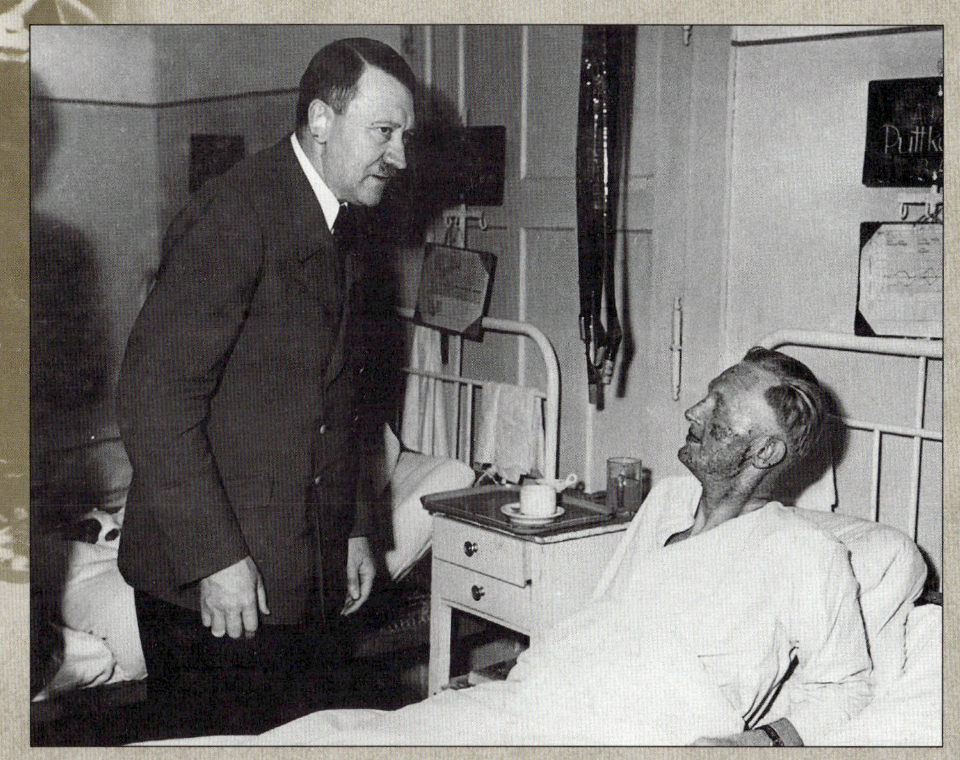

▶ *Hitler visits Admiral Puttkamer, who was badly wounded by theexplosion. Three members of Hitler's staff died. Hitler had a special wound medal struck for those who survived the bomb blast of July 20. It was awarded to 24 recipients.*

▶ *Erwin von Witzleben, a bomb plot conspirator and a retired field marshal, while on trial. He was not allowed a belt or braces and so in the courtroom struggled to hold up his trousers, for which he was berated by the court president, Freisler.*

◀ *Roland Freisler, President of the People's Court that tried those implicated in the plot. An ardent Hitler supporter, he screamed at the accused and tried to humiliate them.*

▲ US fighter-bombers, such as these P-47 Thunderbolts, were crucial in driving back German counter-attacks and disrupting enemy movements in Normandy.

resistance to the drive on Cherbourg meant that it took him longer than expected to develop his strategy and build up his forces, and thus as July wore on US casualties rose. And as the Americans tried to batter through the bocage, there were some complaints that Montgomery was making GIs pay in blood for his pursuit of glory.

Patton was equally critical of Bradley's slowness to break through, commenting: "Sometimes I get desperate over the future. Brad and [Courtney] Hodges [commander designate of First Army] are such nothings. Their virtue is that they get along by doing nothing. I could break through in three days if I commanded. They try and push all along the front and have power nowhere. All that is necessary now is to take more chances by leading them with armoured divisions and covering their advances with air bursts. Such an attack would have to be made on a narrow sector, whereas at present we are trying to attack all along the line."

OPERATION GOODWOOD

Bernard Montgomery then launched Operation Goodwood on July 18 in an attempt to outflank Caen from the east. Three British armored divisions, with almost 900 tanks, backed up by 10,000 infantry, 700 guns, and 2000 heavy bombers, were to smash through the weakened German lines and break into open country.

The Germans weathered the massive bombardment, and an improvised line of Tiger tanks and 88mm flak guns ripped the British attack force apart. Confusion reigned in the British ranks, and the attack stalled without breaching the German lines. Some 270 burning hulks of British tanks littered the battlefield. While the result was a tactical defeat for the British, it doomed the German defences in Normandy. Rommel's panzer reserves had to be committed to hold the line for the next crucial two weeks as the Americans gathered their strength to strike, and Caen was now in Allied hands.

At almost the same time, Rommel was hospitalized after his staff car was strafed by British Typhoon fighter-bombers and a group of German officers planted a bomb in Hitler's East Prussian headquarters as part of an attempted assassination plot. The Führer escaped the explosion but emerged from the ruins of his map room even more convinced of the need to stop his generals retreating any more. Von Rundstedt had already resigned and his successor as Commander-in-Chief West, Field Marshal Günther von Kluge, now had even less freedom of maneuver. The defense of Normandy was being directed personally by the Führer.

THE BOCAGE BATTLE

Holding the German line opposite Bradley was Waffen-SS General Paul Hausser, who had been drafted in to lead the German Seventh Army after its commander, Colonel-General Friedrich Dollman, died of a heart attack at the end of June. Hausser was no blindly loyal Nazi, but a cunning and determined veteran commander with a reputation for being able to improvise skilfully in times of crisis. On the Eastern Front he had commanded the élite II SS Panzer Corps during the battles of Kharkov and Kursk in 1943, at times ignoring Hitler's questionable "fight to the last man and bullet" orders when he thought they would leave his troops threatened with annihilation by Soviet encirclements.

Although he lacked the tank resources of Panzer Group West, later renamed Fifth Panzer Army, under Heinrich Eberbach, which was facing the British and Canadian armies, Hausser deployed his slender forces with great skill to maximize their capability to delay and confound the Americans. His troops turned every village and hedgerow into a fortress, defended by machine guns, mortars, and anti-tank rockets. The bocage terrain, with its impenetrable networks of sunken roads, thick hedges, dense woods, and picturesque villages, was a nightmare to attack.

American tanks and infantry could not maneuver around the German defenses, but had to take each German strongpoint in a slow set-piece attack. Often before the Americans had even been able to consolidate their success, they were driven back by a snap German counterattack and the Americans had to begin the process all over again.

▼ *A German Panzer IV tank of the Hitlerjugend SS panzer Division with its crew. The female names seen in white were written by the young crew, and were probably the names of sweethearts back home in Germany.*

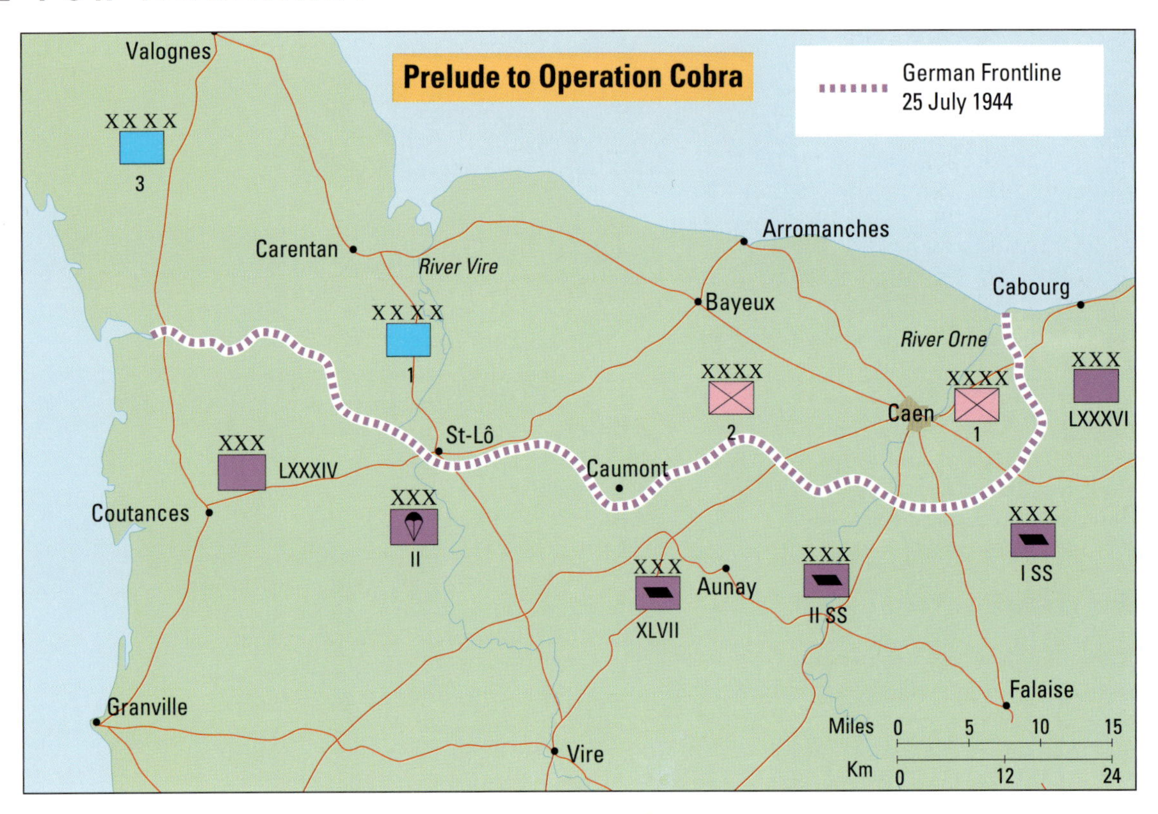

▲ *The disposition of German and Allied forces on the eve of Operation Cobra.* *(See page 192 for map key)*

The first phases of Bradley's campaign in France were conducted in a methodical fashion that reflected his approach to battle. In the days after D-Day, the US Army had concentrated on joining up its two bridgeheads by capturing Carentan at the base of the Cotentin Peninsula on June 12. Over the next two weeks Bradley concentrated on taking the port of Cherbourg, but by the time US troops had reached the city the key dockyards had been systematically demolished by the German defenders and put out of action.

A SLOW, BLOODY ADVANCE

While Bradley's troops were pushing north to Cherbourg, Rommel had a free hand to reinforce his defenses opposite the American sector, pushing II Parachute Corps and LXXXIV Corps into the line opposite Bradley's men. The attack on Cherbourg exhausted the troops taking part, so the newly arrived VIII Corps under Troy Middleton was pushed into the line to help bolster the attempt to achieve a breakout to the south. The experience was very traumatic for the "green" GIs pushed into action for the first time during Bradley's new offensive.

VIII Corps attacked southward on July 3 against the German LXXXIV Corps and immediately found itself bogged down in heavy fighting. The rate of advance was measured in yards and a high price was paid in blood. The 79th Infantry Division lost 2000 men in five days and Middleton's other divisions fared little better. In 12 days of fighting VIII Corps' butcher's bill had risen to 10,000 with little to show for it. Bradley threw VII Corps into the meat grinder on July 4. It attacked across rain-sodden ground and lost 1400 men on the first day and 750 on the following day. Eleven days later, the corps had barely moved the frontline more than 3 miles (5km) south, though had accrued 8000 casualties doing so.

On July 7 it was the turn of XIX Corps to advance, and Bradley assigned a tank division to it in the hope that the armor would be able to open a way forward. The result was little better after the tanks became jammed in the narrow, hedge-lined roads and could not maneuver around the German strongpoints. In five days XIX Corps only managed to advance 6 miles (9.6km).

The only bright point for Bradley in this dismal period was the defeat of a counterattack by the German Panzer Lehr Division on July 11, which was driven back with heavy losses.

Bradley was a methodical and determined man who picked himself up from these setbacks, and a new plan was crafted to seize the town of

St-Lô and defeat the German II Parachute Corps. After a massed artillery barrage, XIX and V Corps surged forward on July 12 in a pincer attack. In a six-day battle, Bradley fed three divisions into the contest against the battered remnants of the German 3rd Parachute and 352nd Infantry Divisions. The weight of firepower overwhelmed the German defenses, and on July 18 American GIs entered St-Lô to find the town totally devastated. This victory cost Bradley another 6000 casualties, bringing his losses over the past 17 days to 40,000 men killed or wounded. His front had advanced less than 7 miles (11km). Many of Bradley's divisions were shattered by this bloody experience, with the long-suffering 90th Infantry Division recording 150 percent casualties among its frontline officers and 100 percent losses in its combat riflemen during the first six weeks of the Normandy campaign.

The one ray of sunshine was the fact that Hausser's battered divisions were in even worse shape than Bradley's troops. Unlike the American First Army, the German forces in Normandy had not received any significant reinforcements during July. Hitler's continued belief that another Allied landing was to be made in the Pas de Calais ensured that the Fifteenth Army, the last uncommitted German force in the West, was kept back from the Normandy Front.

A massive Soviet breakthrough on the Eastern Front—Operation Bagration—meant the German armies had to fight on with whatever resources they had at hand. The divisions manning the Normandy Front boasted little more than a couple of thousand frontline troops to hold their positions. Ammunition and fuel were in short supply because of incessant Allied bombing of German lines of communication (even food had to be transported to frontline troops at night due to Allied air superiority). Hope certainly seemed to be in short supply among the Germans in Normandy.

OPERATION COBRA

Morale among Bradley's divisions was clearly shaken by its bruising battles. Something drastic needed to be done to break through the German lines. Even before his attacks were running out of steam around St-Lô, Bradley was planning a major push to achieve a

▼ ***Moving up behind a hedge in the bocage, three US troops fire on the enemy. The soldier on the far left is firing a fragmentation grenade from his rifle.***

decisive breakthrough. This was dubbed Operation Cobra. It was more than just another thrust through the bocage. The firepower of 2500 heavy bombers and fighter aircraft was to be concentrated on a narrow section of front, and then six divisions, including two armored units, were to roll over the debris of the German defenses.

The objective was the town of Avranches at the gateway to Brittany. After Bradley's tanks had reached this objective, Patton's Third Army would be fed into the battle to swing westward and seize the vital Brittany ports. At the same time, Lieutenant-General Courtney Hodges would take over command of the First Army and swing eastward to roll toward the River Seine and complete the defeat of the German forces in Normandy. At this stage, a deliberate breakthrough and methodical advance was envisaged, not a dramatic breakout. Only as the battle developed would senior Allied commanders see the potential to encircle and trap the German armies facing them if they acted decisively.

To oversee this vastly expanded American effort, Bradley would be elevated to command the Twelfth Army Group, in theory putting him on a par with Montgomery himself. Eisenhower, however, would not have his headquarters fully established on the continent until late August, leaving Montgomery effectively in charge of the high-level conduct of the final stages of the Normandy campaign.

BOMBERS FIND THEIR TARGET

Bradley briefed his commanders on July 12, and over the next 12 days the preparations for Cobra were put in place. A 6-square-mile (15.5-square-kilometre) section of the front to the west of St-Lô, along the road to Périers, was selected as the bombing target, and July 24 was set as the start

▼ *Waffen-SS General Paul Huasser. He was a cunning and sophisticated commander, but ultimately unable to stem the tide of US armor.*

▼ ▶ *General Günther von Kluge. He later became a field marshal, and took his own life after fearing Hitler suspected him of treason.*

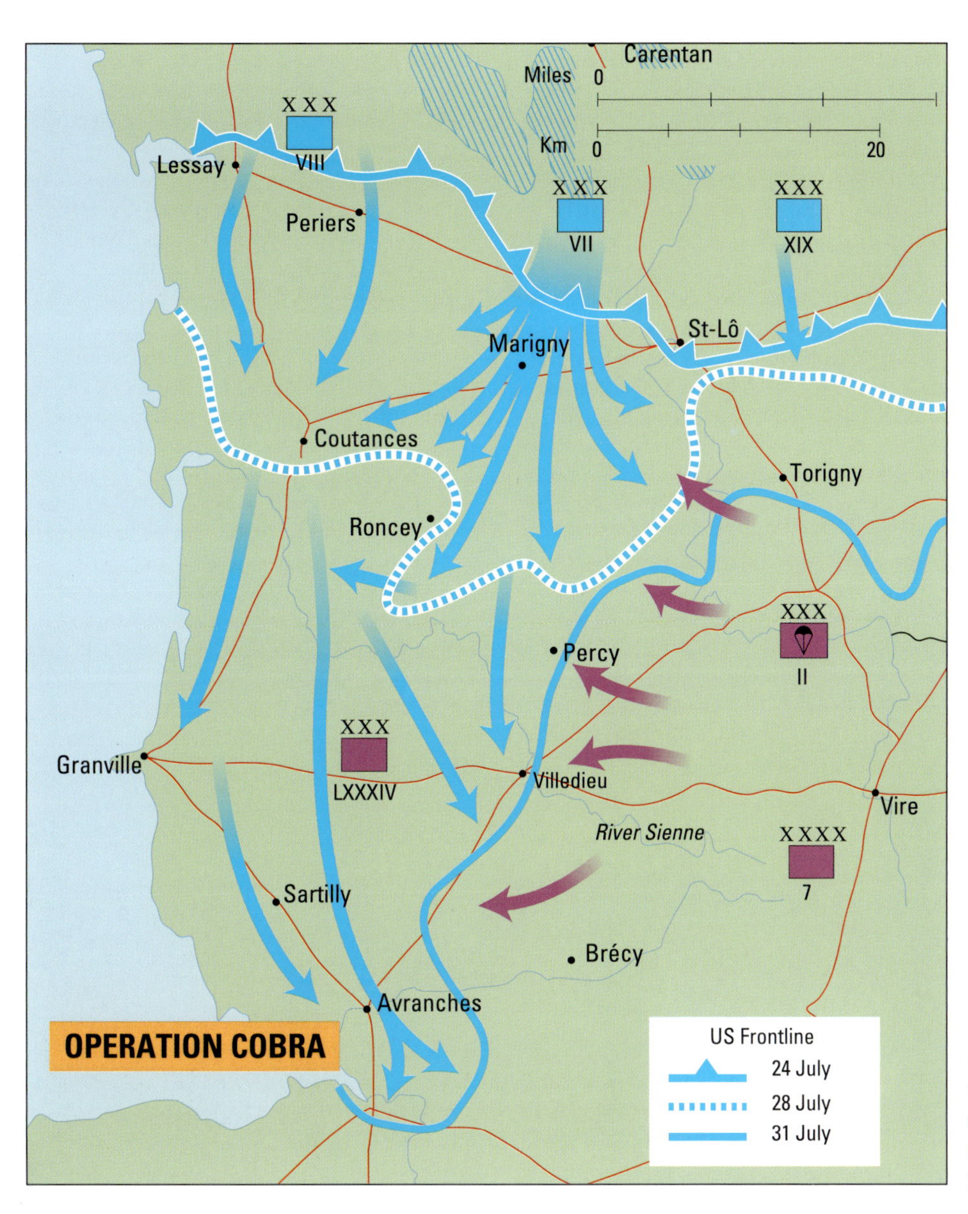

◀ ***The progression of Operation Cobra as it advanced toward Avranches in July 1944. (See page 192 for map key)***

date. The key frontline defenses would be saturated by some 5000 tons (5100 tonnes) of high explosive, napalm, and white phosphorus. The Allied air commanders were worried about the danger of hitting their own troops and they proposed a 9000ft (2750m) safety margin, but Bradley insisted on half this distance. To ease the margin of safety, high-flying heavy bombers would hit the southern fringe of the target box, leaving low-flying fighter-bombers to strike at targets nearer the American lines.

When Allied commanders found out about the July 20 Bomb Plot against Hitler, they realized the urgency of launching Operation Cobra. For George Patton kicking his heels in his command post far behind the front, the tension was clearly too much and he charged into Bradley's command tent, demanding: "For God's sake Brad, you've got to get me into this fight before the war is over."

The first wave of bombers took off on the morning of July 24, but soon the target was obscured by cloud, leading to the raid being canceled. Some 500 aircraft did not receive the recall message and dropped 700 bombs on the target area. Many landed behind US lines, killing 25 and wounding 130 GIs. The raid also alerted the Germans to the fact that a major attack was brewing and their retaliatory artillery bombardment of US staging areas caused heavy casualties and confusion among the assault units.

The following morning the Allied air forces returned in strength to do the job properly. More than 1500 B-17 and B-24 heavy bombers, supported by a further 380 medium bombers and 550 fighter-bombers, dropped 4150 tons (4200 tonnes) of bombs on the target box. The sheer weight of bombs threw up a huge cloud of debris that obscured the targets and led the final wave of aircraft to miss their targets. More than 100 American soldiers were killed and 490 wounded in this attack.

However, the effect on the Germans was devastating, with more than 1000 killed by the bombing alone. In the target zone itself, three battalion command posts were demolished and a regiment was wiped out. The brunt of the bombardment fell on the remnants of the Panzer Lehr Division. Its commander, the veteran Fritz Bayerlein, estimated that 70 percent of the troops in the target area were either killed, wounded, stunned, or driven mad. As the surviving Germans emerged from their ruined command posts or bunkers, they were strafed by USAAF Thunderbolts and Mustangs, further adding to the confusion and panic among the demoralized defenders.

The bombing of the American frontlines had thrown the assault troops into some confusion, and it took time to get the first GIs to advance into the moonscape caused by the bombing. A handful of German machine-gun nests survived and were able to slow the American advance to a snail's pace. Bradley and his commanders were momentarily afraid the attack had failed.

On the other side of the front, the Germans were also in crisis. Their lines were only holding together by a slender thread. There were no reserves left after Hausser sent his last two battalions to bolster the threatened sector. They proved of little use after US fighter-bombers strafed them as they moved in daylight and decimated their advancing column.

Fortunately the VII Corps commander, Major-General J. Lawton Collins, was made of sterner stuff and decided that he had to commit his two armored divisions to crush German resistance once and for all. His lead tanks had been fitted with improvised hedge plows, called Rhinos, that allowed them to smash through the bocage terrain and restore their freedom of maneuver. On the second day of the attack, "Lightning Joe" Collins' troops had all but rolled over the German defenses. The Panzer Lehr Division was as good as annihilated and some 600 American tanks were heading south unopposed.

On July 28, Hausser decided to throw his final card into the battle. He pulled the 2nd SS Das Reich Panzer Division and 17th SS Götz von Berlichingen Panzergrenadier Division out of the front against VIII Corps and sent them in to hit Collins' columns in the flank. The result was a disaster for

▼ *US troops with a destroyed enemy artillery piece after it was attacked by aircraft from XIX Tactical Air Command near Marigny.*

the Germans, with the panzer columns devastated by Allied airpower as they maneuvered to intercept the American formations. A brief tank battle ensued that temporarily halted VII Corps, but on the strategic level the movement of the two Waffen-SS divisions had completely unhinged the German defenses in western Normandy

VIII CORPS STRIKES

Troy Middleton's VIII Corps had arrived in Normandy a month before as the advance guard of Patton's Third Army, only to find itself attached to Bradley's First Army for the vicious battles in the bocage. His infantry divisions had certainly been blooded in those deadly duels with Hausser's Seventh Army, but he had yet to commit his armor.

Once Hausser moved his panzers eastward to counter the American breakthrough, Middleton launched the 4th and 6th Armored Divisions forward. The weakened German line broke under the combined weight of some 300 Shermans rolling forward, and the remnants of three German infantry divisions were cut to pieces. The road south was open.

On July 28 the "Super Sixth" advanced south through Lessay and headed down the main road to Coutances. Three miles (5 kilometres) to the east, the 4th Armored moved through Périers and also had Coutances in its sights. All that blocked their way was the debris of German columns that had been shot to pieces by Allied fighter-bombers. By the evening they were through Coutances and heading south toward Avranches. Combat Command B of the 4th Armored took Coutances in a flanking attack. In the wake of the American tanks came the 79th and 8th Infantry Divisions, who followed close on the heels of the 6th and 4th Armored Divisions, respectively.

During July 28, General Patton was summoned to Bradley's headquarters to be told that in three days' time the Third Army would be activated and unleashed into Brittany. In the meantime, he would be given interim command of Middleton's troops so he could secure his jumping-off points around Avranches.

Without hesitating, Patton drove down to Middleton's headquarters and put the latter in the picture about his intentions. Early the next morning, Patton headed south to Coutances to get a feel for the battle and encourage his armored spearheads forward. Quickly the troops of VIII Corps got to know what it meant to be under Patton's command. He found the 6th Armored halted at a river while their officers studied a map. Ignoring a group of German troops nearby, Patton strode into the river to test its depth. Finding it was not at all deep, Patton unleashed a torrent of expletives to get his tank crews moving. Patton's next target was a battalion of the 90th Infantry Division whom he found digging foxholes. "It is stupid to be afraid of a beaten enemy," he shouted at the cowering troops. Suitably invigorated with fighting spirit, Patton's spearheads spent 29 July motoring at full speed toward the town of Avranches.

The 6th Armored saw action for the first time that day, when Combat Command A, supported by its divisional artillery, forced a crossing of the River Sienne west of Coutances,

EYEWITNESS REPORT

"July 29th: Raining—moved out at 07:28 hours. Went down St-Lô-Périers highway through Périers. All towns and villages in shambles. Périers almost flattened—people streaming back to their former homes if they can find them. Bivouacked about 6 miles (9.6 kilometres) outside of St-Sauveur Lendelin. Here we go again, moved into new bivouac area 4 miles (6.5 kilometres) north of Coutances. We are taking nearly 1000 prisoners a day. We lost a halftrack, and the men are missing. General Wood led the attack personally.

July 30th: Battalion is the spearhead of drive south. Traffic is pretty heavy. We moved out at 08:25 hours traveling south through Coutances, most of city is destroyed. We bivouacked about 3 miles (5 kilometres) north of Cérences. Ate then moved out and bivouacked again. Jerries shelled our position, moved out. Used T5 (halftrack) to rout out some Jerries, who wouldn't come out. I got one with my machine gun. He was trying to circle us. Moved back in old position. Bivouacked 4 miles (6.5 kilometres) up road. Infantry flushing out hedgerows on either side of us. Haven't had a chance to shave for three days. Got five hours' sleep finally—still eating K rations."

Corporal Albert O. Maranda, who served in the 4th Armored Division's 94th Armored Field Artillery Battalion

by fording the shallow stream and scaling the bluffs beyond at twilight after clearing moderate resistance on the north bank. 6th Armored advanced 26 miles (42km) on its first day in combat. The divisional plan stipulated a development in two columns, with Combat Command A following Combat Command B across the river and then advancing on the left flank. During the following 48-hour period the division swept along the Atlantic coast. The city of Granville was not defended, but Bréhal was surrounded by many strongpoints. More than 800 prisoners were captured during the division's advance.

PRISONERS ON THEIR OWN

The German front was collapsing all around Hausser. He himself had to dodge past an American tank to get back to his headquarters. However, that too was soon surrounded by US troops. To the west the remnants of the German LXXXIV Corps, including the two Waffen-SS panzer divisions, were trapped between VIII and VII Corps at Roucy. Hausser made his own escape during the night and ordered his trapped troops to break out to the west. They managed to fight their way past the American columns in the darkness, but left 4000 prisoners and hundreds of burnt-out vehicles behind them. In front of Patton's spearhead was nothing but confused and defeated German units fleeing for their lives. XIX Tactical Air Command's fighter-bombers roamed ahead of the American columns strafing any German traffic they could find. The biggest problem for 4th Armored was what to do with all the prisoners it was taking. In the end they were simply disarmed and ordered to march north on their own to find a prisoner-of-war camp.

On the evening of July 30, the 4th Armored's Combat Command B rolled into Avranches and found the town deserted by the Germans. However, it was soon attacked from the north by a column of several hundred German troops who had been bypassed in the retreat. After a brief firefight the Germans surrendered, but when another group of Germans attacked, the prisoners escaped from the tank company guarding the northern approaches to the town.

A large group of Germans managed to escape westward through Avranches during the night, but with daylight US fighter-bombers appeared. Their support ensured the 4th Armored remained firmly in control of the town.

▼ ***US troops enter the French town of Coutances. The 4th Armored Division's Combat Command B had taken the town on July 29.***

▲ ***US tanks and infantry in jeeps advance down a road near Coutances. Most of the buildings have been destroyed by artillery fire.***

ROUNDING UP PRISONERS

A series of Allied mopping-up attacks rounded up hundreds of German prisoners scattered around Avranches. During July 31, fighter-bomber pilots returning from a routine patrol reported that the key bridge over the River Sélune at Pontaubault was undefended, and thus John Wood ordered an immediate attack to seize this golden opportunity.

The Germans, realizing the danger to their position in Brittany, had dispatched a battalion, backed up by assault guns, to secure the bridge before the Americans could get to it. Wood's men were quicker. After his Shermans rolled over the bridge they turned southeast to confront the approaching German column. After a brisk exchange of fire, the outgunned Germans beat a hasty retreat to St-Malo. During the day the 4th and 6th Armored Divisions captured 4000 prisoners between them and the follow-up infantry bagged another 3000 Germans. This was a significant part of the 20,000 captured during the six days of Operation Cobra. In four days of breakneck advance VIII Corps' total casualties amounted to only 700 killed and wounded. It was a far cry from the bocage fighting.

ADVANCE TO GLORY

That evening Patton gathered his staff in the "Lucky Forward" command post to announce that they would assume full operational control of VIII Corps on the next day, ready for the advance into Brittany. The role of the Third Army would, however, remain secret from the world for as long as possible in order to maintain the fiction that Patton was still being held in southeast England, waiting to lead the invasion of the Pas de Calais and thus distract the German Fifteenth Army from the Normandy Front. The American general was in a feisty mood, and concluded his speech in true George Patton fashion.

"There's another thing I want you to remember. Forget this goddamn business of worrying about our flanks, but not to the extent we don't do anything else. Some goddamn fool once said that flanks must be secured and since then sons-of-bitches all over the world have been going crazy guarding their flanks. We don't want any of that in the Third Army. Flanks are something for the enemy to worry about, not us. I don't want to get any messages saying that, 'We are holding our positions'. We're not holding anything! Let the Hun do that. We are advancing constantly and we're not interested in holding on to anything except the enemy. We're going to hold on to him by the nose and we're going to kick him in the ass; we're going to kick the hell out of him all the time and we're going to go through him like crap through a goose. We have one motto: L'audace, l'audace, toujours l'audace! [Daring, daring, always daring!] Remember that gentlemen."

HITLER'S FOREIGN LEGIONS

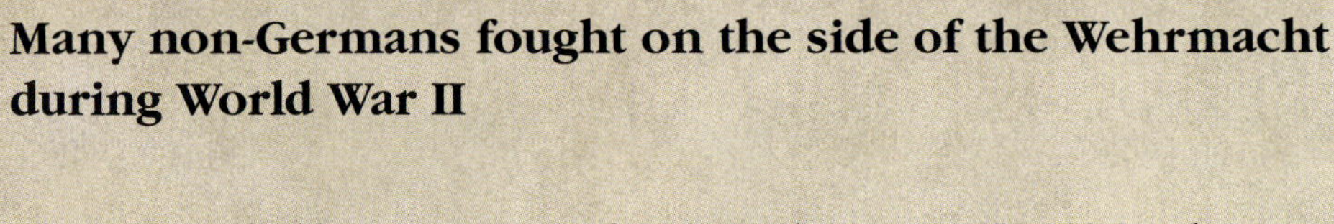

Many non-Germans fought on the side of the Wehrmacht during World War II

The Waffen-SS had been a tiny part of the Wehrmacht in 1939, but by 1945 39 Waffen-SS divisions had been created, 25 of which contained a strong foreign element. Heinrich Himmler, head of the SS, was happy for "Aryans" to join: he said of Estonia, for example, that: "The Estonians really do belong to the few races that can, after the segregation of only a few elements, be merged with us."

In Western Europe there were many individuals prepared to throw in their lot with Germany: 50,000 Dutch, 40,000 Belgians, 20,000 French, 6000 Danes, and 6000 Norwegians joined up. And in spite of Nazi racial theories, Bosnian Muslims, Albanians, Ukrainians, and Russians also formed part of this army within an army.

Those who joined the Waffen-SS did so for a variety of motives—some, no doubt, out of sympathy with Nazi aims, but many because it offered a way out of difficult circumstances back home, and others because they were caught up in a complex situation—such as the Cossacks who were persuaded to fight against Yugoslav and Italian partisans.

Those individuals who joined the Waffen-SS faced a very difficult set of choices in 1945, as Nazi Germany tottered toward defeat. Many in Western Europe would find it very difficult to return to their former lives, and so fought on to the end in Berlin. In Eastern Europe many tried to return to their communities, while others fought the Red Army as partisans even after the defeat of German forces.

◀ ***A member of the 7th SS Freiwilligen Prinz Eugen Mountain Division, formed in 1942 from ethnic Germans (Volksdeutsche) from the Balkans. There was much discussion in Nazi circles about which groups in occupied countries did or did not qualify as "ethnic Germans."***

▼ ***French volunteers to the Waffen-SS swear their oath of allegiance, which was to the Third Reich and "to unconditionally obey the Commander-in Chief of the Armed Forces, Adolf Hitler." The so-called "Charlemagne" Division of French speakers was formed in 1945, and some of its members fought to the end in Berlin in April of that year.***

▲ *A Norwegian ski trooper of the Waffen-SS, carrying ammunition for his unit's machine gun and also armed with an Eihandgranate 39 grenade. The first foreign unit of the Waffen-SS was the Standarte Nordland, made up of Danes and Norwegians, and the second was Standarte Westland, composed of Dutch and Belgians.*

▼ *Infantry and panzer officers of the Wiking Division confer on the Eastern Front in 1944. (Note the divisional cuffband of the officer on the right of the photograph.) Wiking was considered the best of the foreign formations within the Waffen-SS. Originally formed as the 5th Motorised Division under Felix Steiner, it was composed of volunteers from Scandinavia, Finland, Estonia, the Netherlands, and Belgium.*

▼ *Fritz Klingenberg (on left) discusses troop movements with Oberstgruppenführer Paul Hausser (on right), who had helped establish the Waffen-SS. Klingenberg fought with the SS Das Reich Division and then took over the 17th SS Panzergrenadier Division Götz von Berlichingen, which contained many Volksdeutsche members. He was killed in action in March 1945. Klingenberg won renown for his audacious capture of Belgrade in 1941, one of the first major successes of the Waffen-SS.*

▲ *Latvian recruits to the SS take cover behind a knocked-out T-34 tank early in 1944, during the retreat from Leningrad. They are part of III SS Panzer Corps. This formation eventually became trapped in the Courland Pocket in 1945. Although some Latvians managed to escape to the forests, where they hid away from the Red Army, most died in that last year of the war.*

Hard Fighting in the Bocage

The fight in Normandy's bocage country illustrated the problems American commanders had experienced since the US Army first entered combat in North Africa in 1943. While General Bradley and others had counted upon the overwhelming superiority and numerical advantage of American arms, fighting the Germans in the hedgerows demonstrated that war was still the domain of the infantryman and his supporting arms.

GERMAN DEFENSES

The elaborate German defenses in the hedgerows presented American infantry and combined-arms commanders with problems that often negated the "school solution" of overwhelming the enemy with fire and maneuver, with little consideration given to the need for a unified combined-arms doctrine.

Indeed, as the German defenders in the hedgerows reminded the attacking American soldiers time and again, it was the defender and not attacker that decided when, where and how the battle would proceed. By selecting the hedgerow country of Normandy to make its first stand against the US First Army, the Wehrmacht briefly immobilized the overwhelming

▼ *The beginning of Operation Cobra, July 25, 1944: the moment when the Normandy campaign changed from an infantryman's fight to a great armored charge across an 4.5-mile (8-km) front into the heart of France.*

American advantage in tanks, vehicles, and other mechanized assets and forced the US Army to fight on its terms and over terrain of its choosing.

The result was that the Americans had to fight for nearly every hedgerow, that the Germans had transformed into a mini-fortress. The hedges had to be dealt with by set-piece assault teams in a laborious and time-consuming process that delayed General Bradley's desire to avoid the attrition-style of warfare of World War I.

The figures to the right show that Field Marshal Montgomery's later statement that the battle of Normandy "was fought exactly as planned before the invasion" is incorrect. No planner prior to the landings could have

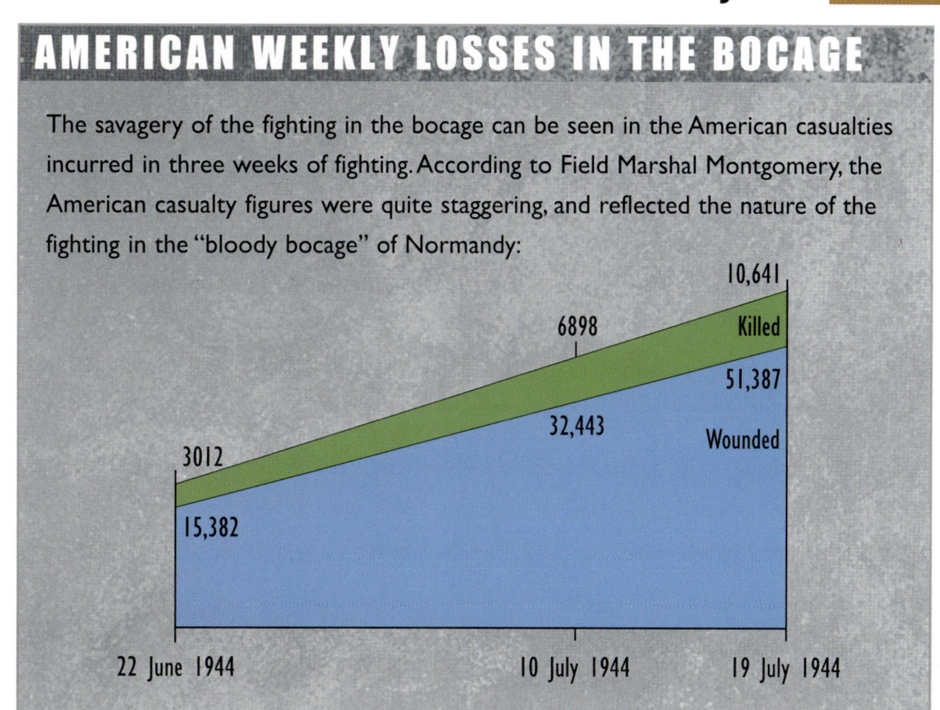

▼ ***To the east of the US First Army, the British VIII and XXX Corps south of Bayeux began their own push south in Operation Bluecoat.***

▲ ***With the roads out of St-Lô now free of Germans, the armored columns of VII Corps began heading for the next major road junction, at the town of Coutances.***

foreseen the difficulties faced by American troops in the bocage country, and if they did then the troops were needlessly thrown into the battle unprepared for the ordeal of combat ahead. General Bradley was more correct in his summation that the only alternative for the Allies (British and American forces) was to "smash through" the German frontline defenses, since only a "breakout" would effect a rupture of the enemy lines to enable the American and British forces to utilize their advantages in mobility in a war of maneuver.

While the debate between Montgomery and Bradley continued on in the battle of the postwar memoirs as to whose methods were instrumental in the defeat of the German Army during the battle for Normandy, the fact remained that the fighting in the bocage country once again brought to the fore the importance of combined arms and the requirements of modern mechanized warfare. This was a fact that had become apparent once in the bocage, as it showed that American commanders had neglected to prepare their forces adequately for combat in northwest Europe. While the prewar US Army field regulations made specific mention of the need to train troops in combined-arms warfare, the fact remained that the lessons of the débâcle at Kasserine Pass in February 1943 had not been completely absorbed by American field commanders, specifically General Bradley himself, as the GIs prepared for Overlord. In fact, General Bradley made little mention or reference to the lessons of Kasserine Pass as applied to preparing the US Army for its grim ordeal in northwest Europe. Indeed, what occurred in the bocage country only reinforced the fact that combined-arms training had been seriously neglected in preparing the US Army for combat in France. This proved to be decisive for both the way the campaign was fought in the hedgerows and throughout the remainder of the campaign in France and into Germany.

The need for more effective tank-infantry teams was among the most vital lessons learned in the bocage fighting, particularly as US forces began to approach the Siegfried Line. While US commanders became absorbed in the planning and execution of the breakout from Normandy and the rapid movement across France, there was agreement in the after-action reports that the experience gained in Normandy demonstrated the need for closer cooperation between the different combat arms.

In a tactical sense, the First Army proved initially ineffective in its first major battle with the main elements of the Wehrmacht during the fighting in the hedgerows. The elaborate German defenses in the Normandy farmland demonstrated that it was the rifleman, with supporting arms backed up by an excellent logistical and support system behind him, that won battles, and not grand strategy. In the bocage fighting, the common denominator between the Americans and Germans was the emphasis the fighting placed on individual combat skills, with advances measured hedgerow by hedgerow and not by large sweeps made or arrows drawn on a map board in a command post or combat operations center.

As for the Germans, only their adoption of elaborate defensive tactics in the hedgerows had averted what they later admitted could have been a total disintegration of their defenses in Normandy. Only by constantly shifting its forces over terrain that channeled the US First Army's broad-front strategy did the Wehrmacht avoid total defeat. Nonetheless, the fact remained that the inability to bring sufficient forces to bear greatly hindered the Germans from capitalizing on their success by concentrating their forces against the American armies in the bocage. Had the Germans been able to concentrate any part of their forces against any one of the American divisions in the area outside of St-Lô, they just might have turned the course of battle in any one sector. However, they were forced to contain local thrusts to relieve pressure on their own frontline units.

▼ *General Patton took command of VIII Corps and on July 30 launched a drive south, taking Avranches — and these prisoners — on the same day.*

LACK OF SPIRIT

One other factor significantly contributed to the German defeat in the battle of the bocage, and that was the lack of aggressiveness displayed by some units in making wholehearted offensive efforts. There was solid evidence for this, at least in the views held by Rommel and the other senior German officers concerning the results of Panzer Lehr's attack of July 11, 1944. This was also noted in the US Army's official history, which stated that there was some German dissatisfaction at the high command echelons with overall panzer effectiveness. Fighting spirit was the vital prerequisite for success, and there were signs that it was eroding at troop level.

Part of the "lack of spirit" can be attributed to the shortages the Germans experienced in both men and materiel. Although German troop morale was good, courage alone could not compensate for materiel disadvantages. In short, the Germans could not meet the Allied rate of fire because their transportation system had been degraded by incessant night-and-day bombing by Allied aircraft, as well as being the target for raids by the French resistance.

HEAVY LOSSES

Costly in men and materiel as hedgerow fighting was for the Allies, it was equally expensive for the Germans, who simply could not replace or replenish their forces in a way the First Army could. In an official report issued from OB West in the autumn of 1944, the German high command reported that it had lost 150 Mk IV tanks, 85 Mk V Panthers, 15 Tiger Is, 167 75mm assault guns (Mk IIIs and Mk IVs), and almost 30 88mm dual-

▼ ***First Army M-10s pass through Fontainbleu on the open road to Paris, August 23.***

purpose guns between June 6 and July 9—more than enough to equip an entire Waffen-SS division.

The price in manpower for the Germans was even more staggering. Between June 6 and July 11, at the start of General Bradley's drive toward St-Lô, OB West lost some 2000 officers and 85,000 enlisted men. In the St-Lô-Cotentin sector, the 243rd Division alone lost over 8000 men, while the 352nd lost 8000 officers and men. Panzer Lehr lost some 3140 officers and enlisted men. By 17 July, total German casualties had risen to about 100,000, of which 2360 were officers.

Despite Field Marshal von Kluge's desperate attempts to constantly reinforce the depleted units in Normandy, he sometimes wondered whether or not OKW truly appreciated the tremendous consumption of forces that was the consequence of the days of major battles his divisions were forced to face during the fighting in the hedgerows.

GERMAN LOSSES: BATTLE OF NORMANDY

Field Marshal Montgomery in his memoirs provided a rough estimate of the German losses during the battle for Normandy:
– Corps and Divisional Commanders Killed or Captured: 20
– Army Commanders Wounded: 2 (Rommel, Hausser)
– Supreme Commanders Dismissed: 2 (von Rundstedt, von Kluge)
– Divisions Eliminated or Mauled: 40
Total Losses (estimate): 300,000
Guns Captured or Destroyed: 3000
Tanks Destroyed: 1000

While the battle in the hedgerows was an infantryman's war, von Kluge and other German commanders, including the former commanding officer of OB West, Field Marshal von Rundstedt, correctly saw Germany's only chance of repelling the US First Army was with an active mobile defense. Field Marshal von Kluge wanted "more tanks" to act as the "spine" for the German infantry to deal with any further Allied breakthroughs.

Unfortunately for such a strategy, Germany was now scraping the bottom of the barrel in order to stave off defeat in the East and the West. As the fighting in the bocage country ended, Field Marshal Montgomery's Twenty-First Army Group and General Bradley's First Army laid the foundation for the Allied victory in northwest Europe, forcing the Germans to concede that the Wehrmacht could never hope to match the Allies in terms of men and equipment, despite its superior tactical and operational abilities.

The Germans, nevertheless, did their best to contain the American breakthrough in Normandy. General Dwight D. Eisenhower acknowledged in his final report on the operations on the Cotentin Peninsula that for six weeks there followed, "a grueling struggle to secure a lodgment area of sufficient depth in which to build up a striking force of such magnitude as to enable us to make full use of our potential material superiority. The process took longer than we expected, largely owing to the adverse weather conditions which repeatedly interrupted the flow of men and stores across the Channel. The enemy fought tenaciously to contain our beachheads, though he was at no time able to collect the strength to constitute a serious offensive threat".

Tactically and operationally, General Eisenhower also acknowledged that, due to the Wehrmacht's shortage in infantry, its leaders came to depend upon the use of tanks in a defensive role to strengthen its defenses. This in turn prevented the Germans from using their qualitative advantage in tanks in more mobile operations, something that Field Marshal von Rundstedt had advocated long before the Allied landings in Normandy. It also prevented the Germans from pulling their armor back to be used once an Allied breakthrough occurred. In one sense, General Eisenhower's comments gave credence to Field Marshal von Rundstedt's earlier conclusions prior to D-Day that a more mobile defense would have been the best way to defeat the landing, as opposed to Rommel's desire to fight from fixed positions around the beachhead.

As for the fighting in the bocage country of Normandy itself, the view of Lieutenant-General Dietrich von Choltitz perhaps best summarized the fighting for both the American and German soldiers, when he commented that the battle in Normandy in the summer of 1944 was "a monstrous bloodbath", the likes of which he had not previously seen in 11 years of war. For the ordinary American GI, meanwhile, who through sheer endurance overcame the elaborate German defenses in the hedgerows of Normandy, combat in the bocage country brought with it a renewed respect for his German adversary — a respect that remained with him throughout the war.

Breakout and the Falaise Pocket

By the end of July the Americans had broken through the German line, thanks to Operation Cobra, which overwhelmed the worn-out frontline defenses. Hitler ordered six panzer divisions to counterattack and seal the front.

After almost two months of continuous fighting, these divisions were little more than weak regimental battle groups. Allied fighter-bombers caught the German tanks in the open and the attack collapsed in chaos. This was the cue for Lieutenant-General George Patton to launch his recently activated Third Army into action, breaking through and racing eastward for the Seine River.

Patton was controversial but talented. He was an expert in fast-moving armored warfare. His Third Army had arrived in France after D-Day, and was fresh. Patton pushed his armored units south and west along the coast. The retreating Germans had no chance to establish a new frontline.

Patton's men entered Brittany on July 30. On that same day, Montgomery opened a new attack to the southwest of Caen. Montgomery's new attack was intended to prevent German units from moving westward to deal with Cobra. Patton's armored units were

▼ *British troops watch a farmhouse burn in the Normandy village of Christot in June 1944. The Allies had to fight hard to advance through Normandy.*

now moving through Brittany without any real resistance. He asked Allied commanders for permission to turn back to the east, and was ordered to drive behind the Germans toward the Seine River. The German forces on the Normandy Front would have to retreat to avoid becoming surrounded.

By August 7, Patton's units had reached the Loire River, some 60 miles (96km) south of their starting point. The German generals in Normandy argued for a retreat. Hitler instead ordered a counterattack against the town of Mortain. The town stood at the western edge of the fast-developing bulge in the German line. The Germans began Operation Lüttich on August 7. They soon captured Mortain. By the next day, however, the attack was over. The attackers could not overcome US resistance backed by Allied ground-attack aircraft. The Allies could now push ahead with their plan to close the escape routes of the German forces.

THE FALAISE POCKET

Hitler forbade his troops to even contemplate retreat. Patton's tanks were now closing a huge trap around the German forces that were being driven into a pocket south of Caen. By mid-August the remnants of more than 20 German divisions were pinned into the pocket, with the only escape route being a narrow corridor to the east. On August 20 the pocket was locked shut. Allied aircraft and artillery pounded the pocket for days until resistance ceased. There was no formal surrender or breakout. Individuals made their own choices. The scene Allied troops found as they combed the ruins of the German Army in Normandy was truly apocalyptic. They found 567 tanks, 950 artillery pieces, 7700 vehicles and the bodies of 10,000 Germans and the carcasses of tens of thousands of horses. Some 50,000 Germans surrendered, and 20,000 others made their escape on foot through the Allied

▲ In the days after the D-Day landings, supplies pour ashore from large landing craft to reinforce the Allied bridgehead. Barrage balloons fly overhead to deter German air attacks.

THE LIBERATION OF PARIS

The liberation of Paris represented tangible proof that the Allies were winning the war in western Europe.

There was fear on the Allied side that the Germans would fight hard in the French capital, and that such fighting might leave one of the great world capitals in ruins. The Allies originally planned to bypass the city and isolate any German garrison. Hitler had, in fact, decided soon after D-Day that Paris should be destroyed rather than fall back into Allied hands: he ordered that, if it fell, the French capital should be left a "field of ruins".

As the German armies in northern France were defeated in the Falaise Pocket, there was wrangling about who should be allowed to enter Paris first, and anxiety about what the Germans were planning. In Paris itself, strikes began on August 18, after which Resistance fighters began attacking German troops.

Fortunately, the commander of the garrison of Paris, General Dietrich von Choltitz, refused to carry out Hitler's orders of destruction and set about negotiating a truce with Paris Resistance fighters (this was difficult in itself, as the resistance was split into various factions, some supporting de Gaulle but many being anti-Gaullist communists). There was street fighting as Resistance fighters tried to take on the Germans. Although a truce of sorts was agreed, violence continued. The Germans burnt down the Grand Palais (held by Resistance forces) on August 23.

General de Gaulle was insistent that the capital of France must be liberated only by French troops. Eisenhower reluctantly agreed to this, with the proviso that the liberation should involve other Allied detachments also. In the event, the French 2nd Armoured Division under General Philippe Leclerc won a race to the capital on August 24 (disobeying orders to do so), and de Gaulle himself attended the first of several victory parades in the capital on August 25. That same day, Von Choltitz himself surrendered.

The relief of the Parisian population was almost palpable as French troops moved in to the capital. There were painful scenes as collaborators were attacked, but in general the atmosphere in the city was one of joy that the Nazi yoke was lifted at last.

▲ *Members of the German administration of Paris surrender to Resistance fighters. On August 16 the Germans executed 35 young Resistance members in the Bois de Boulogne to the west of the city—an act that outraged the public. During the confused fighting of August 17–24 the Germans held many strongpoints, but were not able to clear the streets of Resistance barricades.*

▼ *A Resistance barricade set up on Rue de la Huchette in the 5th Arrondissement. The German garrison had some tanks, and could probably have attacked more of the barricades than it actually did. The Swedish Consul General in Paris, Rauol Nordling, helped broker limits to the fighting that certainly helped the Resistance more than the Germans.*

Cœur de notre France
Symbole des libertés humaines

L'ECHO D'ALGER

PARIS EST LIBÉRÉ
par les Forces Françaises de l'Intérieur
après quatre ans, trois mois et huit jours d'oppression

MARSEILLE seconde ville de France est délivrée

La France entière et l'Empire ont salué avec une joie délirante la libération de la Ville Lumière

Les Nations alliées se sont associées à l'enthousiasme du peuple français

Ce qu'on verra demain...

Le salut du gouvernement au peuple de Paris

Ce qu'on ne verra plus...

Le général Kœnig annonce la libération de PARIS

DÉLIVRANCE !

À ALGER

LA DÉLIVRANCE DE PARIS fait éclater l'enthousiasme patriotique

QUELQUES DÉTAILS SUR LA MAGNIFIQUE ATTITUDE DES F.F.I.

UN APPEL du Gouvernement à la population parisienne

Adresse du général d'armée CATROUX gouverneur général de l'Algérie

Les mêmes méthodes qui permirent aux Allemands d'amener notre défaite pourront un jour se retourner contre eux et nous apporter la victoire

LES INFORMATIONS ... MARSEILLE PAR LES TROUPES FRANÇAISES

▼ *Evidence of the often fierce street fighting that took place in the days before the German surrender: a French flag flies over a barricade on a Paris street. There were about 20,000 Resistance fighters in Paris able to take on the Germans, although they were only lightly armed.*

▼ *Charles de Gaulle walks down the Champs Elysees in front of the Arc de Triomphe. His belief that French troops should liberate the city led General Leclerc, commanding the French 2nd Armoured Division, to disobey orders from his US superior and race into the French capital before any other Allied forces.*

▲ *"Paris is freed by the French Forces of the Interior" screams this headline in a newspaper published in French Algeria. The headline simplifies a mass of complex issues. First, the French Forces of the Interior were de Gaulle's wing of the Resistance, and the communists who formed an equally important Resistance organization certainly did not recognize his authority. Secondly, in spite of the fact that there had been fighting in Paris before Allied regular forces arrived, the liberation was achieved by regular forces from outside.*

ring. Of the 38 German divisions committed to the Normandy Front, 25 had ceased to exist. The German Army had lost almost half a million men.

There were now only 70 German tanks and 36 artillery pieces between the Normandy Front and the Rhine. What remained of the German forces in France were in full retreat from the victorious Allied forces. Additional landings in southern France in mid-August completed the rout of Hitler's armies in the West. For a month the pursuit was unrelenting, and by mid-September almost all of France and Belgium had been liberated.

Montgomery argued for a narrow advance into Germany, but Eisenhower, the supreme Allied commander, maintained a broad-front strategy which gave the Germans some respite. In addition, a fuel crisis forced the Allies to rein-in their tank columns to regroup and reorganize before they could begin the final offensive to smash into the heart of Hitler's Reich.

Now the Allies broke out from Normandy and poured toward the western border of Nazi Germany, pursuing a dispirited enemy.

LANDINGS IN SOUTHERN FRANCE

Allied morale, on the other hand, was high. It was increased by news that Allied troops had landed in southern France on August 15. Operation Anvil had been planned to take place at the same time as D-Day. It had been delayed, however, because not enough landing craft were available to support both operations.

Operation Anvil aimed to protect the flank of the Allied armies in northern Europe. It was also planned to open the port of Marseilles as a supply base from the Mediterranean. The landings met with almost instant success. The German troops in the region were generally poor. By nightfall on August 15, some 95,000 Allied troops had come ashore in southern France; only 183 soldiers had been killed during the landings.

The Allies forced the Germans to flee north up the valley of the Rhône River. By August 28, they had defeated most of the German troops stationed in southern France. They had suffered relatively few casualties themselves.

On September 11, the southern invasion force linked up with Patton's Third Army outside the city of Dijon. From then on, the Allies could drive toward the German frontier from the Swiss border to the North Sea along an unbroken front. After Falaise, Montgomery's Anglo-Canadian armies started moving along the coast of northwestern France, heading toward northern Belgium.

GEORGE PATTON (1885–1945)

Patton first made his name during the Allied landings in North Africa in 1942. His career was controversial, however. His thirst for publicity led to clashes with other senior officers. In Sicily in 1943, he slapped two soldiers who had shell shock. Patton was sidelined and only returned to active duty in July 1944. From then until the end of the war, he led the US Third Army in a series of fast-moving offensives. He reacted very quickly to block the German advance in the Ardennes. Patton's troops were also among the first across the Rhine. At the end of the war, Patton was very outspoken about sensitive political issues. His opinions cost him control of the Third Army. He then took charge of the Fifteenth Army. Patton died from injuries after an automobile accident in 1945.

◀ ***Patton was as effective as he was controversial, commanding great loyalty among many of his soldiers.***

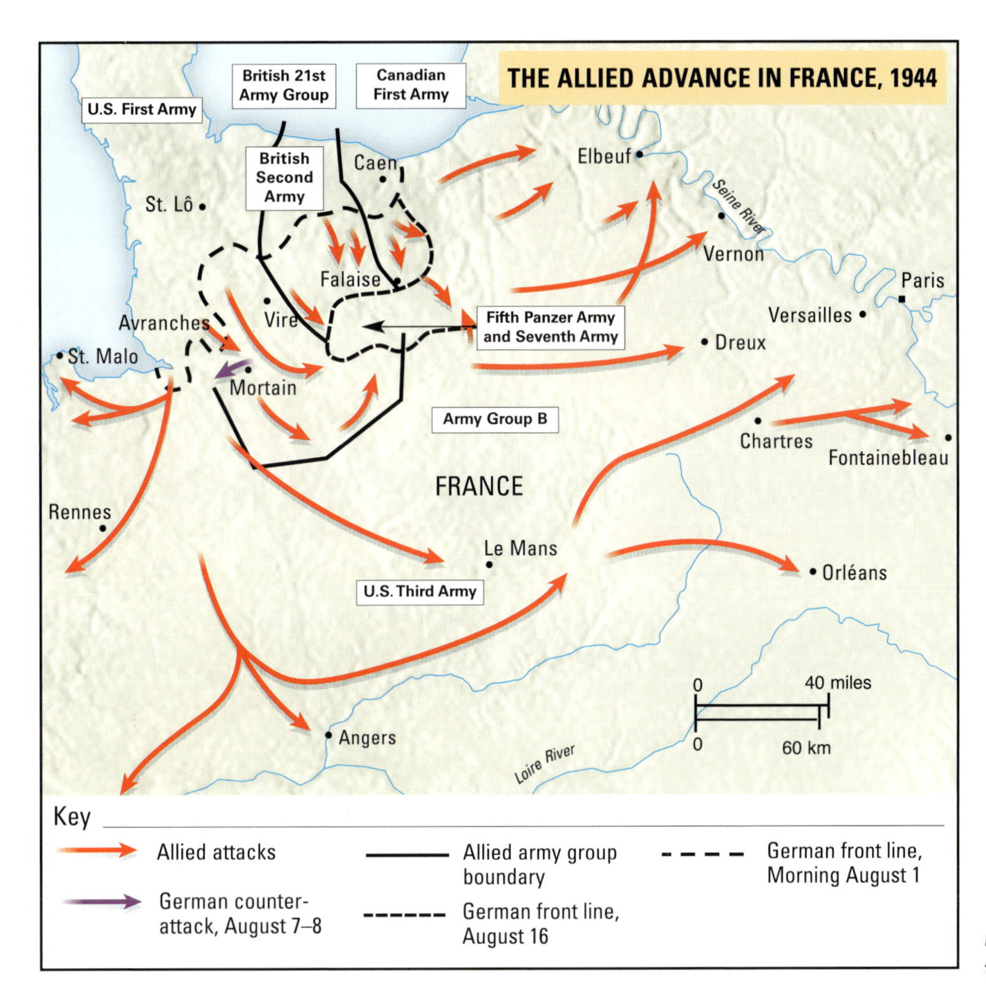

◀ ***The Allied breakout from the bridgehead in Normandy during the summer of 1944.***

PARIS IS LIBERATED

US forces followed a parallel course toward southern Belgium, Luxembourg and eastern France. The first big prize of the Allied advance was Paris. On August 19, as the Allies approached, citizens in the French capital rose up against its German garrison. Five days later, the Allies entered the capital amid scenes of great joy. The first troops to enter the city were the Free French 2nd Armoured Division.

THE ALLIED ADVANCE STALLS

In the excitement, some Allied commanders began to hope that the war might be won before the end of the year. By early September, however, the rush toward the German border was grinding to a halt. Allied troops were tired. Their worn-out vehicles were in urgent need of maintenance. The main problem, however, was keeping the armies supplied.

The Germans had wrecked many ports as they retreated. Other ports, such as Brest in Brittany and Antwerp in Belgium, were still occupied by German forces. The Allies were therefore still being largely supplied from the Normandy beaches. The beaches now lay some 300 miles (480km) behind the troops. The huge strain on supplying the armies was unlikely to improve with the onset of winter weather.

In spite of being five years into a long and bloody war, the Wehrmacht had put up an amazing fight in Normandy. While some of the German Army's generals were disaffected with the Führer and were actively plotting to kill him, the rank and file of the fighting troops still believed in Germany's cause. Rommel's infectious enthusiasm rubbed off on the troops being trained to repel the invasion. He was famous for his victories against the British and Americans in North Africa, and many of his troops, along with the divisional officers, were convinced of the logic of Hitler's claim that if the Allied invasion could be thrown back into the sea, then Germany would be able to turn its attention eastward to finish off the Soviets. "When the enemy invades in the West it will be the moment of decision in this war," said Rommel. He was right—but it was the Allies who were victorious.

MONTGOMERY vs THE AMERICAN GENERALS

Field Marshal Bernard Montgomergy was a difficult character who came into conflict with his allies.

▲ *Dwight D. Eisenhower (left) with the commander of the British 7th Armoured Division, General George Erskine. Erskine was sacked by Montgomery after the British failure to break through at Villers-Bocage in June 1944, which drew criticism from senior US commanders.*

For all his success on the battlefield, Montgomery managed to be unpopular even among his subordinate officers in the British Army. For example, as a corps commander he made few friends when, after the retreat from Dunkirk, he ordered that all officers, even older ones in office jobs, should undergo an intense physical fitness regime.

He was ruthless in sacking any subordinates he considered not up to the job, and criticized openly many of his contemporaries in the British Army, including his superior in North Africa, General Sir Harold Alexander.

Montgomery first encountered his US equivalents in 1942, when American forces invaded French North Africa. He then worked closely with Americans in planning the invasion of Sicily, where his insistence on changing the original plan for the landing was of great importance. During the fighting on Sicily, General George Patton's American forces managed to race around the north of the island while the British were floundering against strong German defenses in the south, confirming Patton's belief that Montgomery was a plodding, overcautious commander.

The big clash came in northwest Europe after D-Day. Montgomery initially commanded all the ground forces that were landed, and made it clear that he would like to continue this command—even though it was always planned that Dwight D. Eisenhower would take over this role. During the fighting to break out from Normandy, Montgomery's troops stalled around Caen, while the Americans eventually broke out further west. There was then a furious argument as Patton, in command of the US Third Army, demanded to be given priority for his thrust to Lorraine. Eventually, Eisenhower allowed Montgomery to undertake Operation Market Garden into Holland, which proved a failure.

Finally, during the German counterattack in the Ardennes in December 1944, when Montgomery was given command of all forces to the north of the incursion, his attitude so incensed the US commanders that they demanded he be removed. He barely hung onto his job.

To the Americans, Montgomery lacked any brilliance and was astonishingly rude; to Montgomery, the US commanders were barely professional. After the war, the debate continued in various sets of memoirs.

▼ *Brothers in arms, but also squabbling siblings: from right, Montgomery, Bradley and Patton. On the left is General Sir Miles Dempsey, commander of the British Second Army during the campaign in northwest Europe.*

▲ *General Omar Bradley, commander of the US First Army in Normandy and then 12th Army Group. He blamed Montgomery for moving his forces too slowly to close the "Falaise Pocket" on the German armies retreating from Normandy.*

▲ *The senior commanders who directed the Overlord landings. Seated front left is Air Chief Marshal Arthur Tedder, Deputy Supreme Commander under Eisenhower. He had worked closely with Montgomery in North Africa during 1942 and 1943, and had little regard for him, finding him arrogant and difficult to work with. During the disputes that arose in 1944, Tedder advocated Montgomery's removal from command.*

◀ *General George C Marshall, US Army Chief of Staff and effectively the most senior American military man directing the European war. He and Roosevelt clashed repeatedly with the British high command, who wanted a strategy that suited Britain's imperial ambitions, especially in concentrating on the Mediterranean theater.*

◀ *George S. Patton, a man who believed Montgomery was a plodding infantry general who did not understand the dynamics of armored warfare. In 1944, Patton believed Eisenhower had "sold out" to the British by agreeing to let Montgomery take the lion's share of resources for his Arnhem operation. Patton believed he himself could win the war by crashing over the German border if he was allowed to. As one of his seniors wrote: "When we get moving, Patton is the man with the drive and imagination to do dangerous things fast."*

Arnhem

SEPTEMBER 1–3

WESTERN FRONT, *FRANCE/BELGIUM*

The British Guards and 11th Armored Divisions, which are both part of the British XXX Corps, reach Arras and Aubigny. The Canadian II Corps, part of the Canadian First Army, liberates the port of Dieppe.

On the 2nd, XXX Corps is instructed to slow its advance in order to await a projected paratroop drop. With the eventual cancellation of the drop, the corps resumes its advance at the original speed. The 32nd and 5th Brigades of the Guards Armored Division meanwhile begin a race to reach the Belgian capital, Brussels, which is won by the 32nd Brigade on the 3rd. On the same day, the British XII Corps becomes bogged down in fighting German defenders around the French town of Béthune.

SEPTEMBER 3

WESTERN FRONT, *FRANCE/BELGIUM*

The US First Army takes Tournai, crushing three German corps in the process. The British Second Army liberates Brussels.

SEPTEMBER 4

WESTERN FRONT, *BELGIUM*

The British Second Army liberates the port of Antwerp.

SEPTEMBER 5

WESTERN FRONT, *FRANCE*

US Third Army spearheads cross the Meuse River. General Karl von Rundstedt is made Commander-in-Chief West by Hitler with orders to counterattack the Allies and split their advancing armies apart. However, von Rundstedt's resources for such an undertaking are scant.

SEPTEMBER 8–13

WESTERN FRONT, *BELGIUM/HOLLAND*

The British 50th Division crosses the Albert Canal at Gheel. On the 10th, the British Guards Armored Division advances to De Groot.

Three days later, the British 15th Division crosses the Meuse-Escaut Canal.

SEPTEMBER 17

WESTERN FRONT, *HOLLAND*

Operation Market Garden, General Bernard Montgomery's plan for an armored and airborne thrust across Holland to outflank the German defenses, begins. The British 1st Airborne Division lands near Arnhem, the US 101st Airborne Division near Eindhoven, the US 82nd Airborne Division near Grave and Nijmegen, while the British XXX Corps advances

▶ *The Allied troops who liberated Brussels enjoyed something similar to a Roman triumph on the streets of the city.*

▲ ***British paratroopers in action near Arnhem. The enemy is close, as indicated by the acute angle of the mortar tube.***

from the Dutch border. The 82nd lands without difficulty and takes the Maas and Maas-Waal Canal bridges, but then encounters heavy resistance at Nijmegen. The 101st Division also takes its bridges, but the British paratroopers discover their way to Arnhem is blocked by German units. Only one battalion, under Lieutenant Colonel John Frost, manages to reach the bridge, where it is quickly cut off.

SEPTEMBER 19–21

WESTERN FRONT, *HOLLAND*
Forward elements of the British XXX Corps reach US paratroopers at Eindhoven, but at Arnhem all attempts to break through to the troops fail. On the 20th, the bridge at Nijmegen is captured by a combined force drawn from the US 82nd Airborne Division and the British XXX Corps. The next

▲ ***Allied vehicles rumble across the bridge at Nijmegen, Holland, during the disastrous Operation Market Garden.***

▲ *A PIAT antitank weapon waits for enemy armor on the outskirts of Arnhem as the Germans close in on the British.*

day, the British troops at Arnhem are overwhelmed. The remainder form a defensive perimeter on the northern bank of the Neder Rijn, around the village of Oosterbeek.

SEPTEMBER 22

WESTERN FRONT, *FRANCE*

Boulogne surrenders to the Canadian II Corps; its garrison of 20,000 men is taken into captivity.

SEPTEMBER 22–25

WESTERN FRONT, *HOLLAND*

Outside Arnhem, the British XXX Corps' advance is slowed by German resistance. The Polish Brigade drops south of the Neder Rijn near Driel. On the 23rd, attempts by the Poles and advance troops of XXX Corps to cross the river are driven back. Evacuation of the surviving paratroopers begins two days later, leaving 2500 of their dead comrades behind.

SEPTEMBER 23

AIR WAR, *GERMANY*

The RAF makes a night precision raid on the Dortmund to Ems Canal, which links the Ruhr with other industrial centers. A total of 141 aircraft are involved, the canal is breached, and a section drained; 14 bombers are lost.

SEPTEMBER 23–30

WESTERN FRONT, *FRANCE*

The Canadian 3rd Division invests the port of Calais, which is defended by 7500 men. Following heavy artillery and bomber attacks, and the use of armor, Calais surrenders on the 30th.

OCTOBER 3

AIR WAR, *BRITAIN*

The German bombardment of Britain with V2 long-range heavy rockets has resumed from new launch sites dotted across Holland.

OCTOBER 9

WESTERN FRONT, *BELGIUM*

Although the Allies captured Antwerp on September 4, they have not been able to use the great port because there are German units on both sides of the Scheldt estuary. Therefore, the Canadian First Army commences operations to eradicate the enemy presence in this area.

OCTOBER 14

POLITICS, *GERMANY*

Field Marshal Erwin Rommel commits suicide with poison. Implicated in the July assassination plot against Hitler, he has killed himself, under pressure, to save his family from arrest. He is to be given a state funeral as part of the charade to maintain the illusion that he was an uncompromising Nazi.

OCTOBER 21

WESTERN FRONT, *GERMANY*

The city of Aachen surrenders to US forces following a 10-day siege.

NOVEMBER 8

WESTERN FRONT, *BELGIUM*

The Canadian First Army completes the clearing of the Scheldt estuary. It takes 41,000 prisoners during the

▲ ***Beaten but defiant, these British paratroopers are led into captivity at the end of Market Garden: 2500 of their comrades were killed in the operation.***

operation at a cost of 12,873 men killed, wounded, and missing.

NOVEMBER 9

WESTERN FRONT, *FRANCE*
General George Patton's US Third Army (500,000 men and 500 tanks) crosses the Moselle River on a broad front toward the heart of the Reich.

NOVEMBER 12

AIR WAR, *NORWAY*
RAF Lancaster bombers from 9 and 617 Squadrons sink the German battleship *Tirpitz* in Altenfiord, killing 1100 of its crew when the ship capsizes.

HOME FRONT, *GERMANY*
The Nazi women's leader, Gertrud Scholtz-Klink, appeals for all women over 18 to volunteer for service in the army and air force to release men for the front.

▶ ***A British paratrooper in cover on the outskirts of Oosterbeek. The failure of XXX Corps to cross the Neder Rijn doomed the airborne operation.***

Part 3 | Chapter 1
ARNHEM

Market Garden

By the beginning of September, the Allied armies in France and Belgium had largely outrun their supply lines, which stretched all the way back to the Normandy beaches.

By the beginning of September, the Allied armies in France and Belgium had largely outrun their supply lines, which stretched all the way back to the Normandy beaches. The Germans had destroyed or still held every port on the French Atlantic coast, and the approaches to the huge Belgian port of Antwerp were still covered by German guns. With only a fraction of the needed supplies coming ashore, the Allied armies could no longer advance into Germany on a wide front. The newly promoted Field Marshal Montgomery convinced the Allied supreme commander, Eisenhower, to allow him to drive into Holland to seize bridges over the Rhine, and then turn right to advance into Germany's industrial heartland of the Ruhr.

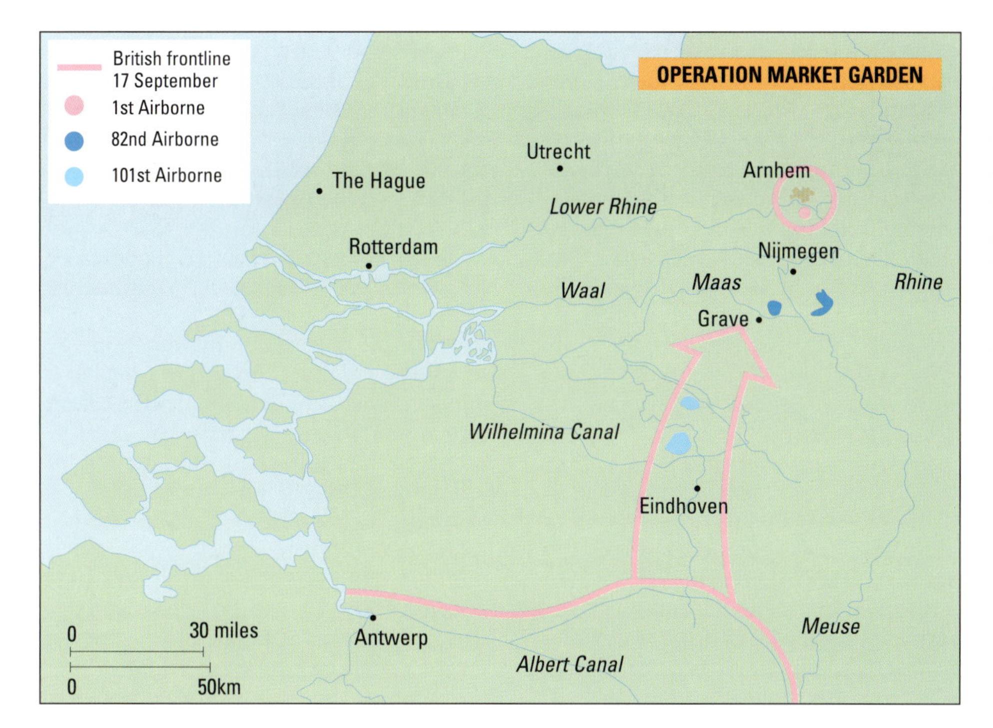

◀ ***Montgomery's Operation Market Garden, which aimed to finish the war by the end of 1944. The colored shaded areas represent the drop zones for the three airborne divisions that took part. The pink circle represents Montgomery's main objective. (See page 192 for map key)***

▼ ***British paratroopers captured by the Hohenstaufen Panzer Division during the bitter battle for Arnhem.***

MULTIPLE AIRDROPS

The normally cautious Montgomery now came up with a very ambitious and daring plan to capture the strategic bridge across the Rhine at Arnhem with a parachute drop by the British 1st Airborne Division. The US 82nd and 101st Airborne Divisions would also be dropped to seize the bridges across the Waal and Maas rivers, as well as the Willems and Wilhelmina canals, to allow the tanks of the British XXX Corps to motor 64 miles (103km) up from Belgium to relieve the troops on Arnhem bridge. In total some 35,000 Allied paratroopers and glider-borne troops would be dropped in the largest airborne operation in military history. Lieutenant-General Brian Horrocks predicted that his XXX Corps would be in Arnhem in 60 hours. Eisenhower faced the very real possibility of stopping his broad front sweep across northern Europe and therefore having to extend the war into 1945. To avert this he supported Montgomery's suggestion that his drive through Belgium toward the port of Antwerp should have priority, even though this meant closing down the advances of various US armies to the south of the Anglo-Canadians. Brussels fell on September 3 and Antwerp was captured 24 hours later with its facilities largely intact. While the Allies had gained a port close to the front, it was actually of little use as Antwerp lies some distance inland. Access to the sea in 1944 was blocked by German-laid mines in the Scheldt River and occupied islands at the mouth of the Scheldt estuary.

OPERATION MARKET GARDEN

The Allies were nevertheless tantalizingly close to the German border and did not want to give their enemy a breathing space in which to recover and reorganize. Both Montgomery and Bradley suggested to Eisenhower that they alone be given all the available supplies for a single thrust into Germany to bring about victory.

Montgomery's uncharacteristically bold plan, Operation Market Garden, was selected. It first called for Anglo-American and Polish airborne forces to carve out a narrow corridor through southeast Holland along the line Eindhoven, Nijmegen and Arnhem to the German border. An armored spearhead would then pour along this route to take the Ruhr, Germany's most important industrial area, without which it could not maintain its war effort. It was vital for the success of the operation that the airborne forces capture a number of bridges intact, not least the one over the Rhine at Arnhem, and that the ground forces keep to a strict timetable.

In the first week of September 1944, Willi Bittrich's II SS Panzer Corps was ordered to move to a reorganizing and refitting area north of the Dutch town of Arnhem. The unit had been in action continuously for just over two months, and was now desperately in need of a quiet period to get itself ready for battle again.

Plans were already in train to bring Bittrich's two divisions, the Hohenstaufen and Frundsberg, back up to operation strength, and Arnhem seemed like a good place to begin this time-consuming task. There they would be safe from Allied attack. Any sightly wounded personnel were sent to hospitals in Germany in order to recover, and those in need of training were sent on courses laid on in specialist depots.

Remaining in the Dutch barracks which had been taken over by the Waffen-SS corps were probably no more than 6000 men, who were equipped with whatever tanks, artillery, and vehicles they had managed to bring with them out of France. No longer worthy of the title "division," the Hohenstaufen and Frundsberg were dubbed divisional *Kampfgruppen*. It was doubtful if the whole of the corps would be able to put more than 30 tanks or assault guns into the field.

Walther Harzer's Hohenstaufen was then ordered to move to Germany to be rebuilt there. Before it left, it was to hand over its remaining operational vehicles and heavy weapons to Heinz Harmel's Frundsberg, which was to remain in Holland. At the same time as this reorganization process was under way, contingency orders were issued stating that the two units should be prepared to dispatch "alarm" Kampfgruppen to crisis zones.

Not believing intelligence reports that the Allied advance had run out of steam, Harzer decided to keep hold of many of his precious remaining tanks and heavy weapons until the very last minute, in case he had to send his men into battle. He simply ordered their tracks to be removed so they would be officially classed as non-operational, meaning they would be exempt from the transfer instructions.

The conventional organization of both divisions had all but collapsed. Instead, the remaining troops were grouped into a number of ad hoc Kampfgruppen. Harmel gutted his panzergrenadier heavy weapons companies to form the division's only anti-tank gun company. Likewise, all the armored halftracks in the division were grouped in a reconnaissance battalion to provide him with a powerful strike force. The artillery regiment's self-propeled gun drivers and crews were all transferred to the panzer regiment, and all the infantry were combined into three weak panzergrenadier battalions.

THE FRONT AT EINDHOVEN

What new equipment had arrived—mainly 15 Panzerjäger IV self-propelled guns—had been dispatched to the Dutch-Belgian border, under the command of Kampfgruppe Hienke. This was formed around one of Frundsberg's panzergrenadier battalions, an engineer and reconnaissance company. Hohenstaufen was ordered to provide an additional panzergrenadier battalion for this force, which was helping to build up the front south of the Dutch city of Eindhoven. It was increasingly involved in a series of inconclusive engagements along the border, and was sent into action in a futile attack against the Neerpelt bridgehead on September 15, in which three of the Panzerjäger IVs were knocked out.

In Arnhem's Tafelberg Hotel, Field Marshal Walther Model was trying to patch together his hopelessly undermanned and under-equipped army group in order to defend the northwest border of Germany. He had a

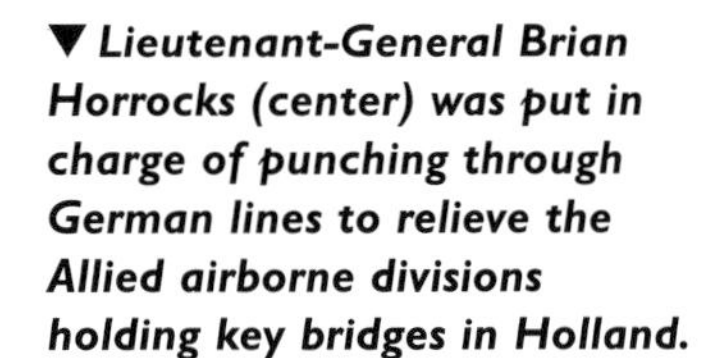

▼ Lieutenant-General Brian Horrocks (center) was put in charge of punching through German lines to relieve the Allied airborne divisions holding key bridges in Holland.

▲ ***German prisoners captured by American paratroopers during their assault on Nijmegen.***

reputation of being a great improviser and, after his successes on the Eastern Front, was nicknamed the "Führer's Fireman." Even at this point of the war, he was ultra-loyal to Hitler and could still be counted on to follow the Führer's orders to the letter. He was sitting down to lunch on September 17 with his staff when hundreds of aircraft were heard flying overhead. Operation Market Garden had begun.

When RAF reconnaissance Spitfires photographed German tanks near Arnhem, the deputy commander of the First Airborne Army, Lieutenant-General Frederick "Boy" Browning, ignored the intelligence. Other Allied intelligence officers were equally quick to dismiss the idea that the remnants of II SS Panzer Corps could put up serious resistance. The party was on, and nothing was going to spoil the show—except Bittrich's panzer troops.

Allied bombers and fighter-bombers hit targets all over southern Holland during the morning of September 17, but the veteran Waffen-SS men took little notice. They had been bombed and strafed on a daily basis for the past two months, so the experience had lost its novelty. Harzer even went ahead with a ceremony to present the Knight's Cross to the commander of his reconnaissance battalion, SS-Hauptsturmführer Viktor Graebner. After 13:00 hours, when the first British paratroopers started to land to the west of Arnhem, Bittrich swung into action, alerting his troops with a warning order that was issued at 13:40 hours. With these brief orders he set in train the German counteroffensive that was to defeat Operation Market Garden. Harzer was ordered to assemble his Kampfgruppen and move with "absolute speed" to contain and defeat the British airborne Oosterbeek landing. Meanwhile, the Frundsberg Division was to race south and hold the Nijmegen bridges across the Waal in order to prevent reinforcements from reaching Arnhem.

Within minutes of receiving their orders, Waffen-SS units sprang into action. Harzer's men began moving into the town by whatever means they found: trucks, tanks, halftracks, cars, trams, even bicycles. SS-Obersturmbannführer Ludwig Spindler, commander of the division's artillery regiment, was given command of the Kampfgruppe that would hold the western edge of Arnhem. At the same time the division's tank, artillery, and reconnaissance units began getting the vehicles that had been deliberately put out of action to stop them being transferred to the Frundsberg Division into some semblance of working order. In two hours, 400 men and 40 vehicles were rolling out of their camp toward Arnhem town center. They had orders to move ahead of the Frundsberg and secure Nijmegen bridge.

On the drop zones west of Arnhem, 8000 British troops were forming up and preparing to move off to their objectives. Within minutes, Krafft's trainee NCOs were in action, fighting in the forests around the British drop zones, delaying their advance for vital hours. One British airborne unit, the 2nd Battalion, the Parachute Regiment (2 PARA), slipped past Krafft's men and was soon marching into the town center. Minutes before 2 PARA reached Arnhem bridge, Graebner's column raced across the huge structure and within an hour the men were in Nijmegen. An improvised Luftwaffe and police Kampfgruppe had already secured the strategic bridge and Graebner had little to do. The Frundsberg Division was equally quick off the mark, and its reconnaissance battalion, under SS-Sturmbannführer Brinkmann, was on its way to Nijmegen. As the column of armored halftracks approached Arnhem bridge, it came under fire from British paratroopers. 2 PARA now held the northern edge of the bridge and several blocks of buildings nearby.

Harmel was away in Berlin arranging for new equipment for his division, so his chief of staff, SS-Sturmbannführer Paetsch, issued orders for the units heading to Nijmegen to be diverted to an improvised ferry across the Rhine that had been established upstream from Arnhem at Pannerden. Brinkmann was ordered to do whatever he could in order to contain the British on the north bank of the Rhine and prevent further Allied reinforcements from reaching the bridge. He set about his task with relish.

Far to the south, Kampfgruppe Heinke was soon in action against XXX Corps' Guards Armoured Division as it pushed up the main road toward Eindhoven. Artillery barrages and air strikes smashed the German paratroopers defending the road, and when the Waffen-SS Panzerjäger IVs tried to help, several were knocked out. British Shermans were soon streaming northward.

▼ Captured Waffen-SS men are put to work by their British captors during the early phase of Market Garden.

Heavy fighting now raged all around Arnhem as Harzer threw more and more troops into action to stop the British establishing a firm base. Speed of response was more important than strength or coordination. It was imperative that the British be denied the chance to establish themselves in firm positions. Spindler first threw two companies of artillerymen, fighting as infantrymen, into action during the evening of September 17. Two bigger infantry Kampfgruppen then joined the battle. The following day, two more Kampfgruppen arrived, along with the first tanks and assault guns from the Hohenstaufen, as well as army units. The battle for Arnhem bridge burst into life on the morning of the 18th, when the British paratroopers heard a column of tracked armored vehicles approaching their position.

Graebner, being an aggressive and self-confident officer, had heard that British troops had cut him off in Nijmegen and, on his own initiative, had returned to clear the bridge for reinforcements. This was to be a coup de main raid to take the British by surprise and scatter them by shock action. Waffen-SS armored halftracks, Puma armored cars, Volkswagen jeeps, and Graebner's captured British Humber scout car raced over Arnhem bridge at 30mph (48km/h), with Waffen-SS troopers training their machine guns and rifles on the high buildings overlooking the elevated highway. Two vehicles got across the bridge unscathed and then the British Paras opened fire. Machine guns, mortars, PIAT bazookas, Sten guns, and rifles raked the column. One halftrack took a direct hit and veered out of control before turning over. Other vehicles went out of control, crashing into each other and effectively blocking the road. Two vehicles crashed over the side of the elevated road. A handful of Waffen-SS men in the tangled wreckage tried to return fire. For almost two hours the carnage continued, until at last the remnants of Graebner's force pulled back to safety at the southern edge of the bridge, leaving 12 wrecked vehicles behind. Scores of the reconnaissance men were dead, including their commander.

PRISING OUT THE PARAS

The British Paras were not going to be removed easily. Army panzers were brought up to reinforce Brinkmann's Kampfgruppe, and a determined effort was launched to blast out the British. As the battle was raging at Arnhem bridge, Spindler was continuing his effort to hold the 1st Airborne Division, which was pushing eastward to help their comrades in the center of the town. Spindler's force had grown to 1000 men in several independent Kampfgruppen, backed by 30 tanks. An ad hoc division of army and Waffen-SS units was also trying to build a front to block the British move westward and to seal them in at Kessel. The Germans were closing in.

During the morning of September 18, Harmel returned to Arnhem and quickly received his orders from Bittrich, who declared: "Schwerpunkt

▲ The British Guards Armoured Division spearheaded the drive to relieve the airborne troops trapped north of the Rhine at Arnhem. These men are members of the Irish Guards.

▲ ***German armor was brought up finally to "liquidate" the trapped British paratroopers holding Arnhem bridge.***

(main effort) is south." No effort was to be spared to hold Nijmegen bridge and prevent a link-up between the British tanks and their airborne troops.

All night his troops had been laboring to get the Pannerden ferry working and, by late morning, Waffen-SS engineers on trucks and riding bicycles at last reached Nijmegen. They immediately began preparing it for demolition. At midday, SS-Hauptsturmführer Karl Heinz Euling arrived to assume command of the bridge defense Kampfgruppe. Soon, armored halftracks, mortars and four Panzerjäger IVs were rumbling over Nijmegen bridge. Artillery batteries were established on the north bank of the Waal to provide support.

LAYING THE TRAP

When American paratroopers edged into Nijmegen they were met with a heavy barrage of German artillery and mortar fire, sending them scurrying back to seek cover. More Frundsberg reinforcements arrived during the day, and Euling's men began laying minefields and barbed wire, as well as building field fortifications. Harmel set up his command post on the north bank of the Waal, from where he could observe the key bridge. Model relayed to him the Führer's orders that the bridges were not to be blown but held to allow a German counterattack to restore the front along the Dutch-Belgian border. Harmel was having none of this nonsense, though, and was determined to order the bridge to be blown if British tanks attempted to cross. Late in the afternoon, German observation posts south of Nijmegen reported British tanks operating with the American paratroopers.

Throughout the afternoon and into the night of September 18/19, fighting raged in Arnhem. Tiger tanks were brought up to blast the paratroopers on Arnhem bridge and the army's 280th Assault Gun Brigade arrived to support Spindler's drive against the main British force. Slowly, the Germans were becoming more organized and effective. A concerted defense line was established and the first counterattacks were launched. Losses were heavy on both sides, with most German Kampfgruppen suffering 50 percent casualties. The German armor was decisive, allowing the outnumbered Waffen-SS Kampfgruppen to stand off and deliberately blast the British out of their positions.

The date September 20 signified the decisive phase in the battle. The Guards Armoured Division had linked up with the 82nd Airborne Division and planned to seize the Nijmegen bridge during the day. Harmel had some 500

Waffen-SS troopers in the town, fighting alongside a similar number of Luftwaffe, army, and police troops. 88mm and 37mm Flak guns were emplaced in order to protect the large road ramps leading up to the bridge, and the Panzerjäger IVs were also in the town.

ALL-DAY BOMBARDMENT

British guns bombarded the German positions throughout the day, and American paratroopers and British Grenadier Guards edged into the suburbs of Nijmegen. The bombardment knocked out the key 88mm Flak guns that provided the main defense of the bridge approach routes. In the afternoon 40 British tanks moved up to the riverbank and started to fire smoke shells onto the far bank to the west of the bridge. A battalion of US paratroopers then raced forward with canvas assault boats and set course for the northern bank of the Waal. German mortars and 20mm Flak guns raked the boats, killing or wounding half the Americans, but the survivors kept going through the maelstrom. Once ashore, they scattered the few old men and boy soldiers holding the rear end of the bridge.

As the river assault was under way, a squadron of British tanks rushed the southern edge of the bridge. Several tanks fell to Panzerfaust fire from the Waffen-SS men. The tanks just kept moving and, within minutes, were up on the bridge, machine-gunning the Frundsberg engineers who were still placing demolition charges. American paratroopers followed close behind.

Watching horrified from his command post, Harmel immediately ordered the bridge to be blown. The engineer officer kept pressing the detonation switch. Nothing happened. Artillery fire had damaged the initiation cable; Nijmegen bridge was in British hands. Harmel was dismayed; the road to Arnhem seemed open, yet the Shermans just stopped. They had run out of fuel and ammunition and needed replenishment. Also, more infantry were needed to clear the villages along the single road north to Arnhem, otherwise German guns would be able to pick off the British tanks with ease.

DASH FOR FREEDOM

The vital British infantry were still stuck in Nijmegen, fighting Euling's men. During the night the Waffen-SS officer gathered 100 or so of his remaining men together and made an escape bid. As they listened to more British tanks rolling over the Nijmegen bridge, Euling led his men on the walkway underneath it to the north bank and safety. They had put up determined resistance and delayed the British at a decisive moment in the battle. The price for this success was high. More than 260 German bodies were found in the ruins of Nijmegen.

On Arnhem bridge itself, meanwhile, 2 PARA was on its last legs. Out of ammunition and with almost every soldier dead or wounded, including its commanding officer, Lieutenant-Colonel Johnny Frost, the battalion

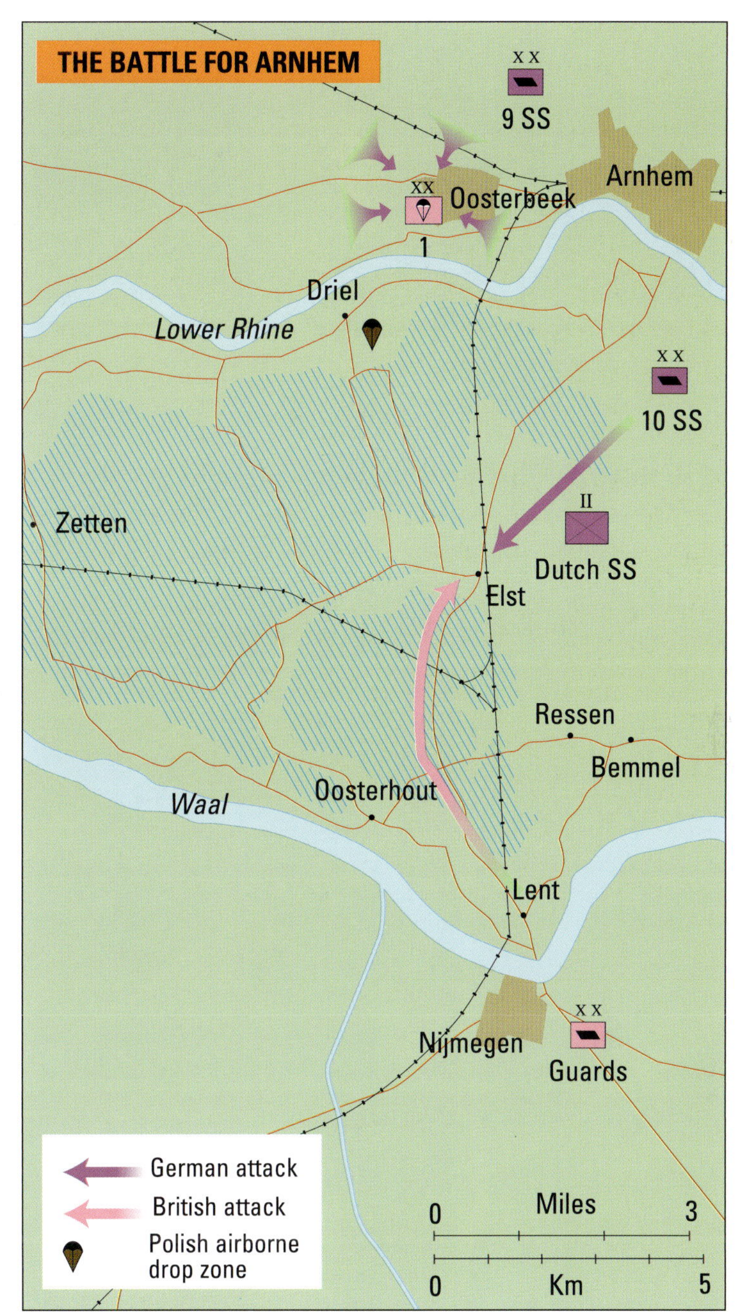

▲ ***While Waffen-SS troops attacked British airborn troops at Oosterbeek and Arnhem, more SS troops were holding up British tanks to the south, effectively blocking the relief of the British paratroopers.*** *(See page 192 for map key)*

EYEWITNESS REPORT

"My job as chief intelligence officer was to try to evaluate what the enemy reactions were going to be and how our troops ought to deal with them. The British airborne troops were going to be dropped at the far end of the operation at Arnhem—it was across the third bridge, so there were three bridges that had to be captured before you got to the British airborne troops. I became increasingly alarmed, first of all at the German preparations, because there were intelligence reports that there were two SS panzer divisions right next to where the British troops were to be dropped. These were the star troops of the German Army, the 10th and the 9th SS Panzer Divisions. They had been very badly mauled in Normandy and were refitting in this area. These were the best fighting troops in the German Army and they had heavy tanks. Airborne troops in those days had absolutely nothing… They had limited supplies of ammunition, and they could not fight heavy armor because they didn't have the weapons to do it."

Brian Urquhart
Senior British intelligence officer discussing Arnhem

surrendered during the morning of September 21. They had no idea that XXX Corps' tanks were now only 10.5 miles (17km) away. Thus ended what had been an epic battle.

Even before the remains of Graebner's vehicles had been removed from Arnhem bridge, reinforcements were on their way to help Harmel block any further move north by the British armor. Four StuG IIIs and 16 Panzer IVs of Frundsberg's Panzer Regiment had been ferried across the Rhine on September 20 and, by the early hours of the following morning, had set up a "stop line" north of Nijmegen. The whole of the "island" between Arnhem and Nijmegen was low-lying marsh or prone to flooding. Any kind of movement off roads was impossible for tanks or wheeled vehicles, and very difficult for infantrymen. Harmel skilfully placed his forces to dominate the road from Nijmegen to Arnhem. British fears about being picked off on the raised road by German anti-tank fire were found to be fully justified when the Guards Armoured began advancing at 11:00 hours. When the first Irish Guards Sherman reached the outskirts of the village of Elst, a high-velocity 75mm round blew the tank's tracks off. More guns opened fire and four tanks were soon blazing on the road, which was now blocked. British infantry tried to attack across the open fields but were soon pinned down by Harmel's artillery. At midday on September 21, eight Panther tanks led columns of Frundsberg panzergrenadiers across Arnhem bridge and moved to join Harmel's depleted Kampfgruppe north of Nijmegen bridge. With the arrival of these reinforcements, any chance the Allies had of reaching Arnhem was doomed.

OUT OF ARNHEM

Harzer's troops continued to press back the eastern flank of the British force east of Arnhem. He ordered his Kampfgruppe to form small penetration teams, each led by a couple of StuG IIIs, to push forward into the British lines. In addition, more guns were brought up to blast the British positions.

South of the Rhine, a brigade of Polish paratroopers was dropped just behind the Frundsberg's "stop line." With customary promptness, Harmel reorganized his small Kampfgruppen to contain the new landing. A battalion of sailors was thrown in to hold the Poles and 16 88mm Flak guns were positioned to cover the road from Nijmegen. Batteries of Nebelwerfers were brought up to stop the Poles massing for infantry attacks. Every attempt to break through his line was rebuffed with heavy losses.

The Germans were not content just to block the Allied advance south of Arnhem. XXX Corps relied on supplies coming up the single road from Belgium to ensure it could keep pushing north. Model was determined to cut this road, which was known as the "corridor."

The Waffen-SS Kampfgruppe that had been brushed aside in the first XXX Corps attack south of Eindhoven had been re-equipped and reorganized by September 22. Its Panzerjäger IVs led a major attack on the corridor at Veghel that briefly cut XXX Corps' lifeline. American paratroopers counterattacked, driving them off, but for several hours the corridor was closed. II SS Panzer Corps had more valuable time to beef up its "stop line" south of Arnhem.

KING TIGERS FOR BITTRICH

A "final attack" was ordered by Bittrich for September 25. Four Hohenstaufen Kampfgruppen made good progress, thanks to heavy King Tiger support, and one unit broke through the now depleted defenses and overran a British artillery battery. Realizing that his 1st Airborne Division was on its last legs, Montgomery authorized its withdrawal during the night. After swimming across the Rhine to a precarious bridgehead held by the Poles, by dawn just under 2500 men had escaped.

Bittrich's men advanced cautiously through the ruins of the Oosterbeek Kessel. They rounded up some 6000 prisoners, the majority of whom were wounded, and buried more than 1000 dead British soldiers. The Americans lost another 3000 men and XXX Corps lost 1500 men, as well as 70 tanks. Bittrich's men were in awe of the fighting qualities of their British opponents, and the formalities of the Geneva Convention were generally observed during the battle. There were no accusations of the premeditated killing of prisoners that had sullied the reputation of Waffen-SS units in Normandy and later in the Ardennes.

The German losses were equally heavy. Some 8000 German casualties were recorded for all the units engaged during Market Garden, from Eindhoven to Arnhem. In the Arnhem area, more than 3000 casualties were inflicted on German units and 1725 of these were dead. The majority of these casualties were incurred by Bittrich's units.

Bittrich's men, however, had defeated Montgomery's daring bid to end the war by Christmas 1944. The prompt reaction of the Waffen-SS panzer corps had ensured the key bridge at Nijmegen was defended and then the road to Arnhem blocked. This was the vital ground of Market Garden. Bittrich had spotted this in his orders which were issued within minutes of the first Allied paratroops landing. For the next week, he ensured his Schwerpunkt remained firmly in German hands. No matter how bravely the British paratroopers fought in Arnhem, they had been doomed from the moment Harmel's Kampfgruppe took up defensive positions on Nijmegen bridge on September 18.

▼ ***Vicious street fighting raged as the British 1st Airborne Division tried to hold onto its precarious bridgehead north of the Rhine.***

The Battle for Lorraine

The British were eager for a push along the Channel coast to Belgium, to clear out the German V-weapon sites that were still causing thousands of casualties in London and southeast England.

Montgomery proposed that his armies receive the bulk of the supplies flowing across the Normandy beaches to allow them to push on into the Netherlands, and then hook right into the Ruhr, the heartland of German war production. Patton and other American commanders were lobbying hard for the bulk of the scarce supplies of fuel, food, and ammunition to go to the US armies driving hard for the German border at Metz, and then on to the River Rhine itself.

Initially, Eisenhower decided to compromise, and give neither set of rival commanders their wish. He opted for what he called a "Broad Front"

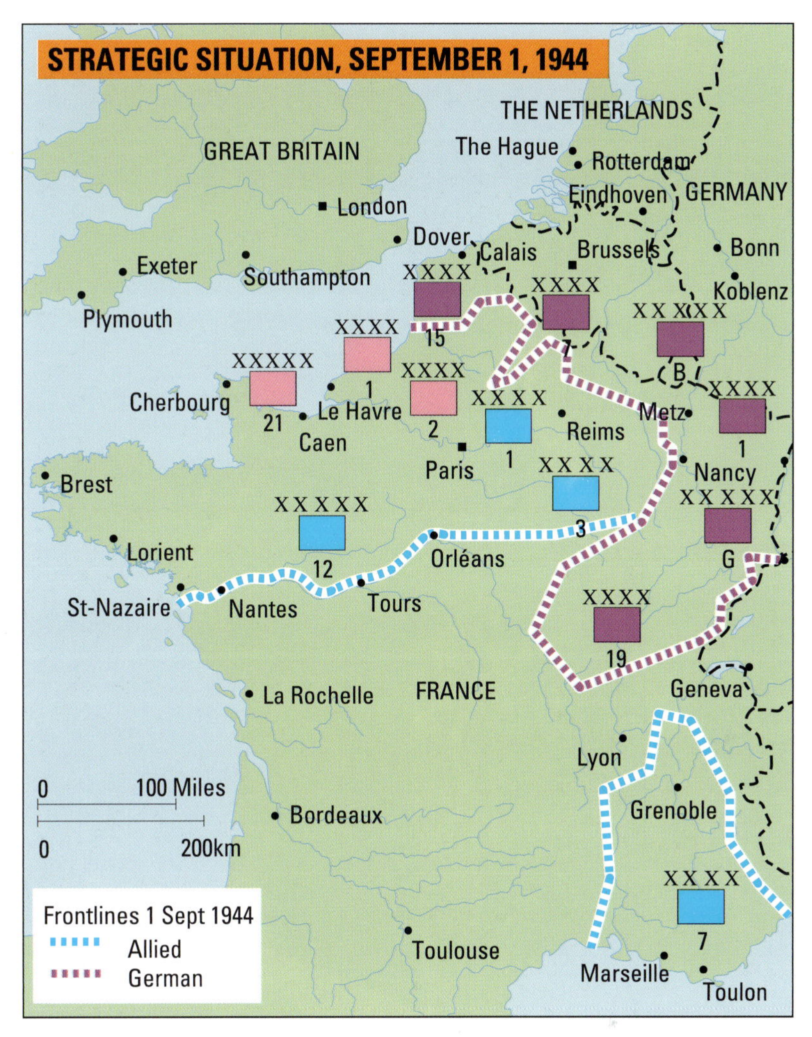

▲ ***The strategic situation in France on September 1, 1944. The Allies had pushed on to the border with the Low Countries, and the US Seventh Army was driving up from the south. (See page 192 for map key)***

strategy. British and US armies would receive equal shares of supplies, particularly fuel, and advance in line abreast across France to the German border. According to Eisenhower, this would keep the pressure on the Germans along the whole of the Western Front and prevent them regrouping to launch a flanking counterattack against an exposed Allied spearhead. As far as Patton was concerned, this was nothing less than a "sell-out" to the British.

In spite of Patton's bluster, the supply problems facing the Allied troops in France at this time were immense. The German campaign to hold or sabotage the English Channel and west-coast ports had denied the Allies access to a means to bring huge cargo ships into port for unloading. Everything the Allied armies needed, from tank shells to fuel and toothpaste, had to be brought ashore across the Normandy invasion beaches using the man-made Mulberry harbours.

The rapid advance to the Seine put the ability of the Allied logistics chain to deliver these supplies to frontline units under great strain. Patton's Third Army was at the extreme limit of these supply lines. Its equipment was worn from a month's continuous action, and its men were in urgent need of a rest.

Patton was given the line of Metz–Strasbourg as his objective on August 24, 1944. Emergency measures were put in train to resupply the Third Army in time for the new offensive. XIX Tactical Air Command opened its forward airfields south of Paris to accept aircraft bringing in fuel, rations, mail, and other vital supplies. More than 250 C-47 Dakota transport aircraft of IX Troop Carrier Command flew into the recently captured Luftwaffe airfields on August 25 alone, and the effort peaked the following day when 606 Dakotas flew .977 million kilograms (2.15 million pounds) of fuel and rations to Patton's troops. The so-called "Red Ball Express" system was instituted to speed supplies to the front. This involved 6000 trucks moving along dedicated one-way roads to and from the Normandy bridgehead. Patton also turned a blind eye to unofficial "foraging" by his supply chiefs, who went on "raids" to US First and Ninth Army depots to "liberate" fuel for the Third Army. Even with these measures, though, Patton's troops remained desperately short of supplies. Indeed, only the capture of a huge German train with 37 wagons of fuel at Sens allowed XII Corps to refuel its tanks.

For the new offensive Patton was allocated seven divisions, under the control of XII and XX Corps. At this time XV Corps was still fighting north of Paris under First Army control, and VIII Corps was to be reassigned to the Ninth Army after it had completed its mission in Brittany.

XX Corps' orders were to strike out northward from its bridgeheads at Fontainebleau and Montereau to seize Reims, before swinging eastward to advance level with XII Corps, which was to attack due east from Troyes toward the Marne River. The offensive began on August 26 in the face of minimal resistance. The 4th Armored Division led the XII Corps advance,

◀ ***Troops of the Third Army continue their assault across the Meuse River in September 1944. Although Patton's forces were unable to continue their thrust into Germany, Patton made sure his men were constantly probing the line.***

▲ *General Patton visits one of his units at the front. He was determined to punch a hole right into Germany, despite all the difficulties he faced.*

motoring more than 50 miles (80km) to capture Vitry-le-François to cross the Marne River. It then headed on to Châlons, with the 80th Infantry Division close behind, before grinding to a halt when its tanks ran out of fuel. Scavenging secured more than 100,000 gallons (378,500 liters) of German gasoline, allowing XII Corps to head toward Commercy on the River Meuse. The 4th Armored's rapid advance took the German defenders on the Meuse totally by surprise.

In the XX Corps sector the 7th Armored Division led the way, advancing in six columns on a broad front to seize bridges over the Marne River south of Reims. The Germans managed to blow several bridges ahead of the 7th Armored, but it threw pontoon bridges across the obstacles blocking its way and was soon outflanking Reims to reach the Aisne River. Following up behind, the 5th Infantry's 11th Regiment was able to formally take the historic city of Reims on August 30.

The 7th Armored then swung east and headed toward Verdun. Driving through the Argonne Forest in heavy rain, the division joined up with French Resistance fighters to clear away the

EYEWITNESS REPORT

The official history of the 134th Infantry Regiment described the heroics of Sergeant Raymond M. Parker during the fighting around Nancy.

"An assistant squad leader, Parker, cut off from his own unit, found himself with some machine gunners who were separated from their leaders. His instinct was to fight with whatever means might be at hand, and he lost no time in organizing a pair of makeshift machine-gun squads and getting the guns into action. But machine guns invite fire and death as well as dispense it, and enemy reaction soon exacted its toll; but then Parker himself manned one of the guns until his ammunition was exhausted. His means for defense eliminated, Parker soon fell into the hands of the Germans. It was only a temporary captivity, however, for the sturdy sergeant saw a fleeting opportunity and dived into the inky darkness and ran toward the river. His first major obstacle was the Canal de l'Est, which ran in a concrete bed just along the northeast bank of the river. There was no time for hesitation, and he plunged into the water, reached the opposite side with a few quick strokes, and scrambled up the concrete bank. Without pause, he made for the river itself, and after a long swim – with a river current now to be fought – he made good his escape."

scattered German roadblocks that tried to hold up the advance. On the afternoon of August 31, the 7th Armored was in Verdun and its tanks had taken control of a key bridge across the Meuse River. German air raids failed to destroy the bridge, and XX Corps was soon across in strength.

Patton was well positioned to strike for the River Moselle and the towns of Metz and Nancy. He hoped to strike fast and take them before the Germans had time to fortify them and block the route to the Siegfried Line or West Wall, a system of pillboxes and strongpoints built along the German western frontier in the 1930s and reinforced during the 1940s.

Now, however, the supply lines to the Third Army finally ran dry, stranding Patton's tanks without fuel. Patton had to wait for almost a week for extra fuel supplies to be brought forward before he could launch his troops forward again to seize a bridgehead over the Moselle. "Its not the Germans who have stopped us, but higher strategy," fumed Patton.

On September 2, 1944, Patton traveled to the headquarters of the US Twelfth Army Group for a conference of senior American military commanders in northwestern Europe. What he heard horrified the Third Army commander. The precarious logistical situation of the Allied armies in France dominated the meeting. Eisenhower announced that he had decided to give Montgomery priority for fuel and ammunition over the coming weeks to allow him to clear up the Calais area and tidy up his supply lines. The idea of a knock-out blow into Germany by the Third Army before the winter was off the agenda. Patton would only be allowed to launch a "reconnaissance in force" to cross the River Moselle and launch a limited attack on the Siegfried Line. Even this limited action was only to be launched when fuel was

▼ US soldiers from Patton's Third Army cross the Moselle River. By the end of September 1944, the Allies were driving on toward Germany itself.

available. A disillusioned Patton dubbed his commanding officer's decision "a fateful blunder".

Patton returned to his headquarters at La Chaume and resolved to exploit the limited opportunities open to him to the maximum. His plan was to capture the two cities of Lorraine, involving XX Corps, which was to seize the fortress of Metz, and XII Corps, which had Nancy as its objective. His final objective was the Rhine River.

Lorraine was perfect defensive terrain. Its many rivers and rolling wooded hills provided natural defense lines, and meant any attacker needed to prepare his assault carefully. In addition, Hitler had been building up forces in Lorraine. He wanted them to launch a counterattack into the southern flank of the US Third Army and then roll up the American line. Army Group G, under Colonel-General Johannes Blaskowitz, was assigned three panzer and panzergrenadier divisions, as well as four independent panzer brigades, for the offensive. This force mustered some 600 tanks, mostly Panthers fresh from factories in Germany. The scene was thus set for the biggest tank battles the Third Army had faced during the course of its advance across France.

The drip-feeding of supplies to the Third Army meant Patton could only push his troops into battle when ammunition and fuel became available. There would therefore be no Third Army lightning offensive. In line with Eisenhower's "reconnaissance in force" policy, Patton planned a steadily escalating series of attacks to probe the German defenses.

On the northern wing of the Third Army, XX Corps opened its attack with scouting probes toward Metz, prior to a full-scale offensive by the 7th Armored Division northeastwards toward the city on the west bank of the Moselle. This attack kicked off on September 7, and the following day the 5th Infantry Division struck toward the Moselle at Dornot. German resistance was dogged and progress was very slow.

NIGHT FIGHT

With most of XX Corps' armor committed south of Metz, the Germans now decided to launch a spoiling attack north of the city to draw American forces away from their main thrust. The 106th Panzer Brigade was to spearhead this attack, with some 36 Panthers, 11 Jagdpanzer IV/70 self-propelled guns, and 119 armored halftracks. Their crews were green,

P-47 THUNDERBOLT

The P-47 Thuderbolt proved to be an excellent close–support aircraft to support ground forces in Normandy after they were converted from their role as escorts to daylight bombing raids on France and Germany (in which capacity the P-51 Mustang was actually a more effective machine). The aircraft was remarkably resilient. P-47s often came back from combat missions shot full of holes, with their wings and control surfaces in tatters. On one occasion a Thunderbolt pilot, Lieutenant Chetwood, hit a steel pole after flying low to strafe a train in occupied France. The collision sliced 4 feet (1.2 m) off one of the Thunderbolt's wings, yet Chewood was still able to fly back safely to base in England. A typical armament load was six or eight .5in wing-mounted Browning machine guns with 267 or 425 rounds per gun and up to 2500lb (1135kg) of bombs or 10 wing-mounted 5in rockets.

and most had only been in the Wehrmacht for a few weeks. After heavy fighting, some 21 Panthers and tank destroyers, 60 halftracks, and 100 support vehicles were destroyed. Almost 800 Germans surrendered. The 106th Brigade effectively ceased to exist as a fighting force.

South of the city of Metz, fighting raged as troops of the Waffen-SS 17th Panzergrenadier Division counterattacked against the 5th Division's bridgehead over the Moselle at Dornot, held by the 11th Infantry Regiment. The 5th Division lost over 1400 men killed or wounded during this fighting south of Metz.

Patton hoped to push the 7th Armored through the Arnaville bridgehead to try to launch an encircling attack against Metz. Heavy German artillery sank a ferry carrying US reinforcements across the river, and then demolished a pontoon bridge, making it impossible to push any tanks across to support the infantrymen on the east bank. Heavy rain now fell over the battlefield, making it almost impossible to move further supplies up to frontline areas. The attack on Metz had stalled.

THE ATTACK ON NANCY

Farther south, Manton Eddy's XII Corps launched its own attack to take Nancy on September 10. The 35th Infantry Division planned an assault river-crossing when scouts of its 134th Infantry Regiment's 2nd Battalion found an undamaged bridge at Flavigny that appeared undefended. By early evening the battalion was across the river. However, shortly afterward the Germans managed to destroy the bridge with artillery fire, and then the 15th Panzergrenadier Division

▲ *In the suburbs of Nancy, two young French boys watch on in fascination as a US tank crew prepares a well deserved meal.*

▲ ***General Hasso von Manteuffel, pictured here in the center of the photograph. After the disaster at Nancy, Hitler gave von Manteuffel the daunting task of blunting Patton's attacks.***

counterattacked, wiping out the American battalion on September 11.

Farther up river, the 35th Division's 137th Infantry Regiment was thrown into the attack and secured several toeholds on the eastern bank. The GIs held long enough for Shermans of the 4th Armored Division's Combat Command B to cross the river and link up with them late in the evening of September 11. This was just in time, because early the following morning a battalion of Panthers was launched against them. The presence of the American tanks saved the day and the attacking panzers were driven off with heavy losses. The Germans were using up their precious Panthers.

Eddy turned his attention to strike at the north of Nancy, with the 80th Infantry Division pushing two battalions across the River Moselle on September 11. For two days they managed to expand their bridgehead until a night-time counterattack by the 3rd Panzergrenadier Division, backed by 10 StuG III assault guns, drove them back to within 328 feet (100m) of the river bank. A company of Sherman tanks was finally brought up and, just at the last minute, managed to stabilize the situation.

The 3rd and 15th Panzergrenadier Divisions next tried to push the 4th Armored and 80th Infantry Divisions back across the Moselle, but Eddy's men were too strong for them and the two German units only managed to exhaust themselves in the process, losing hundreds of casualties in fruitless attacks. With Nancy in danger of being cut off, Blaskowitz ordered the city evacuated, and in a couple of days it was abandoned.

Wade Haislip's XV Corps had been fighting north of Paris with Courtney Hodges' First Army in late August. It was now heading for the southern flank of the Third Army, to achieve a link-up with the US Seventh Army, which was advancing from the south of France.

Haislip was perhaps Patton's most aggressive corps commander, and he had his sights set on destroying the German LXIV Corps, which was occupying a salient pointing westward to the south of Nancy. After linking up with the Seventh Army on September 10, and completing a continuous Allied front from the English Channel to the Mediterranean Sea, Haislip moved eastward to strike at the Germans.

Blaskowitz now committed his armored reserves in the sector, the 112th Panzer Brigade, with more than 38 Panthers, and 45 Panzer IV tanks of the 21st Panzer Division, backed up by a regiment of infantry. Like its counterpart, the 106th Brigade, the 112th Brigade was a green outfit that was poorly trained and not really ready for combat. The Germans used the cover of darkness to move their tanks into Dompaire but the noise of the column alerted the nearby French troops, who moved their own tanks into hull-down firing positions.

At daybreak, an American forward air controller with the Free French troops started to direct a steady stream of P-47 Thunderbolts into action against the German tanks in villages around Dompaire. Rockets, bombs, and machine-gun fire rained down on the Germans, destroying eight Panthers and prompting several inexperienced crews to abandon their vehicles to seek cover. Under cover of more air strikes the French moved forward to block all the escape routes of 112th Brigade. The 21st Panzer Division now intervened, attacking from the south and threatening to outflank the Free French advance guard. Determined resistance from a handful of Shermans, M10 tank destroyers, and machine gun-equipped jeeps held the German tanks at bay for several key hours and broke up a panzergrenadier attack.

On the afternoon of September 13, the trapped 112th Brigade tried to counterattack out of Dompaire, only to be beaten back with heavy losses to

M18 HELLCAT

The M18 was one of the fastest armored fighting vehicles of World War II, boasting a maximum road speed of 50 mph (80km/h). The vehicle's light weight, its sturdy Christie-based suspension, and a 400hp engine, all combined to provide a high power-to-weight ratio. Its light weight was partly due to its light armor – the intention was for the M18 to utilize its speed and mobility for "shoot and scoot" tactics. The vehicle's light armor was partially offset by the arrangement of sloping armor plates to provide extra protection. It was one of the best all-round tank destroyers of World War II. The M18 carried a five-man crew, as well as 45 rounds of ammunition for the main gun and an M2 Browning machine gun on a flexible ring mount for use against aircraft and infantry. Its main weapon was a 76mm gun.

hull-down Shermans and more P-47 attacks. By the evening the German attack force was in full retreat, after losing almost two-thirds of its tank force. The 112th brigade had lost 34 of its Panthers and the 21st Panzer was reduced to only 17 operational tanks. This débâcle doomed the German LXIV Corps, whose survivors were soon heading for safety at top speed. Within days Haislip's men were at the Moselle.

The loss of Nancy and the defeat of LXIV Corps put Hitler's plans for an all-out offensive against Patton on hold. Blaskowitz was therefore able to persuade the Führer to use the remaining panzer reserves in local counterattacks to restore the situation, using the 11th Panzer Division and the 111th and 113th Panzer Brigades. These new attacks began on September 18. In a series of skirmishes with American scout units, the two panzer brigades failed to make significant gains. The

▼ ***US infantry of the Third Army, supported by armored elements, carry out an assault near the village of Dombasle.***

▲ ***A heavily camouflaged US M10 tank destroyer lies in ambush somewhere in the Lorraine area.***

German attack went in under thick morning fog. Panthers and Shermans blundered around in the fog, opening fire at ranges under 330 feet (100m). Eleven Panthers were lost in these battles as the American tank crews exploited their superior knowledge of the local area and their radio communications to spring repeated ambushes on their opponents.

The battlefield was largely quiet on September 21 as the Germans reorganized their forces for a new attack. Thick fog shielded the 111th Panzer Brigade from Allied airpower, and so the burden of the defense fell on M18 tank destroyers. When the fog finally lifted later in the day, swarms of P-47s were able to interdict for the first time in several days. Their intervention delayed the German column long enough for the 37th Tank Battalion to get into position on the prominent ridge to begin engaging the advancing Panthers. The Germans were caught in a killing zone: pounded with artillery, hit by air strikes, and then engaged by Shermans. By the end of the day the 111th Brigade was reduced to 7 tanks and 90 men from its strength of 90 tanks and 2500 men three days before.

THE SUPPLY PROBLEM

As Patton's men were fighting off the panzer attack, their commander was informed by Bradley that there were no longer enough supplies to continue the Third Army's offensive. The British had launched an airborne offensive into Holland—Operation Market Garden—and they would now receive the bulk of the Allied fuel and ammunition for the coming weeks. XV Corps and the 6th Armored were also being pulled away from the Third Army at the end of the month. On September 23, Patton met his corps commanders to plan how to reorientate his forces for a general defensive battle.

Even before they had time to put their plans into action, the Germans struck again, sending the newly arrived 11th Panzer Division into action against the 4th Armored, while the

559th Volksgrenadier Division and the reinforced 106th Panzer Brigade hit the 35th Infantry Division. The next day, the 11th Panzer threw 50 tanks into action and forced the 4th Armored to pull back to a more defensible line. For three days the battle raged around the Lorraine countryside.

BLUNTING THE PANZERS

Both sides had suffered hundreds of casualties in the vicious fighting, but in the end superior American artillery and airpower won the day. The Germans lost 700 killed and 300 wounded in four days of fighting against the 4th Armored, along with 22 Panthers and 14 Panzer IVs destroyed.

In the fighting around Arracourt the Germans lost 86 tanks and more than 100 were badly damaged. Blaskowitz had paid with his job for his failure to retake Nancy, and on September 29 his successor, General of Panzer Troops Hermann Balck, ordered 11th Panzer out of the line to refit. Patton's troops had held their ground.

In a bloody month of fighting the Third Army had managed to cross the River Moselle and had inflicted heavy losses on the German forces sent to halt its advance. The Germans lost some 220 tanks and 220 assault guns during the fighting—losses which they could ill afford—while Patton had lost 49 light tanks and 151 Shermans. The American losses could be replaced with relative ease. Nevertheless, this had been the Third Army's toughest battle since it broke out of Normandy at the end of July.

Patton's ambition to break through to the Rhine River had proved illusory because of the difficulty of receiving supplies. The month-long battle proved, however, that Patton's men were more than capable of taking on the Germans in a stand-up fight, and refuted criticism that they were only good for chasing defeated units. The Battle for Lorraine was far from over, however. Patton's men would spend another two miserable months locked in frustrating battles to try to batter through the Siegfried Line and across the border into Germany. And all the while, the weather was steadily deteriorating as winter inexorably approached.

▼ Though Patton's Third Army was famous for its armored units, it relied heavily on the skills of its supporting artillery to blunt panzer counterattacks.

Planning the German Counter

In the West, as Allied armies ground to a halt in the fall of 1944, Hitler ordered one final effort to rebuild his battered armies to inflict a decisive defeat on the British and Americans. The attack would punch through the wooded Ardennes region to capture the Belgian port of Antwerp, in a repeat of the 1940s offensive that had been so successful.

The July 20 Bomb Plot had destroyed for good Hitler's trust in the army's generals. He wanted his favorite Waffen-SS general, "Sepp" Dietrich, to command the most powerful armored force Nazi Germany had ever put in the field. At an audience with the Führer in early September 1944, Dietrich was told that he was to command the newly formed Sixth Panzer Army. Although this was nominally an army formation—rebuilt from the remnants of XII Corps that had been badly mauled in Russia during the summer—almost all of Dietrich's key staff officers were old hands from either his Leibstandarte or I SS Panzer Corps days. Dietrich's right-hand man was SS-Brigadeführer Fritz Kraemer who, as chief of staff, took on the role of powerhouse behind his commander's bluster.

As an army commander, Dietrich was perhaps over-promoted. He himself realized that he was no professional staff officer, and he relied on the likes of Kraemer to turn his ideas into concrete plans. Dietrich's true forte was man-management and motivation

of the troops. His down-to-earth bonhomie was exactly what was needed to mold the thousands of new recruits who were now arriving to fill out the ranks of his divisions. Hitler liked him so much because Dietrich never had any ambition, beyond looking after his men. He never felt threatened by Dietrich and, because of their time together in 1920s Munich, the Führer would listen to his views on what was happening at the front.

To fill out his new army, Dietrich was given the two premier Waffen-SS corps headquarters, I SS and II SS Panzer Corps. I SS Panzer Corps boasted the Leibstandarte and Hitlerjugend Divisions, under the command of SS-Gruppenführer Hermann Priess, who had previously commanded the infamous Waffen-SS Totenkopf ("Death's Head") Panzer Division in Russia and was considered a sound tactician, if ruthless, even judging by Waffen-SS standards.

After his success commanding one of Hitlerjugend's panzergrenadier regiments in Normandy, Wilhelm Mohnke, now an SS-Oberführer, was given the honor of commanding the Leibstandarte. Although Mohnke had fought well in Normandy, he was far from popular with his comrades. He had lost a foot in the Yugoslav campaign, so missed fighting with Hausser's SS Panzer Corps in Russia, and he was still considered an "outsider" by many of the Waffen-SS officers who were now regimental and divisional commanders in Dietrich's army. Taking the place of Kurt Meyer, who had been captured in early September, was SS-Standartenführer Hugo Kraas, a highly decorated Leibstandarte Division veteran.

▲ *On paper, the Ardennes attack seemed simple enough: a strike through the forests of the Ardennes to take Antwerp and split the Americans and the British. (See page 192 for map key)*

MANPOWER CHANGES

The victor of Arnhem, Willi Bittrich, remained in command of his beloved II SS Panzer Corps, and he had Walther Harzer at his side as chief of staff. He still had the Hohenstaufen Division, under the capable Sylvester Stadler, but the Frundsberg Division had been replaced by the Das Reich Division. Its commander, Heinz Lammerding, was a rabid Nazi who was considered one of the most stupid officers who ever reached high command in the Waffen-SS. He relied on his chief of staff and regimental commanders to come up with battle plans, and he was loathed for taking credit for their successes. Bittrich's corps, however, was now very strong and considered the most militarily professional in the Waffen-SS.

By the beginning of October, battered Waffen-SS units were garrisoned in old Wehrmacht barracks in northwest Germany, where they began to receive a steady stream of new recruits and new equipment. Thousands of conscripts, ex-Luftwaffe and navy men—as well as a few idealistic volunteers—had to be given the basics of military training and then

◀ *The destruction of communications links hampered the Allied build-up for the invasion of Germany during the fall of 1944, giving Hitler the chance to rebuild his panzer reserves.*

molded into effective fighting units. Under the direction of veteran officers, as well as noncommissioned officers, this process gathered pace during October and into November as more ambitious tank-gunnery training and field exercises were undertaken.

The presence of so many highly decorated combat veterans in the ranks of the Waffen-SS panzer divisions provided a major boost to morale. The newly arrived youngsters were treated to a series of medal parades, in which Normandy veterans were decorated for their heroic actions only a few weeks before.

OPTIMISM AGAINST ALL ODDS

The steady arrival of new tanks, halftracks, artillery pieces, weapons, and uniforms added to the spirit of optimism. If Germany, after five years of war, could still find the equipment to outfit completely four panzer divisions, then the Führer's promises of new wonder-weapons to turn the tide of war might well be true. By mid-November 1944, morale among the divisions of Dietrich's new army was high and still rising.

Hitler ordered that Dietrich's new army would have priority for new equipment coming from the Reich's remaining armament's factories. British and American bombing, however, along with the loss of factories in eastern Poland, meant this was almost the last effort of armament minister Albert Speer's organization.

The reorganization and re-equipping of Dietrich's divisions was nearly complete by the end of November. While the frontline panzer divisions were at between 80 percent and 90 percent strength, there was a severe shortage of Waffen-SS corps-level artillery and heavy tank units. These had to be replaced by army units.

As befitted its status as one of the premier units of the Waffen-SS, the Leibstandarte boasted a formidable complement of tanks and armored vehicles. Its Panzer Regiment was again commanded by Jochen Peiper, who had now recovered from wounds received in Normandy, and fielded 38 Panthers and 34 Panzer IVs in a single battalion. To beef up its firepower, the 501st SS Heavy Panzer Battalion—formed from the old 101st SS Battalion—was augmented with 30 of the monster 70-ton (69t) King Tiger tanks. The division's anti-tank battalion boasted 21 Panzerjäger IVs. The division had the pick of Germany's manpower, and veteran officers considered it to be on a par with previous intakes.

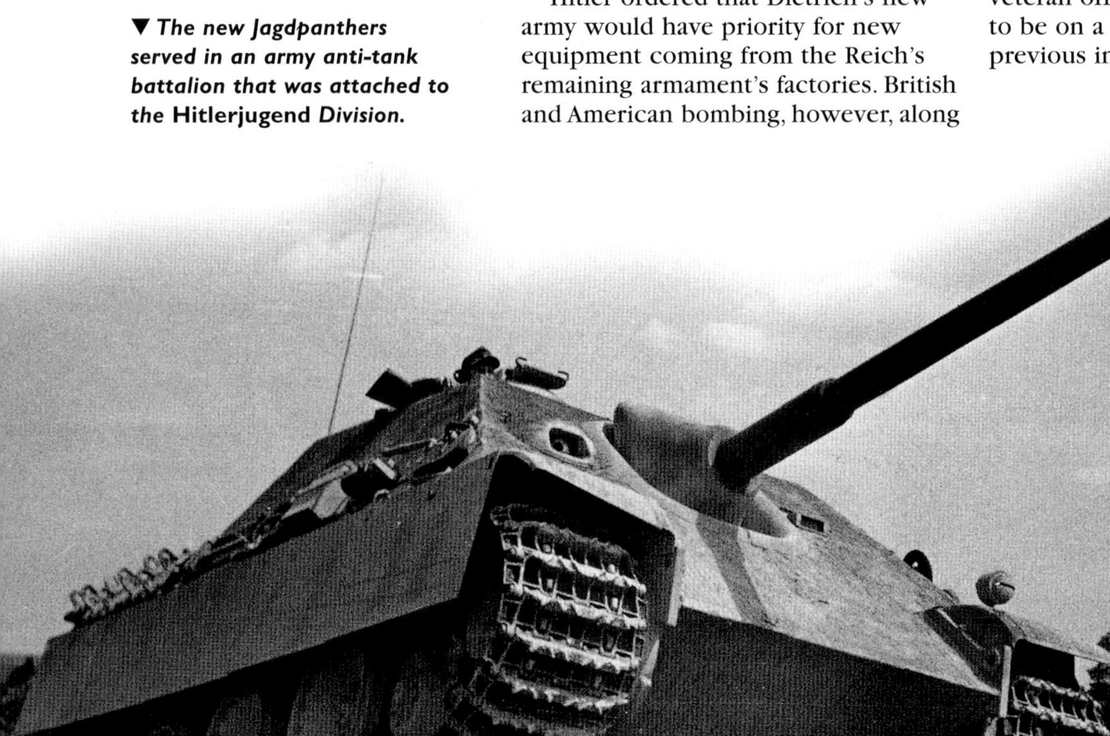

▼ ***The new Jagdpanthers served in an army anti-tank battalion that was attached to the* Hitlerjugend *Division.***

HITLERJUGEND'S MATERIEL

The Hitlerjugend Division was equally powerful, with 38 Panthers and 37 Panzer IVs in its Panzer Regiment, which were grouped in one battalion. It had a strong contingent of self-propeled anti-tank guns, including 22 Panzerjäger IVs, in its own anti-tank battalion. To add to its firepower, the army's 560th Anti-tank Battalion was attached to the Panzer Regiment, with 28 Panzerjäger IVs and 14 of the 88mm-armed Jagdpanthers. It continued to draw its recruits from the ranks of the Nazi Youth organization, which gave it its distinctive character.

I SS Panzer Corps had four army Nebelwerfer and two army artillery regiments attached for fire support.

Bittrich's II SS Panzer Corps was next in line to receive men and equipment, and was not as strong as its sister formation. He only had two army corps-level artillery regiments attached.

The Das Reich Division had 80 percent of its designated manpower strength and a strong complement of armor. Its Panzer Regiment boasted two full battalions, with 58 Panthers, 28 Panzer IVs, and 28 StuG IIIs. The division's anti-tank battalion had 20 Panzerjäger IVs.

The Hohenstaufen was the weakest Waffen-SS division, with only 75 percent of its allocated manpower under arms at the end of November 1944. Its Panzer Regiment had 35 Panthers and 28 StuG IIIs in one battalion and 39 Panzer IVs and 28 StuG IIIs in a second battalion. Anti-tank firepower was provided by 21 Panzerjäger IVs.

Dietrich had an assortment of army artillery, assault gun, anti-tank gun, and heavy tank battalions attached to his army, which, when added to the divisional equipment totals, gave him just under 400 Panzer IV, King Tiger and Panther tanks, 685 guns, 340 rocket launchers, 112 assault guns, and 215 Jagdpanzers.

One of the most unusual units attached to Dietrich's army was the 150th Panzer Brigade, which was under the command of the flamboyant SS-Sturmbannführer, Otto Skorzeny. This unorthodox brigade was intended to infiltrate behind Allied lines, dressed in US Army uniforms and driving American vehicles, in order to spread chaos and confusion. Some 500 Waffen-SS men were attached to this 2800-strong unit.

▲ *Dreadful winter weather proved Hitler's best ally, hiding the preparations for Operation Watch on the Rhine from Allied air reconnaissance.*

THE THREAT TO THE REICH

Building Dietrich's army was the number one priority for the Waffen-SS in the fall of 1944, attracting the bulk of its resources and manpower. The Allied threat to the borders of the Reich was real, however, and a number of Waffen-SS panzer units found themselves dragged into a series of small-scale engagements.

The Leibstandarte Division dispatched two battalion-sized Kampfgruppen to help defend the city of Aachen in early October, when it was threatened by American troops. One of the Kampfgruppe became trapped inside the city when it was encircled. Rather than surrender with the rest of the army garrison, the Waffen-SS men decided to break out. Only eight soldiers made it back to German lines.

In October and November, the fight for Aachen became a battle of attrition as the US Army tried to advance into the Hurtgen Forest and seize the Roer dams that provided power and water for the Ruhr industrial region. Stung that a German city had fallen into American hands, Hitler ordered defenses to be strengthened. The Frundsberg Division was diverted from the effort to build up Dietrich's army to fight in the Aachen region.

The Alsace city of Metz on the French-German border was the scene of a similar bloody campaign during November 1944, as General Patton tried to batter his way onto German territory. The 17th SS Panzergrenadier Division was sent to hold a stretch of the front south of Metz, and it gave Patton's 5th Infantry Division a stiff fight before being forced back to the West Wall at the end of November.

The determined resistance of the Frundsberg and 17th SS Divisions, along with scores of Wehrmacht divisions, was all part of Hitler's deception plan to cover his build-up for what was codenamed Operation Watch on the Rhine after a popular song. The strong defence of Metz and Aachen drew in Allied reserves and diverted their commanders' attention away from the Ardennes region in southeast Belgium.

In September, even before Bittrich's II SS Panzer Corps had defeated Operation Market Garden, Hitler was thinking about launching a counteroffensive in the West. By early October, the Ardennes had been identified as the vulnerable point in the Allied line, with the port of Antwerp as the offensive's objective. The aim was to split the British forces in Holland from the American armies in France.

At the end of the month, Dietrich and the other army commanders who were to lead the offensive were briefed on the details of the plan. Even the

▼ *Nearly four years of bombing meant German industry was reaching the limit of its endurance. The Ardennes attack would use up Germany's last reserves.*

▲ ***US Army Air Force B-17s pounded German factories by day, while the British RAF raided the Reich's cities by night.***

usually loyal Dietrich was incredulous at what was being proposed. The terrain was unsuitable for tanks, the roads were too narrow, their troops were not yet fully trained, and there was not enough fuel. The generals suggested a more modest offensive aimed at cutting off American units in Aachen, but the Führer was adamant. He wanted a decisive attack, that would in one stroke change the course of the war. No argument was allowed.

A major deception program was instituted to ensure that the Allies had no idea where the German offensive would fall. All orders were issued by hand at meetings, or by despatch rider, so Allied radio interception units would not be able to track the movement of headquarters concentrating for the coming offensive. Apart from a few senior commanders, no one was briefed on the full scope of the operation in order to reduce the chance of it being compromised. Halfway through the planning of the attack, its codename was changed to Autumn Mist to further conceal its purpose. Even the Waffen-SS corps and division commanders were not briefed until 10 days before the offensive was due to start, and the troops themselves had no idea of the full size and scope of the operation until 24 hours before they were due to go into action.

The German deception was totally successful, and the Allies were unaware about what was going to happen until the first panzers advanced into the Ardennes region. Surprise was total.

Hitler's greatest gamble finally got under way at 05:30 hours on December 16, 1944. He was relying on his Waffen-SS panzer élite to come forward and save his Thousand Year Reich—or die in the process.

The Battle of the Bulge

DECEMBER 16–22

WESTERN FRONT, *ARDENNES*
Hitler launches Operation Watch on the Rhine. This is the code name for his attempt to break through the US VIII Corps on the Ardennes front, reach the Meuse River, and capture Antwerp, thereby splitting the Allied armies in two. The German units involved in the attack—a total of some 200,000 men—form Army Group B under the overall command of Field Marshal Gerd von Rundstedt. This force includes some of Germany's most renowned veterans, and comprises the Sixth SS Panzer Army, Fifth Panzer Army, and Seventh Army. US forces total 80,000 men.

Surprise is total and there is dense cloud and fog, which negates Allied air superiority, but the Germans fail to take the towns of St. Vith and Bastogne in the initial attacks, which narrows their attack front.

On the 17th, troops of SS Lieutenant Colonel Joachim Peiper's battlegroup

▼ *Abandoned German Panther and Panzer IV tanks in the Ardennes in late December. Shortages of fuel, stubborn defense, and Allied air attacks contributed to the failure of the offensive.*

▲ ***Aided by secrecy and poor weather, the initial assaults of the German Ardennes offensive met with success.***

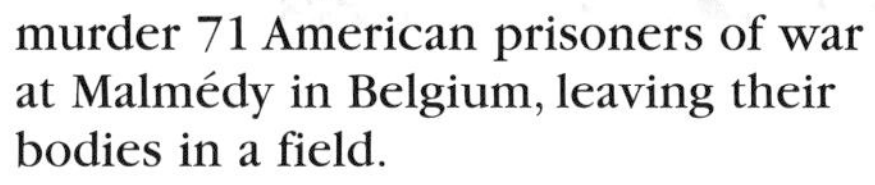

murder 71 American prisoners of war at Malmédy in Belgium, leaving their bodies in a field.

By the 22nd, the Americans at St. Vith, having lost 8000 of 22,000 men, pull back from the town. Meanwhile, however, the men of the 28th Infantry, 10th, and 101st Airborne Divisions continue to hold out stubbornly in Bastogne against one infantry and two panzer divisions. On the same day the Germans mount their last attempt to reach the Meuse.

As part of their sabotage operations, the Germans are using English-speaking commandos dressed in US uniforms to spread confusion behind Allied lines, especially at road junctions and on bridges. However, measures have been taken to defeat these infiltrators, many of whom are later shot as spies.

DECEMBER 24

AIR WAR, *BELGIUM*
The first jet bomber operation in history takes place when twin-engined German Arado 234B bombers raid a factory and marshaling yards. The bombing raid is led by Luftwaffe Captain Dieter Lukesch.

DECEMBER 26

WESTERN FRONT, *ARDENNES*
The US First and Third Armies launch counterattacks against the north and south of the German "bulge" into the Ardennes. The US Third Army's 4th Armored Division relieves Bastogne as Hitler is informed by his generals that Antwerp can no longer be reached by his forces. The only hope of salvaging any sort of victory in the Ardennes is to swing the Fifth and Sixth Panzer Armies north to cross the Meuse west of Liège and come in behind Aachen. However, this presupposes the capture of Bastogne and an attack from the north to link with the panzers—both are increasingly unlikely.

DECEMBER 30

WESTERN FRONT, *ARDENNES*
At Bastogne, General George Patton, his forces swollen to six divisions, resumes his attack northeast toward Houffalize. At the same time, General Hasso von Manteuffel, commander of the German Fifth Panzer Army, launches another major attempt to cut the corridor into Bastogne and take the town. The fighting is intense, but Patton's forces stand firm and defeat the German attack.

Hitler's Last Throw

Field Marshal Gerd von Rundstedt announced the following to his men in the West on the evening of December 15, 1944: "Soldiers of the West Front! Your great hour has arrived. Large attacking armies have started against the Anglo–Americans. I do not have to tell you anything more than that. You feel it yourself. WE GAMBLE EVERYTHING. You carry with you the holy obligation to give everything to achieve things beyond human possibilities for our Fatherland and our Führer!"

The stirring message was read to his attack troops as they moved up to their start-lines in the heavily wooded Eifel region of Germany. At 05:30 hours the following day, 1600 German guns and rocket launchers drenched the American frontline in deadly shrapnel. Then the first attack waves of infantry moved forward to clear a route for the panzer columns, who were to be unleashed to capture their first objective—the bridges across the Meuse—within 48 hours. The panzers would push on to Antwerp and victory.

"Sepp" Dietrich's Sixth Panzer Army was placed on the right flank of the assault and it would be the Schwerpunkt, or main effort, for the attack. I SS Panzer Corps would lead the advance to the Meuse, with II SS Panzer Corps following close behind. Once the vital river crossings were secure, Bittrich's divisions would spearhead the advance on Antwerp.

To help Dietrich reach the bridges before the Americans had time to destroy them, Otto Skorzeny's special forces brigade—with small teams wearing US uniforms taking the lead—was to race ahead of the Waffen-SS panzers and capture them in a coup de main operation. A regiment of Luftwaffe paratroopers was also to be dropped ahead of Dietrich's corps to capture a key road junction.

The sister Leibstandarte and Hitlerjugend Divisions would advance side-by-side towards the Meuse, after army Volksgrenadier divisions had cleared a way through the string of weak American units holding the front along the Belgian-German border. Once unleashed, the two divisions would race through the narrow forested valleys of the Ardennes until they reached the open countryside in the Meuse valley. The region's roads were winding and poorly maintained and, in most places, could barely take single-file traffic. The constricted road network in the Ardennes meant Dietrich's divisions had to be split up into self-contained columns, each of which was assigned its own specific route, or Rollbahn. All told, more than 6000 Waffen-SS vehicles had to be squeezed through the Ardennes road system. The speed of the Waffen-SS advance was determined as much by the commanders' traffic-control abilities as their tactical skills.

The Leibstandarte Division was split into three large Kampfgruppen, centred on the panzer regiment and its two panzergrenadier regiments, and a "fast group" based on the division's reconnaissance battalion. Hitlerjugend was organized in the same way. The most powerful Kampfgruppe was Jochen Peiper's, which had all the Leibstandarte's tanks, its King Tigers, a panzergrenadier battalion in armored halftracks, and a battalion of army howitzers. All told, he had more than 5000 men, 117 tanks, 149 halftracks, 24 artillery pieces, 40 anti-aircraft guns, and more than 500 other vehicles. The success of the offensive would depend on its progress.

The atrocious road network meant that each division was allocated no more than two Rollbahns each, so their Kampfgruppen had to line up behind one another while they waited for the lead troops to blast open a way forward. With little room for maneuver off-road, the lead Kampfgruppe was effectively reduced to relying on the handful of tanks it could place at its head to win through. Behind Peiper's Kampfgruppe followed nose-to-tail columns of tanks and trucks.

◀ ***The US Army's 14th Cavalry Group provided easy pickings for the Leibstandarte, which had smashed into the northern flank of the American defenses.***

▲ ***German film crews were on hand to film the Waffen-SS victories in the early hours of Autumn Mist.***

TRAFFIC JAMS

Although the Germans had amassed more than 3.75 million gallons (17 million litres) of fuel to support the offensive, the jammed road network meant the troops at the front of the convoys could not rely on refueling tankers getting through to them. So Peiper and his colleagues in the lead Kampfgruppe were ordered to seize US petrol dumps in order to maintain the pace of their advance.

Hitler had wanted to launch the offensive in early November, but delays in massing the necessary troops and supplies had put the operation back until December. This brought with it one advantage: the fog, rain, and low cloud that shrouded the hilly Ardennes provided welcome cover from the Allied fighter-bombers that had paralyzed German panzer columns in Normandy in the summer.

▲ Jochen Peiper's Kampfgruppe was boosted by the Tiger II tanks of the army's 501st Heavy Panzer Battalion for its drive westward. Here, one of its tanks passes a column of captured GIs from the 99th Infantry Division.

On the freezing night of December 15, the Leibstandarte moved into its forward assembly areas behind the sector of front held by the 12th Volksgrenadier and 3rd Parachute Divisions. These were units that had been decimated in Russia and Normandy, and then rapidly rebuilt with personnel from rear-echelon units. They lacked heavy equipment and trained infantry commanders. The Hitlerjugend was waiting a few miles to the north, behind the 277th Volksgrenadier Division.

AMERICAN RESISTANCE

The 12th and 3rd Divisions' attacks quickly stalled in the face of very determined, albeit poorly coordinated, American resistance. The attacks were supposed to have captured the town of Losheim and its key road junction in a couple of hours, to allow Peiper's tanks to roar into action as dawn broke. Minefields held up the attack, and the two divisions were still fighting their way through American positions in the early afternoon. When a breach was opened, it was found that a key bridge was blocked and a temporary one had to be built by army engineers.

Furious at the delay, Peiper ordered his own Waffen-SS engineers to begin building their own bridge. It was not until well after dark that his column got into Losheim, where Peiper was dismayed to find the commander of the lead parachute regiment had allowed his men to go to sleep, rather than press on with the advance. The determined Waffen-SS officer "took" the paratroopers under his command and they were soon loaded onto the back of his King Tigers, which pressed on into the night. Several tanks and vehicles were lost when the column ran into a minefield, but Peiper ordered the advance to continue regardless.

PEIPER'S COLUMN PRESSES ON

All night Peiper's men forged on, with two Panthers leading the way until they surprised an American scout company parked up in a village just before dawn. Most of the GIs were captured and subsequently filmed by Nazi propaganda teams accompanying Peiper's column. The weather briefly cleared to allow some American fighters to attack, but they were unable to inflict much damage or delay the column. Running short of fuel, Peiper now made a diversion to raid a large US fuel dump. His tanks were soon being refueled by sullen American prisoners. The Germans turned north toward the town of Malmédy.

When the lead Panzer IVs approached a crossroads in the hamlet of Baugnez, they spotted a column of US soft-skinned vehicles ahead of them. They immediately started firing on the Americans, then raced at full speed toward them. Panzergrenadiers in armored halftracks were close behind. Outgunned, the Americans offered no resistance and, in a few minutes, Waffen-SS men had herded almost 100 stunned Americans into a nearby field. Peiper then passed by in his armored command halftrack and ordered the advance to continue, racing off westward with his lead tanks.

Learning that a US artillery brigade had its headquarters nearby, Peiper set off to capture it and its general. The American general escaped with a few minutes to spare before Peiper's tanks burst into his compound. Back at Baugnez, the captured Americans were being machine-gunned by Peiper's men in an incident that would become notorious as the "Malmédy Massacre," although it occurred several miles outside the town. Peiper and more than 70 other members of the Leibstandarte would later face charges of war crimes for their involvement in the atrocity.

STOPPING AT STAVELOT

Peiper continued to drive his men forward. They kept going even after it grew dark. The Waffen-SS column was unopposed until it approached the village of Stavelot, where the lead panzers were fired upon by a single bazooka rocket. Fearing a tank ambush in the night, the Kampfgruppe pulled back to wait for daylight, not knowing that the village and its strategically important bridge was in fact held by only a few dozen Americans.

Behind Peiper's spearhead, the Leibstandarte's other Kampfgruppe, led by SS-Standartenführer Max Hansen, had already managed to break free and was advancing westward. Containing the bulk of a panzergrenadier regiment and most of the division's Panzerjäger IVs, it was operating slightly to the south of Peiper on a parallel Rollbahn.

THE EISENBORN RIDGE

The Hitlerjugend Division was not faring so well in its attempt to open up the northern Rollbahn and seize the strategic Eisenborn ridge. The US 99th Infantry Division put up stiff resistance and held the attacks by the 326th Volksgrenadier Division. Rather than being used to exploit a breach in the American line, the division's two lead Kampfgruppen had to be committed to the assault action. Although the Waffen-SS Panthers inflicted heavy losses on the few American tanks barring their way, soon GIs with bazookas were picking off the German tanks at an alarming rate. This fierce fighting in a string of border villages allowed time for the Americans to form a firing line with their Shermans, M10 and M18 tank destroyers, and 105mm howitzers in the anti-tank role.

When the Hitlerjugend's Panthers rolled forward on the morning of 18 December, they ran into a hail of well-aimed anti-tank fire. They made it to the American lines, but soon 15 Panthers, 1 Panzer IV, and 2 Panzerjäger IVs were ablaze. A retreat was ordered before more of the Hitlerjugend's valuable armor was lost. Kraas and Dietrich ordered a rethink, and the division's Schwerpunkt was now shifted south in order to try to bypass the strong defense on Eisenborn ridge. More fanatical American resistance was encountered, and the division spent four days trying to batter its way through. Dietrich concentrated four corps artillery regiments to support a large attack on December 21, but the Americans were fighting stubbornly and were not to be moved. When the panzer regiment attacked, it lost 11 more tanks. A further attack on the following day met a similar fate, and the division was pulled out of the line to be re-assigned to push through behind the Leibstandarte Division.

▼ Battle-hardened Waffen-SS troopers cautiously move past vehicles abandoned by US troops holding the line in the Ardennes.

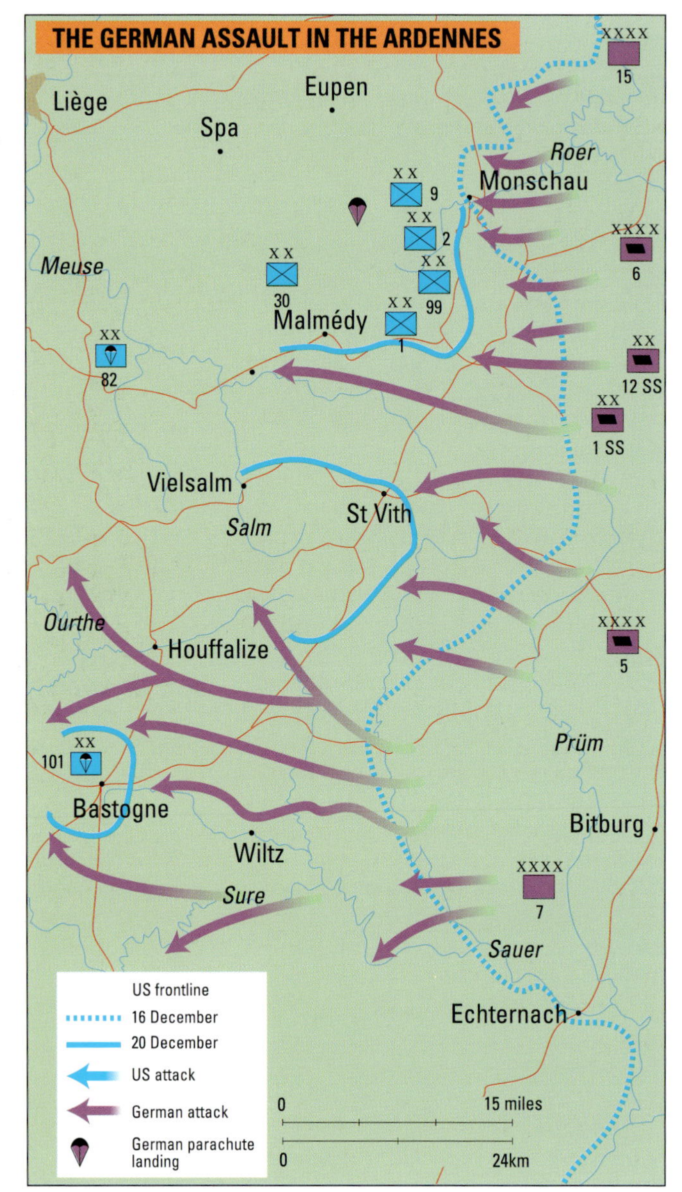

▶ *In the first few days of Operation Watch on the Rhine the Germans had captured more than 7,000 US troops as the panzers broke through the weak American forces holding the frontline in the Ardennes.* *(See page 192 for map key)*

THE LAST PUSH FOR VICTORY

The stalling of the Hitlerjugend's attacks on the morning of December 18 meant that Peiper's Kampfgruppe was now I SS Panzer Corps' Schwerpunkt. Even so, he was still 19 miles (30km) from the Meuse and 48 hours behind schedule. This was not a time to worry about his flanks. Peiper pushed all his tanks forward for one last, desperate lunge for victory.

At dawn that day, Peiper renewed his attack with added vigor. The Panthers rolled at full speed into Stavelot to seize its key bridge. The by-now reinforced defenders knocked out the lead Panther, and Peiper—along with the lead panzergrenadiers—took cover at the edge of the village.

Grabbing a Panzerfaust, Peiper set off to take out the offending anti-tank gun. Another Panther arrived and destroyed the 76mm anti-tank gun before driving over the bridge in a hail of bullets and shells. Their position effectively unhinged, the Americans had no choice but to withdraw to safety. This action left Peiper now in control of the vital bridge.

With time critical, Peiper pressed on to seize his next objectives, the bridge over the River Amblève at Trois Ponts, and another bridge slightly farther south across the River Salm. The bulk of the Kampfgruppe headed for Trois Ponts and a small contingent was sent to the Salm. American engineers were hard at work in Trois Ponts, laying demolition charges on the key bridge and mines on the roads as Peiper's lead Panthers rolled into town just before 11:00 hours.

A well-placed anti-tank gun immobilized the lead tank and, as the following Waffen-SS tanks maneuvered around the wreckage, the GIs pressed the plunger on their demolition charges. The vital bridge disappeared in a massive mushroom cloud. The same thing happened to the assault team sent to capture the Salm bridge, leaving Peiper's route on the main road westward blocked. He therefore turned his troops around, and sent them northward on a side road, which led through the village of La Gleize, in order to bypass the downed bridges.

Two hours later, his Panthers were through the village and heading westward to the crossing at Cheneux. It was undefended and Peiper's tanks were soon across and heading west again. Allied fighter-bombers now swooped down, knocking out two Panthers and a dozen vehicles. The damage inflicted was minor, but the delay proved fatal to Operation Watch on the Rhine. It gave a group of American engineers just the time they needed to plant demolition charges on Peiper's next target, the bridge at Habiemont. As his Panthers arrived at the bridge at 16.45 hours, the structure was blown in front of Peiper's eyes.

Twice in one day his ambitions had been thwarted. He now had to turn his column around and head back to La Gleize to rethink his options. He had only 31 operational tanks: 6 Tigers, 6 Panzer IVs, and 19 Panthers. Once back there, he met up with Gustav Knittel's reconnaissance battalion which had now made its way forward, along with a small convoy of fuel tankers. News also came in that American troops had recaptured Stavelot, so Knittel was ordered to retrace his steps and open up a supply route for Peiper.

After a night spent refueling and reorganizing his tired troops, Peiper launched them into the attack again the following morning. This time he headed northwest toward Stoumont. The first elements of a US blocking force had moved into place in the village during the night, and when his tanks advanced, they were met by 90mm anti-tank gunfire. One King Tiger and four Panzer IVs were hit before German infantry cleared the village. When the advance continued, the panzers ran into a battalion of Shermans emerging out of the afternoon gloom.

His route blocked, Peiper ordered the panzers back to La Gleize. With American columns closing in from four sides, he was effectively trapped. He held out until the evening of December 23, when he was given permission to break out. The majority of his troops were left dead or wounded on the battlefield, along with more then 25 tanks, 50 armored halftracks, and other vehicles. Peiper's desperate lunge for victory had failed.

The remainder of the Leibstandarte Division, led by Kampfgruppe Hansen, was meanwhile making desperate efforts to catch up with Peiper. This soon turned into a rescue mission when the commander of the division's panzer regiment found himself cut off by American reinforcements.

STALLED UNTIL MORNING

Hansen's advance had at first gone well, brushing aside a column of US reconnaissance troops near Recht on December 18. Then it was ordered to push north toward Stavelot, but traffic chaos in the village prevented it moving until the morning of December 19. Ten Tigers and Panzer IVs moved in on the village from the south, but their attack was literally stopped in its tracks when an American M-10 tank destroyer hit the lead King Tiger's side armor, penetrating the monster panzer and causing it to explode. Access to the bridge was blocked.

Knittel's reconnaissance unit mounted its own attack on Stavelot from the west on that day, backed by two of Peiper's King Tigers. His men reached the center of the village but they were too late to stop American engineers blowing the bridge.

▲ *A Waffen-SS panzergrenadier looks over the remnants of an abandoned US column in the Ardennes.*

The following day, Hansen's panzergrenadiers renewed their attack on Stavelot, but they now were ordered to bypass the village from the south and use forest tracks to find a route through to Peiper. The fighting in the village was some of the fiercest of the whole Ardennes campaign and a number of civilians were killed. Later, Leibstandarte men would stand trial for their deaths.

HANSEN BY THE SALM

The move west was more successful and soon Hansen had troops situated overlooking the Salm River. US paratroopers from the 82nd Airborne Division had now arrived in strength, and were starting to build up a strong line, blocking the route through to Peiper. The rescue effort eventually proved futile, and all Hansen's men could do was hold open a bridgehead to receive their beleaguered colleagues. By the time Peiper's men had reached safety on Christmas Day, the Leibstandarte Division had shot its bolt. The destruction of Peiper's Kampfgruppe had ripped the heart out of its offensive power. It would be three days before it was able to take the offensive again.

Skorzeny's 150th Panzer Brigade fared little better than the other elements of I SS Panzer Corps. Only a handful of its sabotage teams were able to penetrate American lines, and none of them managed to seize the vital Meuse bridges. The psychological effect of their presence on the battlefield was far more important than their actual achievements. Indeed, they have entered popular legend after their exploits were immortalized in the Hollywood movie *The Battle of the Bulge*. In the end, Otto Skorzeny's brigade was committed to a half-hearted frontal assault against Malmédy that was easily repulsed, giving the Americans time to destroy the town's vital bridges.

COMMITTING II SS PANZER CORPS

Just four days into Operation Autumn Mist, it was becoming clear that I SS Panzer Corps was stalled. Peiper's Kampfgruppe was stuck at La Gleize and the Hitlerjugend was getting nowhere on the Eisenborn ridge. It was time to commit Bittrich's II SS Panzer Corps to action further south. The rapid advance of Peiper created one opportunity for Dietrich. The US 7th Armored Division and parts of three other divisions were still holding out in the town of St Vith, and were preventing the Germans from securing its vital road junctions. Bittrich's mission was to push his two panzer divisions to the north and south of the St Vith salient, trapping the American force, before pushing westward to the Meuse. It looked good on a map, but Das Reich and Hohenstaufen's Kampfgruppen had to contend with a road network that was hopelessly overloaded. Roads were already congested with units moving to the front, supply columns, and the charred remains of US vehicles. Bittrich's Blitzkrieg soon bogged down.

The Hohenstaufen Division led the northern pincer, pushing through Recht to attempt to seize Vielsalm. They were hoping to block this area, since it would provide the main line of withdrawal for the American troops trapped in St Vith. Under the command of SS-Sturmbannführer Eberhard Telkamp, the Hohenstaufen's panzer regiment went into action on 21 December, but it soon ran into a strong 7th Armored Division Combat Command, equipped with almost 80 Shermans and tank destroyers.

CHRISTMAS CARNAGE

Telkamp had a Panther shot out from under him in his first clash with the Americans. Over the next two days, Hohenstaufen troops pressed forward time and again, only to be rebuffed. The battle came to a climax on Christmas Eve, when Telkamp ordered an all-out effort to break through to Vielsalm. Just as his panzer regiment was forming up to attack, USAAF P-47 Thunderbolt fighter-bombers swooped down in waves and massacred his column. Now the Hohenstaufen's northern pincer was well and truly blocked.

Das Reich had been ordered south of St Vith, but its column was soon halted when the division's tankers were unable to get past road congestion and deliver the vital fuel to the vehicles. The commander of the reconnaissance battalion of Das Reich, SS-Sturmbannführer Ernst-August Krag, was allocated the bulk of his division's scarce fuel on December 21 for the vital task of infiltrating behind the St Vith salient to close the American escape route. The prize was to be the

entrapment of 20,000 American troops. Krag's reconnaissance troopers were reinforced with a company of Panzerjäger IVs and a battalion of Wespe 105mm self-propeled guns.

Using back roads and tracks, Krag managed to slip through the American lines and by the evening of December 23 he was in the village of Salmchâteau, only 2 miles (3km) from Vielsalm. Tanks of the 7th Armored Division were still holding the northern escape route open through that town, but Krag's appearance effectively blocked the southern route out of St Vith. His Kampfgruppe caught the last convoy to leave the town.

In a confused night-time ambush, Krag's Panzerjägers quickly shot up the Americans' M5 light tanks, before his artillery started to rake the escaping convoy. The destruction of the American convoy was complete when Panther tanks of the army's Führer Begleit Brigade attacked it from the south. The remainder of the trapped American force had chosen to use the northern route and managed to get through to Vielsalm by 19:00 hours, when the rearguard blew up the town's bridges.

Denied his prize at St Vith, Bittrich was now determined to push Das Reich forward to exploit a gap in the American defenses at Manhay, which offered a route westward to the Meuse. SS-Obersturmbannführer Otto Weidinger's Der Führer Panzergrenadier Regiment at last received fuel on December 22 and was launched forward with a company of Panzer IVs and StuG IIIs in the lead. It ran into a battalion-sized force of 82nd Airborne paratroopers, artillery batteries, and a platoon of Sherman tanks during the early hours of December 23 at the key Barque de Fraiture crossroads.

When the initial attack was repulsed by the Americans, Weidinger pulled back and brought up his artillery battery to soften up the defenders who were fighting in the woods around the crossroads. After several hours spent bombarding the US position, Weidinger launched a two-pronged attack. With

▼ The surrounded defenders of Bastogne had to rely on parachute drops to keep fighting until George Patton's armor broke through on December 26, 1944.

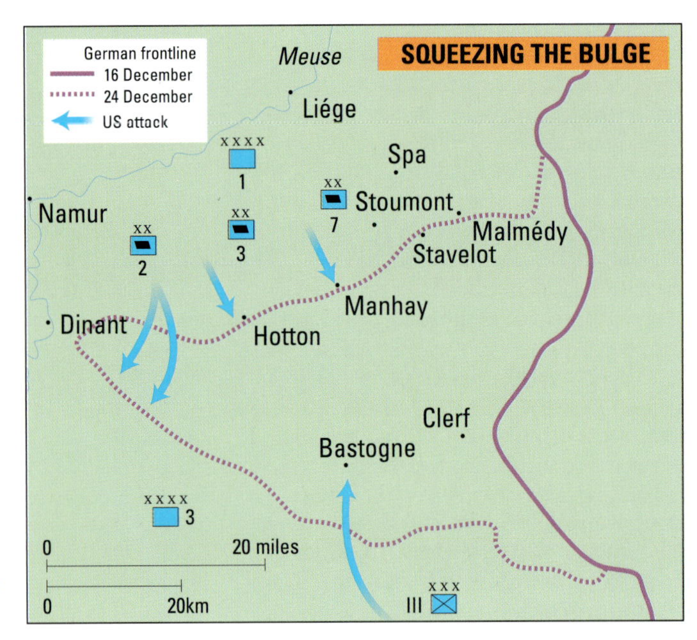

(See page 192 for map key)

◀ ***By Christmas 1944, the German attack in the Ardennes had run out of steam—then the Americans counterattacked.***

Panzer IVs and StuG IIIs leading the way, the Waffen-SS then closed in on the Americans. They were soon almost surrounded, then the German tanks started to pick off the Shermans and 105mm howitzers from long range.

The three surviving American tanks pulled out through the last escape route, leaving the 100 paratroopers fighting on their own amid 34 destroyed tanks and vehicles. The paras were soon being rounded up by the Waffen-SS men. Only 44 managed to escape in the confusion.

The main road to Manhay was now blocked by an American task force, so an infiltration attack was ordered to bypass its positions along narrow forest tracks westward.

AMERICANS AT MANHAY

Waffen-SS pioneers spent the day widening the roads to take the division's Panthers, while Lammerding's two panzergrenadier regiments were brought forward in preparation for the assault. Several fuel tankers had also pushed through the clogged roads, so the Das Reich Division was set to launch a divisional-sized assault.

Setting off just after last light, the Das Reich columns got to within a few yards of the American positions to the southwest of Manhay when American sentries at last realized that something was wrong and started to issue challenges. At this point, it was too late. German commanders fired volleys of flares to illuminate the battlefield and then the Panthers opened fire. Within minutes, 17 Shermans were ablaze and the outlying defenses of Manhay were breached. Hearing firing behind them, the bypassed American task force attempted to intervene, but some well-placed Panzerjäger IVs soon knocked out its lead two Shermans. The task force's commander then ordered his men to "take to the woods, every man for himself!"

The American defenders of Manhay now realized the danger they were in and a retreat was ordered. At this point, a Waffen-SS Panther that had become lost in the night attack just outside the town took a wrong turn on a forest track and drove into the center of Manhay. When the Americans at last realized that they had a German tank in their midst, all hell broke loose. The tank's commander, SS-Oberscharführer Ernst Barkmann, ordered his driver to reverse out of the town as he fired off smoke grenades in order to cover their escape. Gun rounds from the Shermans and machine-gun bullets ricocheted off the Panther's armor as it made a speedy exit.

This single incident turned what had been a well-organized tactical withdrawal into a rout. Hundreds of Americans were streaming north out of the town, at the same time as the remainder of Das Reich's Panthers appeared from the south. Their appearance completed the American rout, and the equivalent of a brigade of troops was now in full flight.

The following day, however, more American tanks arrived to seal the front around Das Reich. The armor was backed by 18 battalions of artillery.

Ordered to press on toward the west, Lammerding's men soon ran into a rock-solid defense. Other American tank columns began to press in against its flanks and, two days later, Das Reich was forced to give up Manhay or face complete encirclement.

TRIPLE PUSH

Three Waffen-SS divisions were now in the line, next to each other, along the northern edge of the German salient or bulge in the US front. Das Reich had pushed the farthest west, and next to it Hohenstaufen had come into line. After being rebuffed at Manhay, Bittrich was now facing two US armored divisions. The remnants of the Leibstandarte were still engaged in fighting the 82nd Airborne Division between Trois Ponts and Stavelot. Fuel shortages, the terrible terrain, and horrendous road congestion—coupled with heavy snow and freezing nights—were preventing Dietrich from being able to concentrate his army's fighting power in order to achieve a decisive breakthrough. Every day that the German advance was stalled gave the Allies precious time, during which they could bring up reinforcements and muster their strength for their inevitable counterattack.

By December 26, the Hitlerjugend Division had managed to battle its way through the grid-locked road systems and it was positioned on Das Reich's western flank, ready to kick-start the stalled Sixth Panzer Army offensive. Most of the division's panzers and artillery were still stuck in jams many miles to the east, so the main responsibility for the attack happened to fall on the 25th SS Panzergrenadier Regiment—helped by Das Reich's Kampfgruppe Krag—by accident rather than design.

THE LOST VILLAGE

The regiment had to attack through a heavily wooded, rugged hillside toward the village of Erezee, which was strongly defended by American paratroopers backed by tanks. It was impossible to get any panzers or armored halftracks through the terrible terrain, so the only fire-support available came from three 75mm anti-tank guns that had to be manhandled by their crews up the hillside into position. The only other defense against American tanks were the Panzerfaust rockets that were carried by every man in the Kampfgruppe.

Starting out early in the evening, the heavily loaded panzergrenadiers had to march through deep snow. It took them five hours to close on their objectives. One battalion stormed into the village of Sadzot, completely surprising its American defenders there, many of whom were trying to keep warm in farmhouses rather than stand outside on sentry duty. The panzergrenadiers soon cleared the village and took many of the defenders prisoner. Surprise was not complete, though, and the Americans managed to get off a radio message calling for help before their command post was overrun. Another panzergrenadier unit pushed on past Sadzot and moved toward Erezee.

Kampfgruppe Krag had tried to advance along the main road to Erezee, via the village of Amonines. It ran into a strong road-block and lost a number of armored vehicles in the dark, so its commander decided that it should turn back.

The Americans now launched their reserve battalion in an attempt to retake the lost village. They were backed by several M5 Stuart tanks, and for several hours the US paratroopers and Waffen-SS men fought it out in the streets and houses of Sadzot. By dawn 40 dead Germans were left in the village and the panzergrenadier battalion had pulled back to the woods on its outskirts.

The 75mm anti-tank guns were now dueling with the American tanks, but the heavy US artillery support kept the Germans pinned down. A stalemate reigned throughout the day, during which the Hitlerjugend began preparations to push forward again during the course of the coming night.

After leaving behind their vehicles, Kampfgruppe Krag was to push forward through the forests to the south of Sadzot, leading two battalions of the 26th SS Panzergrenadier Regiment that had moved up into the line earlier in the day. Their advance was unopposed until they reached the far side of the forest, when heavy American small-arms fire stalled the attack. A counterattack against the 25th Regiment was rebuffed and incurred heavy losses during the morning of December 29. Those losses included the destruction of five Stuart light tanks. In terms of manpower during these clashes, more than 120 US paratroopers were lost, either killed or wounded. But such small successes were of little use.

The German High Command ordered the Hitlerjugend Division to halt its offensive operations during the afternoon and the division was instructed to pull back. This was not so that it could rest and recuperate: it was now to concentrate for a new offensive elsewhere in the Ardennes.

This was the high-water mark of the Waffen-SS advance on the northern wing during Operation Watch on the Rhine. The tide had now turned irrevocably in favor of the Americans. Adolf Hitler's massive gamble in the West had failed miserably.

The fighting in the Ardennes, however, was far from over. For three more long weeks, the Waffen-SS panzer divisions would find that they were going to have many more bitter battles to fight.

▼ ***German troops loot the boots of dead GIs in a wintry Ardennes village.***

BASTOGNE

Although the German attacks took the US Army by surprise, the Americans held firm at Bastogne.

▲ ***An aerial photograph of US armored forces advancing through the snowy landscape north of Bastogne. The woods that covered much of the Ardennes provided cover for anti-tank units. The defenders of Bastogne made good use of this during the fighting of late December.***

Bastogne was a key town in the center of the German Ardennes Offensive. It was a road hub and the Germans needed to occupy it in order to get supplies to the units that were trying to break through to the Meuse River. General Eisenhower swiftly committed reserves to Bastogne: he ordered in the 101st Airborne Division, a formation that had distinguished itself in the Normandy landings. Units from the 101st began arriving in the town on December 19.

The US forces fought off attacks north of Bastogne by the 2nd Panzer Division and then had to resist attacks on Bastogne itself, as the town was cut off by the German forces streaming forward. The biggest attack, which came on Christmas Eve, was fought off with heavy fighting. The soldiers of the 101st combined with M18 Hellcats of the 705th Tank Destroyer Battalion to successfully prevent German armor breaking through.

Although surrounded, the garrison of Bastogne was kept resupplied by air, and air support by ground-attack aircraft also proved vital in hitting German tanks as they moved forward.

Units from the US Third Army managed to make contact with the defenders in Bastogne on December 26, and supply lines were restored on December 27. The German armored units pushing on to the Meuse were forced to halt due to lack of fuel because of the stubborn resistance of the 101st at Bastogne—the 2nd Panzer Division, for example, ran out of fuel near the village of Celles, to the west of Bastogne, and was later comfortably picked off by Allied armored units.

The commander of the 101st Airborne, General Maxwell Taylor, had been away when the unit was ordered forward. His subordinate, Brigadier General Anthony McAuliffe, commanded the division during the deployment to and siege of Bastogne. When McAuliffe received a request to surrender from the surrounding German forces, he exclaimed "Aw, nuts!" and "Nuts" was sent to the enemy as the 101st's written answer—a response that now resonates in the division's history.

▼ ***US infantry in Belgium prepare to counterattack early in 1945. Note the "jerrycan" on the back of the jeep. Petrol was the key to stopping the German advance through the Ardennes, and the town of Bastogne was crucial in stopping supplies getting through to German forward units.***

◀ *The men of the 101st Airborne rejoiced in the nickname 'the battered bastards of Bastogne'. The 101st remained in Bastogne, taking the attack to the Germans, until January 17.*

▲ *US supply lorries enter the town center of Bastogne after the German attacks have been beaten off.*

▶ *An American sergeant, bearded and tired after days of almost non-stop combat, early in January 1945.*

▼ *One of the many waves of Allied supply formations flies into Bastogne. In the foreground, smoke billows from a destroyed German vehicle. The low cloud that had covered much of the battlefield early in the German offensive lifted on December 23 and Allied fighter-bombers were able to dominate the area.*

The Conquest of Germany

◀ *The "Big Three"—from left, Churchill, Roosevelt, and Stalin—meet at Yalta to decide the shape of postwar Europe.*

JANUARY 1–21

WESTERN FRONT, *FRANCE*
In a follow up to the German attack in the Ardennes sector, General Johannes von Blaskowitz's Army Group G attacks the US Seventh Army in Alsace and Lorraine, forming the so-called Colmar Pocket. The Americans retreat in an orderly fashion, although General Dwight D. Eisenhower, commander-in-chief of Allied forces in Europe, orders Strasbourg to be held after the leader of the Free French, General Charles de Gaulle, expresses concern that the loss of the symbolically important border city would affect French morale. The fighting is bitter. It costs the US 15,600 casualties, and the Germans, 25,000.

JANUARY 3–16

WESTERN FRONT, *ARDENNES*
The last German attack against the town of Bastogne is defeated. The Allied counterattack begins: on the northern flank the US First Army attacks the northern sector of the "bulge," while the southern sector is assaulted by the US Third Army. Within the "bulge" itself, Hitler orders a German withdrawal to Houffalize on the 8th. However, in the face of overwhelming Allied superiority in men and hardware the Germans are forced to retreat farther east, and the US First and Third Armies link up at Houffalize on the 16th.

JANUARY 5

AIR WAR, *BELGIUM/HOLLAND*
The Luftwaffe launches Operation Bodenplatte in support of the Ardennes offensive with 1035 fighters and bombers attacking Allied airfields in Belgium and southern Holland. The Germans destroy 156 Allied aircraft but lose 277 of their own, losses the Luftwaffe cannot make good. It is the last major German air attack.

JANUARY 15–26

WESTERN FRONT, *GERMANY*
After the containment of the German Ardennes offensive, the Allies launch a large counterattack against the Germans. In the north, Field Marshal Bernard Montgomery's British 21st Army Group presses into the Roermond area, while farther south General Omar Bradley's US 12th Army Group approaches the upper Roer River.

JANUARY 28

WESTERN FRONT, *ARDENNES*
The last vestiges of the German "bulge" in the Ardennes are wiped out. The total cost to the Germans in manpower for their Ardennes offensive has been 100,000 killed,

◀ *Boeing B-17 Flying Fortress bombers of the US 8th Army Air Force unleash death and destruction on Dresden.*

wounded, and captured. The Americans have lost 81,000 killed, wounded, or captured, and the British 1400. Both sides have lost heavily in hardware—up to 800 tanks on each side. The Germans have also lost around 1000 aircraft. However, whereas the Americans can make good their losses in just a few weeks, for the Germans the military losses are irreplaceable.

JANUARY 28–FEBRUARY 1

WESTERN FRONT, *ARDENNES*
Two corps of General Courtney Hodges' US First Army and one from General George Patton's US Third Army try to penetrate the German defenses northeast of St. Vith, which lies astride the Losheim Gap. Snow and ice inhibit progress, and the Germans manage to fight back hard, thereby slowing the rate of the US advance.

FEBRUARY 4–11

POLITICS, *ALLIES*
Marshal Joseph Stalin, President Franklin D. Roosevelt, and Prime Minister Winston Churchill meet at the Yalta Conference in the Crimea to discuss postwar Europe. The "Big Three" decide that Germany will be divided into four zones, administered by Britain, France, the United States, and the Soviet Union. An Allied Control Commission will be set up in Berlin, and Austria will also be divided into four zones. The capital, Vienna, will be in the Soviet zone and will also have a four-power administration. The Soviet Union will declare war on Japan two months after the war in Europe has ended, while changes to Poland's borders will allow the Soviet Union to annex former Polish areas.

FEBRUARY 5

WESTERN FRONT, *FRANCE*
The German bridgehead on the west bank of the Rhine, south of Strasbourg around the town of Colmar—the Colmar Pocket—is split by units of the French First Army attacking from the south and elements of the US Seventh Army advancing from the north. The elimination of the pocket is essential before the Allies can proceed to cross of the Rhine.

FEBRUARY 9

WESTERN FRONT, *FRANCE*
Following Allied pressure against the Colmar Pocket, Field Marshal Gerd von Rundstedt, German commander-in-chief in the West, convinces Hitler to pull back the Nineteenth Army across the Rhine. The west bank of the river south of Strasbourg is now free of German troops.

FEBRUARY 13–14

AIR WAR, *GERMANY*
The RAF mounts a night raid on Dresden. The 805 bombers inflict massive damage on the city's old town and inner suburbs. The bombing triggers the worst firestorm of the war, in which at least 50,000 people are killed. The raid is controversial, as the city has negligible strategic value, is virtually undefended, and is crammed with refugees. The next morning, the city is bombed again by 400 aircraft of the US 8th Army Air Force.

FEBRUARY 21

WESTERN FRONT, *GERMANY*
The Canadian First Army takes the town of Goch, which ends Operation Veritable, an offensive from the Nijmegen area between the Rhine and the Maas Rivers.

FEBRUARY 23

WESTERN FRONT, *GERMANY*
The US First and Ninth Armies launch Operation Grenade, the crossing of the Roer River, and head to the Rhine. Preceded by a barrage from over 1000 guns, four infantry

▶ *Women help clear rubble from the ruins of the Catholic cathedral in Dresden after the Allied air raids against the city.*

divisions cross the river in the face of sporadic resistance. German reserves have been committed to halt Operation Veritable farther north. By the end of the day, 28 infantry battalions have crossed the river.

FEBRUARY 28

WESTERN FRONT, *GERMANY*
The US First Army begins its drive to the Rhine River, spearheaded by the VII Corps.

MARCH 3

WESTERN FRONT, *FRANCE*
In snow and freezing rain, General George Patton unleashes his US Third Army over the Kyll River toward the Rhine. The attack is spearheaded by the VIII and XII Corps, which make good progress.

MARCH 7

WESTERN FRONT, *GERMANY*
Despite German orders to destroy all river crossing, units of the US First Army manage to capture the Ludendorff bridge over the Rhine River at Remagen. The bridge, having withstood bombs, demolition, heavy usage, and artillery shells, collapses into the river 10 days later.

MARCH 10

WESTERN FRONT, *GERMANY*
Field Marshal Bernard Montgomery's 21st Army Group completes the conquest of the area west of the Rhine River. The group has lost 22,934 casualties, although the Germans have suffered casualties totaling 90,000 men defending the area immediately west of the Ruhr.

MARCH 14

WESTERN FRONT, *GERMANY*
General George Patton's US Third Army crosses the lower Moselle River to cut behind the German Siegfried Line defensive system.

MARCH 22–31

WESTERN FRONT, *GERMANY*
The Allied crossings of the Rhine River begin. The 5th Division of the US Third Army crosses near Nierstein and Oppenheim. By the end of the 23rd, the whole division is over the river. German resistance is negligible.

Field Marshal Bernard Montgomery's 21st Army Group (1.25 million men) begins crossing the river on the 23rd. On the 24th, the US 87th Division crosses at Boppard and the 89th at St. Goer, while farther north the British 6th and the US 17th Airborne Divisions land east of the Rhine.

German units, exhausted by the fighting west of the river, offer only token resistance. By the end of the month the Algerian 3rd Division of the French First Army has crossed the river: every Allied army now has troops on the east bank of the Rhine.

APRIL 2–3

WESTERN FRONT, *GERMANY*
Units of the US First and Third Armies meet at Lippstadt to complete the encirclement of the economically-important Ruhr region.

APRIL 4

WESTERN FRONT, *HOLLAND*
Field Marshal Bernard Montgomery's 21st Army Group begins its offensive to liberate Holland and sweep across northern Germany. As food stocks in Holland are low, this operation is important as the Dutch postwar political attitude toward the Allies will depend on the speed of liberation.

APRIL 11

WESTERN FRONT, *GERMANY*
The US Ninth Army arrives at the Elbe River near Magdeburg. More and more German towns are surrendering without a fight, while Hitler's armies are disintegrating.

APRIL 12

POLITICS, *UNITED STATES*
President Franklin D. Roosevelt dies of a cerebral haemorrhage in Warm Springs, Georgia. Vice President Harry S. Truman takes over as president.

APRIL 14

POLITICS, *ALLIES*
General Dwight D. Eisenhower, Supreme Commander of Allied Armies in the West, informs the Combined Chiefs-of-Staff that the Allied thrust against Berlin takes second place to the securing of the northern (Norway and Denmark) and southern (south Germany and Austria) Allied flanks. The British approve his plans on the 18th.

APRIL 18

WESTERN FRONT, *GERMANY*
All German resistance in the Ruhr industrial area ceases; 370,000 prisoners fall into Allied hands.
WESTERN FRONT, *HOLLAND*
The Canadian I Corps, encountering sporadic resistance, has reached Harderwijk, thus isolating German forces in the west of the country.

▼ ***The Rhine was a formidable barrier, but crossing it was largely a logistical rather than a military problem for the Allies.***

▲ *Hitler and his mistress Eva Braun, whom he married in Berlin just prior to their mutual suicide at the end of April.*

APRIL 20

WESTERN FRONT, *GERMANY*
Nuremberg, the shrine of National Socialism in southern Germany, falls to the US Third Army after a five-day battle. The city had been defended by two German divisions, Luftwaffe and *Volkssturm* battalions, and ringed by anti-aircraft guns, and the German commander had vowed to Hitler that he and his men would fight to the bitter end.

APRIL 23

WESTERN FRONT, *GERMANY*
The last German defenders in the Harz Mountains are captured. Farther north, the British Second Army enters the outskirts of Hamburg.

APRIL 28

POLITICS, *HOLLAND*
The first meeting between Allied and German representatives takes place in western Holland. The Reichskommissar for the Netherlands, Artur von Seyss-Inquart, has offered the Allies the freedom to import food and coal into German-occupied western Holland to alleviate the plight of the civilian population if they will halt their forces to the east. This leads to a cessation of hostilities and saves the country from the ravages of further fighting.

APRIL 29

POLITICS, *GERMANY*
Adolf Hitler, now confined to the "Führerbunker," orders the arrest of Heinrich Himmler, head of the SS, for his attempts to seek peace with the Allies. Hermann Goering's has also attempt to negotiate with the Allies. Hitler writes his "Political Testament," in which he blames international Jewry for the outbreak of the war. He nominates Admiral Karl Doenitz as his successor, and marries his long-time mistress, Eva Braun.

HOME FRONT, *HOLLAND*
The RAF begins dropping food supplies to alleviate the plight of the country's starving civilians.

APRIL 30

POLITICS, *GERMANY*
Adolf Hitler and Eva Braun commit suicide in the Führerbunker in Berlin. Hitler shoots himself, while Braun takes poison. Their bodies are later cremated by the SS.

MAY 1

POLITICS, *GERMANY*
General Krebs, chief of the General Staff of the Army High Command, initiates cease-fire negotiations with the Soviets on behalf of the Nazi leadership in Berlin. The Soviets demand unconditional surrender and the fighting continues.

MAY 2

WESTERN FRONT, *GERMANY*
The British 6th Airborne Division of the 21st Army Group moves into Wismar, just in time to prevent the Red Army entering Schleswig-Holstein.

MAY 3–4

POLITICS, *GERMANY*
The whole of the northwest of the country is under British control. Admiral Karl Doenitz sends Admiral Hans von Friedeburg to Field Marshal Bernard Montgomery's headquarters at Lüneburg Heath to discuss surrender terms. On the 4th, the official German delegation signs the instrument of surrender—covering German forces in Holland, northwest Germany, the German islands, Schleswig-Holstein, and Denmark—to come into effect at 0800 hours on May 5.

MAY 4–5

POLITICS, *DENMARK*
Some 20,000 members of the Danish Resistance movement, organized under the central leadership of the Freedom Council, come out of hiding and take over the key points in the country. Soon, they are in control of Denmark. The first Allied soldiers arrive in the country on the 5th.

MAY 7

POLITICS, *GERMANY*
General Alfred Jodl, acting on behalf of the German government, signs the act of surrender to the Allies of all German forces still in the field. Hostilities are to cease by midnight on May 8 at the latest. In Norway the German garrison of 350,000 men capitulates to the Allies. The German Army Group South surrenders to the US Third Army in Austria.

▼ *A grim-faced Admiral Hans von Friedeburg and Field Marshal Bernard Montgomery finalize the German surrender.*

Part 5 | Chapter 1
THE CONQUEST OF GERMANY

The Allied Counterattack

A week after the start of Operation Watch on the Rhine, the German offensive had well and truly run out of steam. Dietrich's Sixth Panzer Army had been held in check along the Amblève River. To the south, the Fifth Panzer Army had advanced to within 9.5 miles (15km) of the Meuse at Dinant before being turned back by British tanks and Allied fighter-bombers.

General of Panzer Troops Hasso von Manteuffel had managed to surround the American 101st Airborne Division in the town of Bastogne. However, the town was successfully kept resupplied by airlift until a relief column from Lieutenant-General George Patton's Third Army was able to punch its way through from Luxembourg to lift the siege on December 26, 1944.

With huge Allied reinforcements now pouring in to counter their initial penetration, German commanders were convinced that the offensive stood no chance of success. They wanted to pull out the surviving panzer divisions from the line and concentrate them as a counterattack force to help prop up the now threatened Eastern Front. Hitler would have none of this. He

wanted a renewed offensive to defeat the Americans, by cutting off Bastogne again to open a new route for further westward offensives.

GERMAN PROGRESS SLOWS

As the panzers approached the main road south out of Bastogne across open fields, the Americans mobilized two companies of Sherman tanks to block their path. Now the clouds cleared to allow the intervention of Allied fighter-bombers. For more than two hours, the Thunderbolts worked over the panzer column, claiming seven kills and delaying the advance as the tanks were forced to take cover in woods. The American tanks had now taken up ambush positions ahead of the German armor, and were lying in wait when Werner Poetsche, commander of the Leibstandarte Division's panzers, finally got his forces moving again.

Poetsche's command Panther was knocked out by the very first American shot, and soon nine of the panzers were also ablaze. The panzergrenadiers were forced to go to ground until they could pull back under cover of the gathering darkness.

To the south, Kampfgruppe Hansen was led by seven Panzerjäger IVs through the heavy woods surrounding the village of Villers-la-Bonne-Eau at dawn. The Waffen-SS men soon surrounded the defenders in the small village and spent the rest of the morning clearing them out. Early in the afternoon, the advance was pressed forward and, in a few hours, the Kamfgruppe were through the woods on the edge of the main road leading south out of Bastogne. Reinforcements were pushed in at nightfall and the Leibstandarte tried to secure its positions overnight. The news that the eastward attack by their army colleagues had failed did little to raise the Waffen-SS men's sagging morale.

For the next week the soldiers of the Leibstandarte division held on to their hard-won ground against a series of strong US counterattacks, which were backed by tanks and large quantities of artillery. The Waffen-SS panzers found themselves "fire-fighting" small local incursions by American tanks on the fringes of the positions held by the panzergrenadiers. Two precious King Tigers and several other panzers were lost in these widely scattered battles.

◀ ***A Hitlerjugend Panther that was knocked out during the fighting around Bastogne.***

As the Leibstandarte was being brought to a halt south of Bastogne, I SS Panzer Corps was being mustered to the north of the town for a final push for victory. Hitlerjugend and Hohenstaufen had been pulled out of the northern shoulder and sent south, along with the 340th Volksgrenadier Division. Field Marshal Model visited the corps headquarters north of Bastogne on January 2, 1945, in order to put his seal of approval on the plans to smash open the American defenses the following day. Hohenstaufen was to drive in from northwest of the town and Hitlerjugend would attack from the northeast, as the Volksgrenadiers linked them together. Several Volks artillery brigades were mustered to provide fire support, which was fortunate, because the Hitlerjugend's guns were stranded to the north due to lack of fuel.

The Americans, however, were quicker off the draw and put in an attack against the Volksgrenadiers during the afternoon of January 2. As the Americans reached the outskirts of Bourcy, the advanced Kampfgruppe of the Hitlerjugend's panzer regiment was just driving through the village from the north. Eleven Panthers and Panzer IVs immediately engaged the advance guard of the American column, sending it reeling back to its start-line.

At 09:00 hours on January 3, the German attack was launched as planned. Led by 20 Panzer IVs, the Hohenstaufen advanced in the face of heavy American anti-tank fire. The attack stalled in the afternoon when the panzers were caught in open ground. Another attack was attempted in the early evening and suffered a similar fate. The division tried a surprise raid later in the night and successfully penetrated some distance behind American lines before it was eventually beaten back.

▲ ***British armor joined the allied effort, helping to strike into the northern flank of the German forces in the Ardennes.***

ON TO BASTOGNE

In the early afternoon the Hitlerjugend and Volksgrenadiers began to move forward. The Volksgrenadiers were soon bogged down in heavy fighting in large forests. Hitlerjugend's panzer regiment led the division forward along the open ground to the left of the railway track, which headed south into the center of Bastogne. It put 13 Panzer IVs, 7 Panthers and 15 Panzerjäger IVs into action, along with 28 Jagdpanzer IVs and 13 Jagdpanthers of the 560th Anti-Tank Battalion. Panzergrenadiers in armored halftracks were close behind the German armour, and during the afternoon the armada made steady progress, advancing 1.8 miles (3km) despite heavy American artillery fire.

In a night attack, the Hitlerjugend made a further big advance, reaching the edges of the villages of Magaret and

▲ ***Tiger II heavy tanks spearheaded the attack on Bastogne, but made little impact on the American defence lines.***

Bizory on the northern outskirts of Bastogne. Panzergrenadiers and Panzerjäger IVs now pressed into the large Azette wood in front of the town, cutting to pieces a US infantry battalion defending the position.

More attacks were now launched against Magaret and Bizory in the afternoon by the panzer regiment, but they couldn't dislodge the defenders. Wild rumours of enemy breakthroughs caused panic among some US units and some GIs fled into Bastogne. Panzers penetrated the villages, only to be driven back by American Shermans and bazooka teams. The line held.

PANZER PUSH ON HILL 510

Over on the northwestern edge of the American line, the Hohenstaufen panzers were again pushing forward, making local gains as well as overruning a number of trench lines.

During the afternoon of January 5 the Hitlerjugend panzers made one last lunge to capture Hill 510 outside Magaret, which overlooked Bastogne. Heavy American tank and artillery fire soon forced the Germans to pull back from the exposed position. This wall of fire was instrumental in blunting the Waffen-SS attack, making it virtually impossible for the Hitlerjugend men to even contemplate further movement toward Bastogne.

An American breakthrough against the northern shoulder of the German front forced the withdrawal of the Hohenstaufen from Bastogne on January 6. The Hitlerjugend Division was now totally exhausted by its exertions and had to spend the next two days consolidating its hard-won gains. Plans were already in hand to pull the division out of the line when it was called upon to make one last drive to capture Hill 510.

Under the concentrated fire of all the division's artillery and tanks, the Hitlerjugend panzergrenadiers reached the summit of the hill by mid-morning on January 8. Yet again, the Americans massed their artillery fire, which swept the hillside and forced the Waffen-SS men to fall back by midday, leaving some 50 dead behind.

On January, Hitler finally realized that trying to take Bastogne was a lost cause and authorized the withdrawal of the Waffen-SS divisions. The Leibstandarte was at last able to pull out of its exposed salient into the Bastogne corridor, after Patton launched an attack farther to the east aimed at cutting the division's escape route. The order to withdraw had come just in time, and the last Leibstandarte convoys were engaged by American tanks as they made their way eastwards, suffering heavy losses. Artillery and air strikes later joined in to pound the Leibstandarte as it made its escape.

While I SS Panzer Corps was gathering around St Vith, II SS Panzer Corps found itself locked in a bitter battle with US armor advancing southwards. Das Reich bore the brunt of the defensive fighting until the Hohenstaufen could join the fray. They steadily fell back until orders were issued on January 16 for them to be taken out of the line to join their sister

Waffen-SS divisions in Army Group B's reserve. Fuel shortages and general chaos meant this was not actually achieved for several days. Hitler then ordered the four Waffen-SS divisions and Dietrich's headquarters to be withdrawn from the Western Front to be refitted for operations on the Eastern Front, where a new Russian offensive was underway.

Operation Watch on the Rhine was officially over. Hitler's gamble had failed. The Germans lost 33,000 dead, 22,500 missing, and 34,000 wounded. They also left behind more than 600 smashed tanks in the Ardennes. The Americans lost 8600 dead, 21,000 missing, and 30,000 wounded, along with more than 733 destroyed tanks.

The Waffen-SS had spearheaded the operation and made some of the deepest penetrations into American lines. Many senior Waffen-SS officers, such as Dietrich, had been skeptical about its chances of success, but had given it their best shot. No one could accuse them of not trying, but no amount of bravery and tactical flair could make up for the fact that Hitler's plan was too ambitious and the US Army too powerful.

Figures for losses in the Waffen-SS divisions are hard to establish. Dietrich's Sixth Panzer Army lost some 10,000 dead in total. The armored vehicle strength of the Waffen-SS divisions was soon restored to practically its initial capacity thanks to the smooth recovery of wrecked and damaged tanks from the early phases of the battle. Harder to replace were officer and noncommissioned officer casualties that ran to nearly 50 percent in some Waffen-SS units.

OPERATION SOLSTICE

The departure of Dietrich's Sixth Panzer Army—which was soon to be renamed the Sixth SS Panzer Army—did not mark the end of the participation of Waffen-SS panzer divisions against the Western Allies.

In tandem with his plan to strike into the Ardennes, Hitler had long dreamed of pushing into Alsace and reclaiming the border city of Strasbourg. Army Group G was to strike south in Operation North Wind, with the 17th SS Panzergrenadier Division in the lead, in order to outflank the city. The division was rebuilt after being heavily battered around Metz in November 1944 and bolstered with the delivery of 57 StuG IIIs in early December. When the attack began on New Year's Eve, the Waffen-SS division achieved the deepest penetration into American lines until it was halted by strong counter-attacks. Three days of heavy fighting followed in which the division's commander, SS-Standartenführer Hans Linger, was captured when he took a wrong turn near the frontline as he drove in his command Volkswagen.

Hitler now launched Operation Solstice. Its aim was to drive a pincer around Strasbourg from the south and it was to be conducted under the command of Army Group Upper Rhine. The refitted Frundsberg Division was committed to this offensive on January 13, 1945, and its 36 Panzer IVs and 35 Panthers made good progress until the operation ran out of steam a week later. In a final irony, the veteran Waffen-SS general Paul Hausser, who had recovered from his injuries received in Normandy, was placed in command of Army Group Upper Rhine for what would be the final months of the war from January 29.

Soon the needs of the Eastern Front also resulted in Hausser losing the Frundsberg Division. The 17th SS Division was the only Waffen-SS armored unit to remain on the Western Front until the end of the war. By March 25, it had been reduced to some 800 men who were desperately holding the last German bridgehead on the west bank of the Rhine. The Frundsberg managed to escape across the mighty river, but the Americans eventually caught up with the division at Nuremberg, where it tried to mount a series of rearguard actions during early April. It then surrendered to the victorious Allies.

▼ ***After regaining their composure, the Allies began pouring in troops to crush the German "bulge" into the Ardennes.***

Unconditional Surrender

In February 1945, the Allies were ready to begin the conquest of Germany itself. In the west, US and British armies were preparing to drive to the Rhine River and into the German heartland. In the east, Soviet troops were massed along a front that stretched from Lithuania to the Balkans. They would soon also enter German territory. But Hitler was determined to resist to the very end.

PLANS FOR CROSSING THE RHINE

The Allied advance to the Rhine was in some ways as much about personalities as military operations. The Supreme Allied Commander in Europe was US General Dwight D. Eisenhower. His forces were in turn led by three strong personalities. At the northern part of the Allied frontline was the Twenty-First Army Group led by the British Field Marshal Bernard Montgomery. The center of the line was held by the Twelfth Army Group of US General Omar Bradley. To the south, the US Sixth Army Group was led by Lieutenant-General Jacob Devers.

By February 7, the Allied positions stretched from just east of Nijmegen in the Netherlands to the northern border of Switzerland. The Rhine River was the

last significant obstacle barring the advance towards Berlin. Each of the Allied commanders wanted to be the first to cross it.

The Rhine arched out like a bow from the Allied line. Montgomery was the closest, at the top. Eisenhower's plan was that both Montgomery and Bradley would launch a general thrust toward the river. Montgomery would make the main crossing of the Rhine, between Emmerich and Düsseldorf. Bradley, meanwhile, would back up Montgomery's operation. He would attack through the forested Eifel region and cross the Rhine near Koblenz. Then he would push out to help Montgomery surround the Ruhr. The Ruhr was Germany's industrial heart. It contained the country's major coal fields and much of its heavy industry. Its factories included the Thyssen steelworks and Krupp armaments plants. Meanwhile, farther south, Dever's Sixth Army Group would meanwhile move into the Saarland and attempt a Rhine crossing around the city of Mannheim.

LAUNCHING THE RHINE OFFENSIVE

On February 8, 1945, an artillery bombardment along Montgomery's front began the Rhine offensive. The Canadian First Army fought its way into the forested Reichswald area. It met stiff German resistance and had to cross difficult muddy terrain. The Canadians reached the Rhine by February 21. At the Rhine, the Canadians were scheduled to meet up with the US Ninth Army, advancing from the south. However, the Germans blew up dams on the small Roer River.

▼ ***Soviet tanks enter the city of Berlin in 1945. The agreement reached in February 1945 gave the Soviets the task of capturing the German capital.***

▲ ***Troops of the US Third Army keep low to avoid snipers, as they cross the Rhine River in an amphibious DUKW on March 26, 1945.***

The Ninth Army was delayed in the flooded countryside. It did not reach the Rhine until March 2.

Meanwhile, Bradley and Devers were fighting their way east. The US First Army reached the Rhine on May 7, near Cologne. The Germans had by now blown up most bridges across the Rhine. In a surprise attack, however, the Allies captured an intact bridge at Remagen, just south of Cologne. The bridge provided the first major crossing point over the river.

PATTON'S DYNAMIC STRATEGY

The achievements of the First Army were somewhat overshadowed by those of the Third Army, which was part of the Twelfth Army Group. The Third Army was commanded by the controversial General George S. Patton. Of the Allied commanders, Patton had the farthest distance to travel to the Rhine. He attacked the Siegfried Line, a defensive chain in western Germany. His infantry broke through to Koblenz, then headed south. Patton reached the Rhine between Mainz and Worms. The Allies had planned to cross the Rhine on March 23. Instead, Patton's Third Army crossed the river in an amphibious assault the previous night.

Patton had stolen Montgomery's thunder. Montgomery had reached the Rhine by the end of the first week of March. He had then, however, held back around the town of Wesel. Montgomery wanted to build up his forces for the crossing. He assembled more than 250,000 men on the western bank of the river. After Wesel had been devastated by Allied bombers, Montgomery's troops crossed the river as scheduled late on March 23. The Allies had now succeeded in establishing three large strategic points on the eastern bank of the Rhine.

In theory, the Allies still faced strong opposition in western Germany. Three army groups defended the German front line. In reality, however, the German troops were in a desperate state. After months of fighting, some units were at only a third of their normal strength. In order to boost unit numbers, poorly trained reservists had been sent to the front. They included both pensioners and teenagers. Military typists and cooks were also pressed into action.

In Berlin, meanwhile, Adolf Hitler was slowly losing his grip on reality. He refused to accept Germany's impending defeat. He still tried to command his army as if it were at full fighting strength. Hitler had fired his commander-in-chief in the West, Field Marshal Gerd von Rundstedt. Von Rundstedt was replaced by Field Marshal Albert Kesselring. Kesselring was a talented commander, but he did not have the forces to deal with the Allied advance. On a local level, however, many German units fought bravely and skillfully. They remained a formidable enemy.

POLITICAL INFLUENCES

The next objective of the inexorable Allied advance from the west was the Elbe River. The Elbe was only about 45 miles (70km) from the heart of the Reich: Berlin itself.

The Allied commanders expected to push on from the Elbe to the capital. Unbeknownst to them, however, their advance would be halted by a political decision that had already been taken. When the Allied leaders met at the Yalta Conference in February 1945, they had agreed to divide Germany between the Western Allies. The Soviet Red Army would capture Berlin. Eisenhower had decided to halt the US and British advance at the Elbe.

▲ ***Engineers ferry one of the first tanks across the Rhine on a pontoon raft.***

TO THE ELBE

The Allies first had to reach the river, and Eisenhower now revised his strategy to achieve this key goal. He decided that the main advance toward the Elbe would be spearheaded by Omar Bradley's XII Army Corps. Bradley would also take control of Montgomery's US Ninth Army. Montgomery would take the rest of his forces not toward the Elbe but into the north of Germany. Devers's Sixth Army Group would meanwhile push out into southern Germany and Austria.

◀ ***White flags of surrender and confused civilians greet US troops entering a ruined German town in the Rhineland.***

YALTA CONFERENCE

From February 4–11, 1945, the three Allied leaders—Churchill, Roosevelt and Stalin—met at a conference at Yalta in the Crimea, in the Soviet Union.

They discussed a wide range of issues, including the strategy for the final defeat of Hitler. They also decided Germany's postwar future. After Allied victory, the country would be divided into zones of occupation among the four major Allies (France was the fourth power). The most significant discussions were about the political arrangements of postwar Europe. The Soviets would be left in control of large areass of eastern Europe. They agreed to allow free elections there. In reality, however, eastern Europe would be controlled by communist puppet governments from Moscow. The failure of the Western Allies to get better terms for eastern Europe led some later critics to call Yalta the "Western betrayal."

◄ ***Winston Churchill (left), Franklin D. Roosevelt (center), and Joseph Stalin at Yalta.***

By the beginning of April, the Allied offensive was well underway. A large German force in a pocket on the Ruhr River was surrounded by US forces on April 1. Cut off, it surrendered on April 18. Allied formations made rapid advances across the length of Germany.

The Allies met fierce resistance. There were many instances where a small group of Wehrmacht troops was able to hold up far larger US or British units. In the east, however, the Russian offensive was threatening Berlin itself. This disrupted supplies to the troops in the west. The German forces began to collapse. The Allies captured a total of 325,000 German prisoners in the Ruhr Pocket alone. By the end of April, the Allies had cleared almost all parts of Germany west of the Elbe. They had also defeated the Germans in the northern Netherlands.

OVER TO THE SOVIETS

On April 25, 1945, a US patrol met up with Soviet forces near Torgau on the Elbe. The Allies' eastern and western advances had finally come together. Eisenhower's commanders now urged him to continue the advance. They were certain they could reach and take Berlin before the Soviets. In accordance with the decisions taken at Yalta, however, Eisenhower stopped any advance farther east.

THE RED ARMY'S PLAN

The western Allied troops had suffered significant casualties in their campaign since the landings on D-Day. On the Eastern Front, however, the losses were much greater still. The scale was almost incomprehensible. The advance through eastern Europe, from late 1944 until the fall of Berlin in May 1945, cost the Soviets more dead than the British and United States suffered in the entire war in all theatres.

By January 1945, the Soviet dictator Joseph Stalin and his trusted senior commanders had developed their plan for final victory. They would advance toward Berlin in two massive leaps. The first would take the red Army from the Vistula River in Poland to the Oder River on the German border. The second leap would push from the Oder to meet the Allies at the Elbe. On the way, it would capture Berlin.

◀ ***Tanks and trucks of the US Third Army cross the Muhl River in Austria in May 1945.***

▼ ***Members of the 225th Infantry make their way through the ruins of the town of Waldenberg on April 16, 1945. The Wehrmacht had made a stand in the town, which was virtually destroyed by U.S. artillery.***

THE BOMBING OF DRESDEN

The most devastating air raid of the final phase of World War II in Europe occurred at Dresden, cultural capital of Saxony and picturesque city on the Elbe River.

An important communications hub and a center of the arms industry, by mid-February 1945 Dresden, teeming with refugees, was in the path of the Soviet advance, which was nearing the Elbe. In response to a specific request from the Deputy Chief of the Soviet General Staff, General Antonov, to "paralyze the junctions of Berlin and Leipzig," Allied air leaders agreed that the bombing of the city would serve strategic objectives of mutual importance to the Allies and the Soviets: not only would it disrupt road and rail communications in and around the city, it would shatter the German will to resist even further. The Allies were also keen to demonstrate to Stalin that they were lending support to the Red Army in their bombing campaigns. On February 13, two waves of British bombers attacked the city center. There were no flak defenses because the guns had been removed to stiffen defenses against the Red Army, and German fighters were grounded due to lack of fuel. The British aircraft were followed by two daylight raids by US bombers. The continuous waves of bombers created a devastating firestorm that destroyed the whole of the city center and great swathes of the suburbs. One of the city's inhabitants wrote: "Dresden was a single sea of flames as a result of the narrow streets and closely packed buildings. The night sky glowed red."

In the aftermath of the raids, tens of thousand of bodies were piled high and loaded onto lorries or carts for mass burial. However, the city authorities could not dig mass graves fast enough and the stench of rotting corpses forced them to cremate thousands of bodies in the city's old market square.

▲ *In February 1945, at the Yalta Conference, the Russians had requested attacks on communications centers ahead of their advance—Dresden was selected.*

▼ *Whole areas of Dresden were reduced to rubble by the bombers, but trains were back running through the city two days after the first attack.*

◀ *Three of the 527 US bombers that hit the city.*

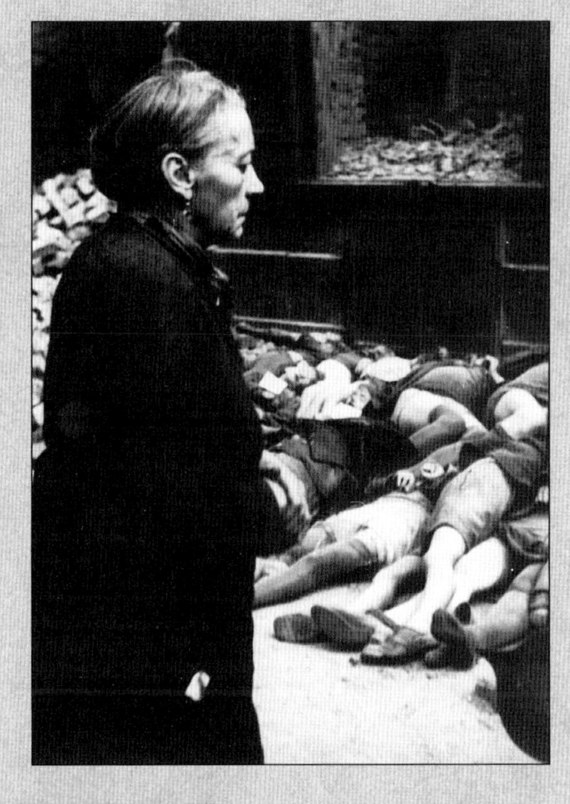

▶ *Afterward came the grim task of identifying the dead, often made impossible if bodies were charred.*

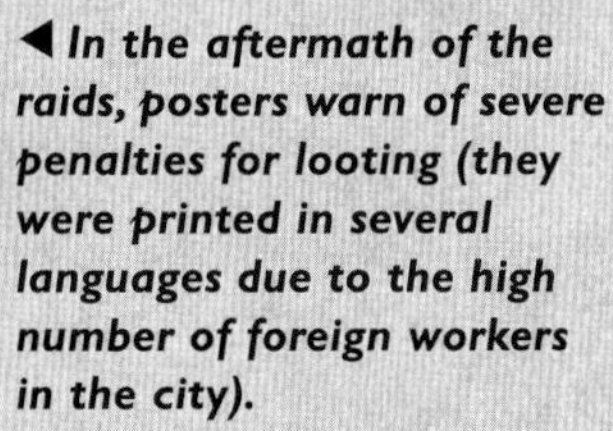

◀ *In the aftermath of the raids, posters warn of severe penalties for looting (they were printed in several languages due to the high number of foreign workers in the city).*

▶ *At the beginning of 1945, Dresden was packed with refugees fleeing from the Red Army (the city's parks were used for camps) and 26,000 Allied prisoners. This resulted in high casualties: up to 70,000 are estimated to have perished.*

EYEWITNESS REPORT

"New command post in the subway tunnels under Anhalt railroad station. The station looks like an armed camp. Women and children huddling in niches and corners and listening for the sounds of battle. Shells hit the roofs, cement is crumbling from the ceiling. Water comes rushing through the tunnels. The crowds get panicky, stumble and fall over rails and sleepers. Children and wounded are deserted, people are trampled to death. The water covers them. It rises 3 feet (1 metre) or more, then it slowly goes down. The panic lasts for hours. Many are drowned. Reason: Somewhere, on somebody's command, engineers have blasted the locks of one of the canals to flood the tunnels against the Russians who are trying to get through them."

From the diary of a German staff officer, describing conditions during the defense of Berlin.

THE OPPOSING FORCES

The Red Army assembled huge forces to launch its advance. Its divisions were arranged into fronts, which were the equivalent of Western army groups. From the Baltic Sea to Yugoslavia, there were 10 fronts in total. The four fronts that would strike directly into the heart of Germany comprised nearly four million men. The offensive would be supported by 10,000 aircraft, 3300 tanks, and 28,000 artillery pieces. The drive to Berlin itself was to be handled by Stalin's two most capable military commanders. Marshal Georgy Zhukov led the 1st Belorussian Front, while Marshal Ivan Konev commanded the 1st Ukrainian Front.

Resisting the Soviets were four crumbling and battle-weary German formations. They were Army Group Center in East Prussia, Army Group Vistula in Pomerania, Army Group A in central Poland, and Army Group South in Czechoslovakia and Austria. The total German strength in East Prussia and Poland was only about 600,000 men. The Germans were further weakened by poor command. Hitler later placed Army Group Vistula under the command of Heinrich Himmler, for example. Himmler might have been the head of the SS, but he was not militarily experienced. Hitler put him in charge because of his political loyalty rather than his combat skill.

THE SOVIETS ENTER GERMANY

The Soviet advance was the largest single offensive of World War II. It began on January 12, 1945. German resistance soon collapsed under waves of artillery fire, air and tank attacks, and infantry assaults. In East Prussia, Army Group Center was virtually wiped out.

East Prussia was the first German territory the Soviets entered. Several million East Prussian civilians tramped west toward the Baltic coast, hoping to escape by ship from one of the ports. In the harsh subzero winter conditions, up to a million of them died. Even those who managed to get on board refugee ships were not safe. Soviet submarines sank many vessels. In only

▼ *Soviet troops look out over Budapest. Hitler had ordered that the city be held "at all costs."*

THE VOLKSSTURM

In September 1944, Hitler created the *Volkssturm* (People's Guard, literally "People's Storm"). He put the new organization under the leadership of his private secretary Martin Bormann and SS chief Heinrich Himmler. The *Volkssturm* conscripted all able-bodied German males between the ages of 16 and 60, who were not already in military service, into home-defense units. Volkssturm soldiers had little military value. They could only train on Sundays, so that they could work the rest of the time, and they had few weapons and little ammunition. Nevertheless, *Volkssturm* members armed with Panzerfaust hand-held anti-tank weapons successfully destroyed many Allied tanks. They played a major role in the city fighting in Berlin. It is estimated that as many as 200,000 *Volkssturm* soldiers died in frontline fighting.

▶ **Volkssturm *surrender. Many were forced to fight or threatened with execution.***

two such sinkings, more than 11,000 people died.

Farther south, the Red Army advanced through Poland. It captured the Polish capital, Warsaw, on January 17. Within two weeks, Konev and Zhukov were amassing troops along the eastern German border on the Oder River. Berlin lay only 35 miles (55km) to the west.

By February 24, Pomerania had been cleared. During February and March, the Soviets consolidated their position. There was little fighting apart from limited attacks into German territory. The focus of the war now shifted south into Hungary.

THE TAKING OF BUDAPEST

The Soviets had captured eastern Hungary in October 1944. The Hungarian capital, Budapest, however, was still in German hands. Stalin launched an attack to take Budapest on October 26. The city was defended by a garrison of 188,000 men. It took the Red Army two full months to surround it. The city was besieged.

In January 1945, Hitler made a decision that reflected how badly he had lost his grasp on military strategy. His army chief of staff, Heinz Guderian, urged him to send every available unit to the Oder. Guderian feared a Soviet thrust into Germany. Instead, Hitler ordered a panzer division from the western front to relieve the Budapest garrison. The panzers were held up by poor weather, however. They reached Budapest on February 13. On that same day, the city finally fell to the Soviets.

On March 6, Hitler launched what would be Germany's final offensive of the war. He believed that an offensive around either side of Lake Balaton to the south would retake Budapest. It would also establish a new defensive line along the River Danube. However, the troops and tanks available for the German offensive were dwarfed by Soviet firepower. By March 15, the Red Army was advancing north up the Danube Valley toward Vienna, the capital of Austria.

THE FALL OF VIENNA

The campaign to take Vienna began on March 16. Mountains and numerous rivers made it difficult to use armor. Using land maneuvers and amphibious actions, however, the Soviets reached Vienna on April 5. Much of the historic center was destroyed before the city fell on 13 April, along with 130,000 German prisoners.

THE STRATEGY TO TAKE BERLIN

The honor of taking Berlin was given to marshals Zhukov and Konev. Zhukov would attack west into the city from

Küstrin, on the Oder. Konev's 1st Ukrainian Front was going to move into the south of Berlin. Another army front, meanwhile, would strike north of the city against Army Group Vistula.

Inside Berlin, Hitler had scraped together almost every available male to defend the city. The total defensive force came to about one million, but many of the defenders were poorly trained. They included, for example, 100 battalions of Volkssturm units, who were little more than civilians. The German defenders also lacked any armored vehicles.

Hitler himself had now retreated into the Führerbunker. The bunker was set deep underground beneath the Chancellery, the political center of Berlin. Hitler stayed in the bunker with his mistress, Eva Braun, and an entourage of his faithful followers. He gave an order that the Soviets "must and shall fall before the capital of the Third Reich." It was a delusory hope. The Soviets had 2.5 million soldiers ready to attack the city. They also possessed the equivalent of one artillery gun for every 13 feet (4m) of ground along 55 miles (90km) of front.

▲ ***Red Army troops enter Vienna, the Austrian capital, in April 1945.***

▼ ***Budapest was left in ruins after the Soviet siege.***

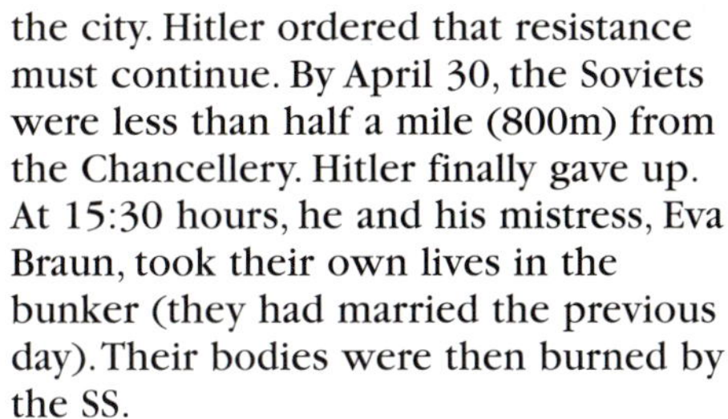

A heavy bombardment on 16 April 1945, began the Battle of Berlin. Soviet troops stormed forward, but they faced desperate resistance. The Russians were also slowed down by the weather conditions. The spring thaw made the countryside outside the city a muddy bog in many places.

Zhukov became stuck against the defenses to the east of Berlin for several days. It took him until April 20 to overcome all German resistance on the west bank of the Oder. Stalin ordered Zhukov to move around to the north of the city. Hitler, however, left his Ninth Army in position on the Oder while Zhukov began to maneuver. Meanwhile, Konev pushed steadily up from the south.

By April 25, Berlin was surrounded. In ferocious fighting, the Red Army made its way into the German capital, clearing resistance street by street. Soviet aircraft bombed strongpoints around the clock. German resistance remained strong. Berliners feared the invaders. They also faced reprisals from their own army. Any male found not fighting risked being picked up by SS squads and hanged from a lamppost.

LAST DAY OF THE REICH

After April 20, Hitler did not leave his bunker. He was losing his reason as his Reich disintegrated around him. By April 27, the Germans held only 15 square miles (38 square kilometres) of the city. Hitler ordered that resistance must continue. By April 30, the Soviets were less than half a mile (800m) from the Chancellery. Hitler finally gave up. At 15:30 hours, he and his mistress, Eva Braun, took their own lives in the bunker (they had married the previous day). Their bodies were then burned by the SS.

The Nazi leadership passed to the commander of the German Navy, Grand Admiral Karl Dönitz. The German High Command now tried to make a peace deal. Their first attempts failed because the Soviets demanded unconditional surrender, which the Germans initially rejected. On May 2, however, the commandant of Berlin, Lieutenant-General Karl Weidling, surrendered the city. The city had lost about 300,000 German and Soviet dead. Five days later, Germany signed its total surrender. The war in Europe was over.

▼ *In 1945, Berlin fell to the Red Army, marking the final stages of the war in Europe.*

FINAL DAYS IN THE BUNKER

From April 20–30, 1945, Hitler lived entirely in the Führerbunker. With him were his mistress, Eva Braun, a large number of high-ranking Nazi officials, and administrative and domestic staff. According to accounts by those present, by this time Hitler was physically and mentally broken. He was prone to furious rages. Even his closest allies began to desert him. On April 23, his close friend Hermann Göring sent a telegram from Bavaria saying that he would take over leadership of Germany if he did not hear otherwise from Hitler. Five days later, Hitler learned that another close friend, Heinrich Himmler, had been conducting secret peace negotiations behind his back. On April 29, Hitler received reports that Russian forces were little more than a block away from the Chancellery above the bunker. He married Eva Braun. The next day, the pair went into a separate room and committed suicide. Braun took cyanide, while Hitler shot himself. Their bodies were later burned.

◀ ***One of the last photographs of Hitler shows him with members of the Hitler Youth in April 1945.***

▼ ***Russian troops look on as the Reichstag, the heart of German government, smolders after the fall of Berlin in 1945.***

▼ *Field Marshal Bernard Montgomery (left) receives the German surrender in northwest Europe on May 4 at Luneberg Heath.*

THE SURRENDER

The death of Hitler and the surrender of Berlin did not bring an immediate end to the fighting in Europe. Admiral Karl Dönitz, who now led Germany, tried to extend the war. He wanted to allow as many Germans as possible to escape Russian occupation. The surrender therefore happened in piecemeal fashion.

Dönitz sent Hans-Georg von Friedeburg to negotiate with Montgomery. On May 4, 1945, the German forces in northwest Europe laid down their arms. Von Friedeburg's next stop was northern France, where he met with Eisenhower's staff. Von Friedeburg tried to arrange a surrender in the west, while continuing war against the Soviets in the east. The Americans rejected the terms.

After negotiations, the Allies allowed Germans 48 more hours to move across into the US–British western zone. At 02:41 hours on May 7, the Germans signed the surrender of all their forces. It became effective at one minute past midnight on May 9. Fighting went on until 11 May in places such as Austria and Czechoslovakia, but the Allies could now celebrate victory in Europe.

▶ *New Yorkers celebrate Victory in Europe (VE) Day on May 8, 1945. Fighting against Japan would go on for another three months.*

◄ *A work party clears rubble in front of the town hall in Saarbrucken, in the Saarland, late in 1945. Much of the rebuilding work in Germany was done by women nicknamed "Trümmerfrau"—"rubble women."*

Key to maps

The key below refers specifically to the maps used on pages 100, 103, 129, 135, 139, 149, 160, and 164. Other maps have their own keys.

Military units – types

infantry

armoured

motorized infantry/
panzergrenadier

parachute/airborne

Military units – size

XXXXX army group

XXXX army

XXX corps

XX division

X brigade

III regiment

II battalion

Military unit colours

German

British and Commonwealth

US

Military movement

atttack/advance (in national colours)

Geographical symbols

road

urban area

urban area/building

trees

Military Units track

marsh

river

railway

bridge